Writing
in a
Second
Language

Insights from
First and Second
Language Teaching
and Research

Bruce Leeds, Editor

Writing in a Second Language:
Insights from First and Second Language Teaching and Research

Editorial director: Joanne Dresner
Acquisitions editor: Allen Ascher
Assistant editor: Jessica Miller
Production editor: Liza Pleva
Compositor: Kim Teixeira

Library of Congress Cataloging-in-Publication Data

Writing in a second language : insights from L1 and L2 teaching and research
    by Bruce Leeds
        p.   cm.
    ISBN 0-201-82589-9
    1. English language—Rhetoric—Study and teaching—Foreign
speakers.   2. Language and languages—Study and teaching.
3. Rhetoric—Study and teaching.   4. Second language acquisition.
I. Leeds, Bruce, 1950–
PE1128.A2W759   1995
808'.042'07—dc20   95-15296
                                                              CIP

ISBN: 0-201-82589-9

1 2 3 4 5 6 7 8 9 10-CRS-99 98 97 96 95

CONTENTS

ACKNOWLEDGMENTS

I wish to thank several people, without whose help and support this book would not have been possible. First, I am grateful to Prof. Harry L. Gradman, chair of the Program in TESOL and Applied Linguistics at Indiana University, not only for his support and encouragement over the years, but for his helpful suggestions during the creation of this book. I would also like to thank my colleagues at IU, Tom Gabriele and Beverly Hartford, for their support and helpful comments.

Thanks are also owed to Allen Ascher at Longman/Addison-Wesley for his unfailing belief in the project from the beginning, and for his encouragement and extremely helpful suggestions throughout the project. I also thank Jessica Miller, Liza Pleva, Kim Teixeira, and Keri Toksu for their untiring assistance in bringing the book to press in its final form.

Finally, I would like to thank the students in my graduate writing theory class at IU, for it was out of that class that the present book took its original inspiration.

INTRODUCTION

When teachers and researchers first began to think about second language (L2) writing in a systematic way, they looked to the work carried out in first language (L1) composition research for guidance and insight. They did this perhaps because of the well-founded intuition that L1 and L2 writing are rooted in a similar reality. For both L1 and L2 writers, writing is a protracted process through which ideas are explored, elaborated, and finally shaped for the reader. L2 writing research has confirmed this essential connection between the two fields, and studies in L1 writing continue to provide L2 theorists with valuable insights. In addition, a large body of work has accumulated in the field of L2 writing, and the questions that researchers are asking today demonstrate a deeper awareness of the unique nature of the L2 writing process.

This text brings together some of the most influential and commonly cited articles from the literature on L1 and L2 writing, giving the reader an idea of the historical and ongoing interaction of L1 and L2 theory. The organization of the text highlights many of the issues that are of central concern to contemporary writing teachers and researchers. What are the similarities and differences between L1 and L2 writing? What is the essential nature of the writing process? In what ways are reading and writing connected? What kind of writing should we be teaching? How does reader awareness affect the writing process? What can we do to help students get started with their essays, and how can we help them when they get stuck? How do experienced writers revise, and how can we teach our students to do the same? How can we respond to students' writing so that they develop their full potential as writers? And how can we evaluate our students' writing in a constructive way?

The authors collected here, representing over a decade of work in L1 and L2 writing theory, address these issues with unusual insight and skill. Given the complex nature of the writing process, however, and the changing needs of our students, it would be unrealistic to look for easy answers to these questions. Teaching writing, like writing itself, is an art. It is the art of helping students find ways to use writing to discover new ideas, and to convey those ideas in a way the reader will not only find acceptable but persuasive. Perhaps the primary value of this book rests in its ability to help the teacher achieve that skill. One thing is certain: The reader will come away from these articles with a deeper appreciation of the complexity involved in writing and the teaching of writing, and of the creativity required to do both well.

1

TRADITION IN L1 AND L2 COMPOSING

In the first essay, Edward P. J. Corbett surveys some of the changes that have taken place in the research and teaching of first language (L1) composition. Graduate programs and conferences have proliferated, and the teaching of writing has become specialized into such areas as second language (L2) writing. Corbett further points out that attention is now being paid to the process as well as the product of writing. In the next essay, Ann Raimes also discusses the shift to a process approach in her discussion of emerging traditions in the teaching of L2 writing. With this shift, she says, have come reactions from teachers who are concerned that the process is being emphasized at the expense of the product. She indicates some of the complex problems that English as a second language (ESL) teachers face, such as choosing the kind of writing to teach, responding to student writing, and recognizing the diversity of ESL students. In the final essay, Ilona Leki offers a bird's-eye view of some of the similarities and differences between L1 and L2 writers. She cautions the reader that the similarities should not obscure the differences, suggesting that the L2 writing teacher encourage students to draw on their L1 writing experience when they can, while at the same time acknowledging their particular needs as L2 students.

Prereading Questions

1. Do you think that writing can be taught? If so, what is the teacher's role?

2. How do you think writing instruction today differs from writing instruction in the past?

3. Discuss your best writing teacher. What was good about his or her approach to teaching writing?

4. What do you think are the main difficulties involved in teaching L2 writing?

Teaching Composition: Where We've Been and Where We're Going

EDWARD P. J. CORBETT *Ohio State University*

To get a clear view of any scene or activity, one needs a room with a view. It is helpful if the room commands an expansive view—at least on three sides. (The blind side provides a convenient excuse if the viewer fails to note some important feature of the scene.) And if the view is to be truly retrospective and prospective, one cannot be stiff-necked.

It takes an ounce of temerity and a pound of arrogance for me to do a survey of the composition scene, because I am not at all confident that I am any more qualified than the next teacher of English to explore the territory. My room with a view has been paid for, as yours has, with a lot of toil and trouble: teaching composition for several years at one or more schools; talking shop with colleagues; listening in on the grapevine, reading the journals and the pertinent books; attending conferences and conventions. But maybe the one experience I have had that most teachers have not had was a six-year tour as the editor of a major composition journal. An editorship sets up a marvelous vantage point from which the view can be as expansive as the one that a forest ranger gets from his mountain-top tower. Even if my eyesight is not 20/20, I can still point out salient features of the landscape to the interested spectator. Despite the myopia of the guide, the survey of the scene, whether retrospective or prospective, can be both fascinating and instructive for the spectator.

THE ENHANCED PROFESSIONALISM OF THE COMPOSITION TEACHER

The most salient feature of the current scene is the enhanced professionalism and the elevated status of the young composition teachers. I specify the *young* composition teachers, because many of the older composition teachers are just serving out their time and have not kept up with all the exciting new developments in composition studies. When I contrast the knowledge and competence commanded by my own graduate students and by the young teachers I hear talk at our conferences and conventions with the folklore and trial-by-error that I relied on when I was their age, I am duly humbled but simultaneously inspirited. The enhanced professionalism of the young composition teachers is due, for the most part, to the formal training they have received in rhetoric and composition; their elevated status is largely due to that enhanced professionalism.

From "Teaching Composition: Where We've Been and Where We're Going" by E. P. J. Corbett, 1987, College Composition and Communication, *38, pp. 444–452. Copyright 1987 by the National Council of Teachers of English. Reprinted with permission.*

What a startling change has taken place in the last twenty years in the way that we prepare our graduate students to teach writing. The English teachers of my generation were mainly, if not exclusively, trained to take over a literature class. They were trained to take over a literature class, not with any special courses in pedagogy but with courses that exposed them to wide and intensive reading of literary texts. Because they usually had to take courses in Anglo-Saxon and Middle English and had to pass qualifying examinations in one or more foreign languages, they also got some formal training in language. But for the teaching of writing, which supported their graduate studies, usually the only training they got was in a rather desultory practicum, which met once a week and which dealt chiefly with the nuts-and-bolts aspects of the writing course.

That situation prevailed in our colleges and universities until early in the 1960s when rhetoric appeared—or reappeared—on the scene. I have always dated the emergence of rhetoric as the rationale for the teaching of composition from the spring of 1963, when the Conference on College Composition and Communication held its annual convention in Los Angeles. At that convention, the word *rhetoric* appeared frequently and prominently in the titles of many of the panels and workshops. That was the convention when two of the most often reprinted talks on composition were delivered: Francis Christensen's "A Generative Rhetoric of the Sentence" and Wayne Booth's "The Rhetorical Stance." In October of that year, Ken Macrorie, the editor of the journal *College Composition and Communication,* published a special collection of some of the papers from that convention under the title *Toward a New Rhetoric.* As I observed in a talk that I gave in May 1986, at a conference of the Rhetoric Society of America at the University of Texas at Arlington,

> Rhetoric remained in the hot spotlight, at least in composition circles, for the rest of the 1960s. By the early 1970s, rhetoric had dropped out of the limelight, but working under much softer lights, a number of turned-on English teachers began to produce some solid scholarship on the old rhetoric and the new rhetoric. That scholarly activity has continued unabated among many composition teachers right up to the present time, and what is most promising about that activity is that it has engaged the interest and the talents of some of the best and the brightest of our young people.

GROWTH OF GRADUATE PROGRAMS IN RHETORIC AND COMPOSITION

I might also have said on that occasion that starting sometime after the mid-1960s, we began seeing the institution of full-fledged graduate programs in rhetoric and composition at many of our universities. We can all tick off a list of the schools that not only have such programs firmly in place but that have produced a number of graduates with specialties in rhetoric and composition—schools such as the University of Southern California, the University of California at Berkeley, the University of Texas at Austin and at Arlington, the University of Illinois at Chicago Circle, the University of Michigan, Ohio State University, Penn State University, Purdue University, the University of Louisville, Carnegie-Mellon University, and Rensselaer Polytechnic Institute. This list does not include the many schools where an English department has instituted two or three graduate courses in rhetoric and composition. In the

January 1986 issue of the *Rhetoric Review,* Gary Tate has given us the most comprehensive listing of graduate programs offered by English departments in rhetoric and composition that we have ever had.

BOOKS ON THE HISTORY, THEORY, AND PRACTICE OF COMPOSITION

It is those courses and those programs which have contributed greatly to the enhanced professionalism of composition teachers in recent years. It is debatable whether the creation of those courses and programs encouraged the production and the publication of certain kinds of textbooks or whether the publication of certain kinds of textbooks fostered the development of the courses and programs. In any case, we now have a number of textbooks that were not even a gleam in some author's or editor's eye back in the mid-sixties. The publication of those texts began back in 1965, with Dudley Bailey's *Essays on Rhetoric* (Oxford), a collection of snippets from primary rhetoric texts from various periods, and Joseph Schwartz and John A. Rycenga's *The Province of Rhetoric* (Ronald), a collection of secondary articles on the history of rhetoric. At about the same time, the Southern Illinois University Press issued handsome facsimile editions of important eighteenth- and nineteenth-century rhetoric texts in its Landmark Series. Some of these texts, such as Richard Whately's *Elements of Rhetoric,* are still in print, and recently the SIU Press has been publishing new titles in paperback, such as *The Rhetorics of Thomas Hobbes and Bernard Lamy*, edited by John T. Harwood, and *Selections from the Rhetorical Works of Alexander Bain,* edited by Andrea A. Lunsford. Now one of the publishers is planning to publish a huge anthology of substantial selections from primary rhetorics from the time of the Greeks to the twentieth century. Just the publication of that much-needed anthology of texts will promote the creation of additional undergraduate and graduate courses in the history and theory of rhetoric.

The production of texts on the theory and practice of composition has proliferated at an even more astonishing rate than that of historical texts in rhetoric. None of the texts that I am about to name existed when I was in graduate school right after World War II, and they were still not available when I first became a director of freshman English in the early 1950s and had to prepare TAs to assume full responsibility for one or more writing classes. Now the TAs have available to them not only formal graduate courses in the teaching of composition but a rich library of texts on the teaching of composition. They have texts on how to teach composition by such veteran teachers and directors of freshman English as William Irmscher (*Teaching Expository Writing,* Holt, 1979), Erika Lindemann (*A Rhetoric for Writing Teachers,* Oxford, 1982), and Arnold Tibbetts (*Working Papers: A Teacher's Observations on Composition,* Scott, Foresman, 1982). Timothy R. Donovan and Ben W. McClelland have edited a volume entitled *Eight Approaches to Teaching Composition* (NCTE, 1980), and Charles Bridges has come out with a collection of essays by veteran writing teachers under the title *Training the New Teacher of College Composition* (NCTE, 1986). Instead of having to scramble for important articles on composition in the bound periodicals in the library, graduate students now have convenient collections of such articles—collections such as Ross Winterowd's *Contemporary Rhetoric: A Conceptual Background with Readings* (Harcourt, 1975), Richard L. Graves's *Rhetoric and Composition: A Sourcebook for Teachers and Writers* (Boynton/Cook, 2nd ed., 1984), and Gary Tate and Edward P. J. Corbett's *Teaching Freshman English* (Oxford, 1967) and more recently their *The Writing Teacher's Sourcebook* (Oxford, 1981).

Then there are the books that represent a particular teacher's philosophy on the teaching of composition, books which have been influential in shaping a composition program at a particular college or university. The following litany of such texts is familiar to most teachers: William Coles, *The Plural Eye: The Teaching of Writing* (Holt, 1978); Ken Macrorie, *Uptaught* (Hayden, 1970); James Moffett, *Teaching the Universe of Discourse* (Houghton Mifflin, 1968); Peter Elbow, *Writing without Teachers* (Oxford, 1973); James Britton et al., *The Development of Writing Abilities (11–18)* (Macmillan Education, 1975); Ann E. Berthoff, *The Making of Meaning* (Boynton/Cook, 1981); Janet Emig, *The Web of Meaning* (Boynton/Cook, 1983); Edward M. White, *Teaching and Assessing Writing* (Jossey-Bass, 1985); Marie Ponsot and Rosemary Deen, *Beat Not the Poor Desk: Writing: What to Teach, How to Teach It, and Why* (Boynton/Cook, 1982); Mina Shaughnessy, *Errors and Expectations: A Guide for the Teacher of Basic Writing* (Oxford, 1977). So voluminous has the library on the teaching of composition become that when the 28-page *Bedford Bibliography for Teachers of Writing,* compiled by Robert M. Gorrell, Patricia Bizzell, and Bruce Herzberg, appeared in 1984, new graduate students who were contemplating doctoral work in rhetoric and composition were at once inspirited and intimidated. They feel both emotions even more sharply now. For 1987 brought the publication of Gary Tate's *Teaching Composition: Twelve Bibliographical Essays* (Texas Christian University Press)—revised and expanded since the ten-essay edition of 1976—and the 1984–1985 volume of the ongoing *Longman Bibliography of Composition and Rhetoric,* edited by Erika Lindemann. New students certainly know that if they decide to make a professional career of rhetoric and composition, they have a lot of rather heady reading to do.

SPECIAL CONFERENCES ON RHETORIC AND COMPOSITION

But there are other resources available to them if they want to steep themselves in the scholarship of the field. In addition to the rich convention programs offered at the annual meetings of the CCCC, there are the special seminars and conferences offered summer after summer at the University of Wyoming and at Penn State, Janice Lauer's Summer Seminar in Rhetoric, offered originally at the University of Detroit and now at Purdue University, and Elaine Maimon's NEH-sponsored conferences on writing-across-the-curriculum at Beaver College. Even more specialized conferences have been staged in recent years: the CCCC Winter Workshops; Joseph Williams's seminars at the University of Chicago; Hans Guth's Young Rhetoricians' Conferences at San Jose State University; the Rhetoric Society of America's conferences at the University of Texas at Arlington; the conferences at the University of New Hampshire; the international conference on Learning to Write that Aviva Freedman and Ian Pringle put together in 1979 in Ottawa for the Canadian Council of Teachers of English. A student could assemble a graduate program in rhetoric and composition simply by attending the conferences sponsored by universities or professional organizations. One of the consequences of all of these special conventions is that a tight-knit coterie of students and teachers has formed. If they continue to meet this way, the cabal may develop a special handshake as a ritualistic form of greeting when they assemble at larger meetings.

The recitation of these lists of persons, places, and titles must be boring for listeners or readers to attend to. But these lists should be enunciated or enscribed, if for no other reason than that our treasury of resources should be recorded, not only for posterity but also for desperate teachers now. You have only to consider how you have been helped repeatedly in your own teaching by something you read in some preserved document from the past.

NEW JOURNALS AND NEW RESEARCH IN RHETORIC AND COMPOSITION

And just think of the new journals on writing that have come into existence in the last twenty years. In his review of "Journals in Composition Studies" in the April 1984 issue of *College English,* Robert J. Connors dealt with fifteen of them, six of which were inaugurated in the 1970s and five of which were launched in the first half of the 1980s. These new journals were created partly because more teachers were writing articles on composition and partly because it had become increasingly difficult to place an article in *College English* and *College Composition and Communication,* the two oldest of the professional journals that regularly publish articles on writing. On the rhetoric side, five new journals have come into existence since the late 1960s: *Rhetoric and Philosophy, Rhetoric Society Quarterly, Pre/Text, Rhetorica,* and *Rhetoric Review.* All these new outlets for scholarly articles constitute further evidence of the growing professionalism of students and teachers who were interested in pursuing studies in rhetoric and composition.

Additional evidence of that growing professionalism can be found in the kinds of research that students and teachers of composition have engaged in and in the published books that have reported on that research. In her article "Toward a Theory of Composition" in one of those books, *Perspectives on Research and Scholarship in Composition,* edited by Ben W. McClelland and Timothy R. Donovan (New York: Modern Language Association, 1985), Lil Brannon groups all the recent research in composition under three main headings: empirical-experimental, phenomenological-ethnographic, philosophic-historical. In a monograph jointly published by ERIC and NCTE, *The Teacher-Researcher: How to Study Writing in the Classroom* (1985), Miles Myers provides guidelines for English teachers engaged in these strange kinds of research. Those who have been reading some of the articles printed in *Research in the Teaching of English* have become acquainted with the kinds of scientific research methods that people trained in the humanities have been using lately in their composition studies. Perhaps the crown jewel of this new kind of research is George Hillocks's *Research on Written Composition: New Directions for Teaching* (Urbana, IL: National Conference on Research in English and ERIC Clearinghouse on Reading and Communication Skills, 1986), which provides the most rigorous metanalysis of composition studies since Richard Braddock, Richard Lloyd-Jones, and Lowell Schoer published their *Research in Written Composition* in 1963. Some of our humanistically trained English teachers have been baffled and even scandalized by these scientific methodologies applied to the art of writing, but I think that ultimately we have to agree that this kind of rigor is more intellectually respectable than the kind of anecdotal, intuitive reporting that characterized many of the articles about experimental practices back in the 1950s and 1960s. In fact, in the last two or three years, some of the well-established graduate programs in rhetoric and composition have added a new course in research design.

CHANGES IN WHAT WE TEACH IN THE COMPOSITION CLASSROOM

What significant changes have taken place in the last twenty years in what we teach and how we teach in the composition classroom? One of the changes in *what* we teach has been the increased attention English teachers have paid to the teaching of business, professional, and technical writing. I can remember the days when the teachers of technical writing constituted a fringe group in the CCCC that was allotted only two or three slots at the annual convention. But with the vocational mood that seized many of our students along about the mid-1970s, there was a dramatic increase in the demand from these students for upper-division courses in the kinds of writing that they would have to do someday in their jobs. With the drop in enrollments in literature courses, many English teachers had to fill out their teaching schedules by taking over the teaching of the special writing courses. They tooled up in a hurry for these assignments, but once they began teaching these courses in business, professional, or technical writing, they discovered how intellectually exciting and personally satisfying such courses could be. Consequently, many departments now have a cadre of fervently dedicated and reliably effective teachers of these courses. I am one of those teachers in my department.

But the development that has *most* excited me since I became a part of academia has been the writing-across-the-curriculum movement. One reason the writing-across-the-curriculum movement became so exciting to me is that I recognized it as being the kind of liberal-arts venture that people like Isocrates and Cicero tried to make of the rhetoric course in the ancient schools. Everyone in the academy becomes, in a very real sense, a teacher of writing, and those who are specially trained to be teachers of writing have to widen their purview and be willing to exercise students in the kinds of writing demanded in a variety of disciplines.

All of us probably know of some school where a writing-across-the-curriculum program is firmly entrenched and notoriously successful. If one's school is contemplating the institution of such a program, one turns to these successful schools for models and for advice. Much as I want this movement to succeed on a large scale in this country, two big questions about it pester my mind: (1) Can an interdisciplinary writing program be made to work in a large state university? (2) Can the willingness of the faculty involved in these programs be sustained over the long haul? Those are crucial questions.

The TESOL program has become a bigger and bigger enterprise in many of our schools because of the great influx of foreign students. It remains to be seen whether this program will continue to grow or whether it will slow down and become a permanent but small operation in our curriculum. That question has been complicated by the whole issue of bilingualism. One of the facts that makes this development such a crucial matter is that right now, in some states in this country, such as California, over 50 percent of the students come from foreign-born families.

An emerging development in what we teach in the composition class is the attention we are giving to the cultivation of thinking skills. Because students are becoming acclimated to the inexorable logic of the computer, they are much more disposed now than they were to submit to some rigorous training in critical thinking and logical reasoning. More attention to the cultivation of reading skills may be the way to provide this kind of training. More and more journal articles and convention talks are beginning to talk about the need to exercise our students in reading and to explore, more than we did in the past, the connections between reading and writing. I predict that the cultivation of reading and thinking skills will become the major thrust of our efforts in the composition classroom in the 1990s.

CHANGES IN HOW WE TEACH COMPOSITION

As for the developments during the last twenty years in *how* we teach in the classroom, one would certainly have to mention the persistence of the free-writing movement, the increased attention paid to collaborative learning, the interest manifested in the use of a wide variety of heuristic procedures, the emerging approach to writing as a meaning-making activity. Each of those approaches has had an influence, for better or for worse, on our teaching practices in the last twenty years, and most of us can tick off the names of the people who have introduced or promoted those approaches. But an adequate treatment of those approaches would require another whole paper.

So I will confine myself to a few remarks about the most prominent development that has taken place in recent years in how we teach in the writing course: the pronounced shift of our attention from the product of writing to the process of writing. That shift was a salutary one and long overdue. But like most good things, the emphasis on process was susceptible to abuse, and eventually, it did get abused. In some cases, the emphasis on process became so extreme that attention to the product virtually dropped out of sight. What we need to do now is redress the balance. The condition of the product of the process should not be ignored, for it is the product after all that represents the bottom line of the writer's efforts. Readers do not care at all about the process that produced the product; they are concerned only with the produced document that they hold in their hands. Can they easily read and understand the document? Is the document free of distracting errors? Does the document say something that is informative or useful or interesting to the reader? Does it fulfill the author's purpose? In short, as teachers of writing, we will have to give due attention to both the process and the product of writing.

A NEGATIVE NOTE ABOUT THE TEACHING OF COMPOSITION

Up to this point, I have been blatantly euphoric in my review of the fortunes of the composition course during the last twenty years. I could be upbeat because I was not dealing with any of the social or political aspects of this course. We all know about the inequities associated with the teaching of this course in our colleges and universities. But the tale about those inequities is the subject for another paper. In conclusion, however, I will introduce a negative note, largely at my own expense.

After all these years of teaching writing, I am beginning to ask myself whether I have done any of my students any good. In assessing my way of teaching, I recognize that I spend most of my time in the classroom talking *about* writing. In terms of the trivium—the threefold way that the ancient rhetoricians said we learned any skill: by precepts, by imitation, and by practice—I spend most of my time giving my students prudential advice about how to write a particular assignment. I do not, of course, neglect the imitation and the practice; my students get plenty of opportunity to learn by observing how others write and by writing and revising. But unquestionably, I spend most of the fifty minutes of a typical class period talking about writing.

Simply out of habit, I have adopted the lazy way of teaching writing. And as a result, my conscience is beginning to bother me after all these years. If I were dragged before the Inquisition, I would have to confess that I do not seem to be doing my students much good.

I do not turn my good writers into excellent writers; and I do not detect that my bad writers are any less bad at the end of the term. It has become increasingly difficult for me to cash my paycheck every month. After all these years, I still believe that writing can be taught, and for that reason, I keep flailing around in the composition classroom. But am I really teaching any of my students how to write? Maybe all of us composition teachers need to ask ourselves that question.

Lately, I have been giving myself the Marine Corps treatment. In Marine boot camp, the Drill Instructors had a marvelously effective way of communicating with their charges. On the parade ground, for instance, if anyone fouled up in the marching formation, the Drill Instructor would halt the platoon, would right-face us, and then while we all stood at quivering attention, he would stride down to the offending recruit, stick the tip of his nose right up against the tip of the recruit's nose, and for the next five minutes, he would subject the poor recruit to his wonderfully varied and emphatic ways of letting him know that he was an asshole.

Well, one morning recently while I was shaving—probably after a period of being conscience-stricken about my repeated failures as a teacher of writing—I stuck this big nose of mine against the tip of the nose reflected in the mirror and shouted at the top of my lungs, "CORBETT, YOU FRAUD!"

Maybe we all need to assess ourselves as teachers periodically. Whatever you appropriate for your teaching from the books and articles you read or from the conferences and conventions you attend, give it a fair trial in the classroom. But from time to time, pause to ask yourself, "Am I doing my students any good?" Try it. You have nothing to lose but your delusions.

Out of the Woods: Emerging Traditions in the Teaching of Writing

ANN RAIMES *Hunter College, City University of New York*

Most good fairy tales, at least the ones that delight us and make us or our children beg for more, begin with looking back to "once upon a time." Since the TESOL organization has now reached its twenty-fifth anniversary, this seems a good way to begin looking at the story of how the teaching of writing to adult (secondary and higher education) nonnative speakers of English has developed since 1966; we can follow it up with an account of the thickets and thorny problems we face as we journey into the woods. Despite false trails, we might still, true to the best endings of fairy tales, be able to find a way out of the woods and live happily ever after. But that last is only speculation. Let's begin by looking back at the trails we've followed up to now, keeping in mind that we might not all have met the same witches, wizards, wolves, or good fairies along the way. Readers should be aware that the author of this article has been teaching ESL for more than twenty-five years, and so her telling of the story is inevitably influenced by the paths she chose to follow.

ONCE UPON A TIME: WRITING INSTRUCTION AND RESEARCH 1966–1991

This brief historical survey delineates four approaches to L2 writing instruction that have been evident in the last twenty-five years. Each approach, at least as it emerges in the literature, has a distinctive focus, highlighting in one case the rhetorical and linguistic *form* of the text itself; in another, the *writer* and the cognitive processes used in the act of writing; in another, the *content* for writing; and in the last, the demands made by the *reader*. The dates given mark the approximate time when each focus first appeared consistently in our literature; no final dates are given, since all the approaches are still, in varying degrees, subscribed to in theory and certainly in practice.

Focus on Form, 1966–

Once upon a time, when the TESOL organization first was founded in 1966, the audiolingual method was the dominant mode of instruction. The view that speech was primary meant that writing served a subservient role: to reinforce oral patterns of the language. So in language instruction, writing took the form of sentence drills—fill-ins, substitutions, transformations, and completions. The content was supplied. The writing reinforced or tested the accurate application of grammatical rules. In the 1970s, the use of sentence combining (O'Hare, 1973; Pack & Henrichsen, 1980), while still focusing on the manipulation of given sentences and thus, according to Zamel (1980), ignoring "the enormous complexity of writing" (p. 89), provided students with the opportunity to explore available syntactic options.

In the early 1970s, too, passages of connected discourse began to be used more often as classroom materials in the teaching of writing. Controlled composition tasks, still widely used today, provide the text and ask the student to manipulate linguistic forms within that text (see, for example, Byrd & Gallingane, 1990; Kunz, 1972; Paulston & Dykstra, 1973). However, the fact that students are using passages of connected discourse does not necessarily guarantee that the students view them as authentic. If the students are concentrating on a grammatical transformation, such as changing verbs from present to past, they "need pay no attention whatever to what the sentences mean or the manner in which they relate to each other" (Widdowson, 1978, p. 116).

It was not only grammatical form that was emphasized in the 1960s and early 1970s. Concern for rhetorical form was the impetus for Kaplan's influential 1966 article that introduced the concept of contrastive rhetoric. His "doodles article," as he calls it (Kaplan, 1987, p. 9), represents the "thought pattern" of English as "dominantly linear in its development" (Kaplan, 1966, p. 4) in contrast to the paragraph patterns of other languages and cultures. It has led to compensatory exercises that offer training in recognizing and using topic sentences, examples, and illustrations. These exercises often stress imitation of paragraph or essay form, using writing from an outline, paragraph completion, identification of topic and support, and scrambled paragraphs to reorder (see, for example, Kaplan & Shaw, 1983; Reid & Lindstrom, 1985).

Formal considerations are also the basis for a great deal of current L2 writing research. Textual features, such as the number of passives or the number of pronouns, are counted and compared for users of different cultures (Reid, 1990). Researchers examine the structure of such features as introductory paragraphs (Scarcella, 1984), the form of essays in various languages (Eggington, 1987; Hinds, 1987; Tsao, 1983), cohesion and coherence (Connor, 1984; Johns, 1984), and topical structure (Lautamatti, 1987). A large-scale study of written composition across fourteen countries established to codify tasks and describe the state of writing instruction has provided a rich database for cross-cultural discourse analyses (Purves, 1988). (For a summary of text-based research, see Connor, 1990.) A form-dominated approach has the largest body of research to inform and support it; it has been with us for a long time and lends itself to empirical research design.

Focus on the Writer, 1976–

The 1970s saw the development of more than sentence combining and controlled composition. Influenced by L1 writing research on composing processes (Emig, 1971; Zamel, 1976), teachers and researchers reacted against a form-dominated approach by developing an interest in what L2 writers actually do as they write. New concerns replaced the old. In place of "accuracy" and "patterns" came "process," "making meaning," "invention," and "multiple drafts." The attention to the writer as language learner and creator of text has led to a "process approach," with a new range of classroom tasks characterized by the use of journals (Peyton, 1990; Spack & Sadow, 1983), invention (Spack, 1984), peer collaboration (Bruffee, 1984;

Long & Porter, 1985), revision (Hall, 1990), and attention to content before form (Raimes, 1983a; Zamel, 1976, 1982, 1983). Zamel (1983) has recommended that teachers not present instruction in the use of thesis sentences and outlines before the students have begun to explore ideas. In response to theory and research on writers' processes, teachers have begun to allow their students time and opportunity for selecting topics, generating ideas, writing drafts and revisions, and providing feedback. Where linguistic accuracy was formerly emphasized from the start, it is now often downplayed, at least at the beginning of the process, delayed until writers have grappled with ideas and organization. Some practitioners even entirely omit attention to grammar, as in ESL writing textbooks that contain no grammar reference or instructional component (e.g., Benesch & Rorschach, 1989; Cramer, 1985).

Research publications on L2 writing processes grew rapidly in the 1980s to inform and support the new trends in instruction (e.g., Cumming, 1989; Friedlander, 1990; Hall, 1990; Jones, 1982, 1985; Jones & Tetroe, 1987; Raimes, 1985, 1987; Zamel, 1982, 1983; for a summary, see Krapels, 1990). However, although we are beginning to discover much about the writing process, the small number of subjects in case-study research limits generalizations, and we are rightly warned that the "lack of comparability across studies impedes the growth of knowledge in the field" (Krapels, 1990, p. 51).

Despite the rapid growth in research and classroom applications in this area, and despite the enthusiastic acceptance of a shift in our discipline to a view of language as communication and to an understanding of the process of learning, teachers did not all strike out along this new path. The radical changes that were called for in instructional approach seemed to provoke a swift reaction, a return to the safety of the well-worn trail where texts and teachers have priority.

Focus on Content, 1986–

Some teachers and theorists, alienated by the enthusiasm with which a process approach was often adopted and promulgated (Horowitz, 1986a), interpreted the focus on the writer's making of personal meaning as an "almost total obsession" (Horowitz, 1986c, p. 788) with "the cognitive relationship between the writer and the writer's internal world" (Swales, 1987, p. 63). Those who perceived the new approach as an obsession inappropriate for academic demands and for the expectations of academic readers shifted their focus from the processes of the writer to content and to the demands of the academy. By 1986, a process approach was being included among "traditional" (Shih, 1986, p. 624) approaches and in its place was proposed what Mohan had already proposed in 1979—a content-based approach. In content-based instruction, an ESL course might be attached to a content course in the adjunct model (Brinton, Snow & Wesche, 1989; Snow & Brinton, 1988) or language courses might be grouped with courses in other disciplines (Benesch, 1988). With a content focus, learners are said to get help with "the language of the thinking processes and the structure or shape of content" (Mohan, 1986, p. 18). It is interesting to note here that the content specific to English courses—language, culture, and literature—is largely rejected (see Horowitz, 1990) in favor of the subject matter of the other fields the ESL students are studying.

The research studies that inform this approach include analysis of the rhetorical organization of technical writing (Selinker, Todd-Trimble, & Trimble, 1978; Weissberg, 1984), studies of student writing in content areas (Jenkins & Hinds, 1987; Selzer, 1983), and surveys of the content and tasks L2 students can expect to encounter in their academic careers

(Bridgeman & Carlson, 1983; Canseco & Byrd, 1989; Horowitz, 1986b). While classroom methodology might take on some of the features of a writer-focused approach, such as prewriting tasks and the opportunity for revision, the main emphasis is on the instructor's determination of what academic content is most appropriate, in order to build whole courses or modules of reading and writing tasks around that content.

This content-based approach has more repercussions on the shape of the curriculum than the two approaches previously described, for here the autonomous ESL class is often replaced by team teaching, linked courses, "topic-centered modules or mini-courses," sheltered (i.e., "field specific") instruction, and "composition or multiskill English for academic purposes (EAP) courses/tutorials as adjuncts to designated university content courses" (Shih, 1986, p. 632–633). With an autonomous ESL class, a teacher can—and indeed often does—move back and forth among approaches. With ESL attached in the curriculum to a content course, such flexibility is less likely. There is always the danger that institutional changes in course structure will lock us into an approach that we want to modify or abandon.

Focus on the Reader, 1986–

Simultaneously with content-based approaches came another academically oriented approach, English for academic purposes, which focuses on the expectations of academic readers (Horowitz, 1986a, 1986b, 1986c; Reid, 1987, 1989). This approach, in which the ESL teacher runs a theme-based class, not necessarily linked to a content course, is also characterized by its strong opposition to a position within a writer-dominated process approach that favors personal writing. A reader-dominated approach perceives language teaching "as socialization into the academic community—not as humanistic therapy" (Horowitz, 1986c, p. 789).

The audience-dominated approach, focusing on the expectations of readers outside the language classroom, is characterized by the use of terms like *academic demands* and *academic discourse community*. Attention to audience was, in fact, first brought to the fore as a feature of the process approach, but the focus was on known readers inside the language classroom, as peers and teachers responded to the ideas in a text. An English for academic purposes approach focuses on the reader, too—not as a specific individual but as the representative of a discourse community, for example, a specific discipline or academia in general. The reader is an initiated expert who represents a faculty audience. This reader, "particularly omniscient" and "all-powerful" (Johns, 1990a, p. 31), is likely to be an abstract representation, a generalized construct, one reified from an examination of academic assignments and texts.

Once the concept of a powerful outside reader is established, it is a short step to generalizing about the forms of writing that a reader will expect, and then an even shorter step to teaching those forms as prescriptive patterns. Recommendations such as the following: "Teachers must gather assignments from across the curriculum, assess the purposes and audience expectations in the assignments, and present them to the class" (Reid, 1987, p. 34) indicate a return to a form-dominated approach, the difference being that now rhetorical forms, rather than grammatical forms, are presented as paradigms.

A reader-dominated approach, like the other approaches, has generated its own body of research: mostly surveys of the expectations and reactions of faculty members (Johns, 1981; Santos, 1988), studies of the expectations of academic readers with regard to genres (Swales, 1990), and identifications of the basic skills of writing transferable across various disciplines (Johns, 1988).

These four approaches are all widely used and by no means discrete and sequential. Certainly the last three appear to operate more on a principle of critical reaction to a previous approach than on cumulative development. In all, our path through the woods of writing instruction is less clearly defined now in 1991 than it was in 1966. Then there was one approach, form-dominated, clearly defined, and relatively easy to follow in the classroom. Now teachers have to consider a variety of approaches, their underlying assumptions, and the practices that each philosophy generates. Thus, leaving the security of what Clarke and Silberstein call the "explicitly mandated reality" (1988, p. 692) of one clear approach, we have gone in search of a new theoretical approach or approaches to L2 writing instruction.

INTO THE WOODS: THICKETS AND THORNY ISSUES

Once we have left the relative safety of a traditional form-dominated approach and set off into the woods in search of new theories, our progress is hampered by many thickets and thorny issues. These we have to confront and negotiate before we can continue our journey. Particularly thorny are five classroom-oriented issues that arise in our literature and in teachers' discussions frequently enough to trouble L2 writing instructors, issues that in my more than twenty-five years of teaching have provided cause for reflection and uncertainty: the topics for writing; the issue of "real" writing; the nature of the academic discourse community; the role of contrastive rhetoric in the writing classroom; and ways of responding to writing. These areas, difficult to negotiate, will be described as discrete items, each posing its own set of problems. A word of caution is in order, though: Readers should not expect to find here miracle solutions or magic charms to lead the way past these thickets and out of the woods.

The Topics for Writing

One of the major problems teachers face is what students should write about. Topics for writing are an integral part of any writing course, and the four approaches outlined above lead to what can be a bewildering array of topics for teachers. In a form-dominated approach, topics are assigned by the teacher; since the interest is in how sentences and paragraphs are written rather than in what ideas are expressed, each piece of writing serves as a vehicle for practicing and displaying grammatical, syntactic, and rhetorical forms. For this purpose, almost any topic will serve. In a writer-dominated approach (usually called a process approach), the students themselves frequently choose the topics, using personal experience to write about what concerns them, or responding to a shared classroom experience, often a piece of expository writing or a work of literature (Spack, 1985). In a content-dominated approach, topics will be drawn from the subject matter of either a particular discipline or a particular course, supplied either by the content teacher when content and writing course are linked in the adjunct model (Snow & Brinton, 1988) or by the language teacher in theme-based EAP courses. And in a reader-dominated approach, the model is one of the writing-across-the-curriculum movement, with language teachers examining what other disciplines assign and training students how to respond to those assignments by "deconstructing" (Johns, 1986a, p. 253) the essay prompt and by following a model of the appropriate form of academic writing.

The problem of whether to teach personal or academic writing has surfaced frequently in recent years (Mlynarczyk, forthcoming) and has no easy solution. Approaches that focus on rhetorical form and on the reader's expectations look to the larger community for guidance. ESL instruction is seen as a service "to prepare students to handle writing assignments in academic courses" (Shih, 1986, p. 617). For EFL students and for international students in the United States, who will probably only write in English as part of their educational requirement and not at all thereafter, this might be suitable. However, the purposes are different for the many ESL immigrant and refugee nonnative speakers in secondary and college classrooms. This last group, a rapidly growing one, Leki (1990) equates with native speakers of English, who, she says, are "more likely to write for many different contexts in the course of their professional lives" (p. 14). For native speakers—and, by extension, certain large groups of ESL students—Hairston (1991) rejects the idea that writing courses should be "service courses" taught for the benefit of academic disciplines, since "writing courses taught by properly trained teachers do have important content: learning how to use language to express ideas effectively" (p. B1).

"Real" Writing

A great deal of the recent controversy about the teaching of writing has centered not only around the topics students write about but also around the dichotomy of process and product. Horowitz initiated lengthy debate (see Braine, 1988; Hamp-Lyons, 1986; Horowitz, 1986a, 1986b, 1986c; Liebman-Kleine, 1986; Reid, 1984; Spack, 1988; Zamel, 1983) by questioning the effectiveness of the process approach with its focus on the writer. In particular, Horowitz (1986a) criticized what he termed the "cavalier view" (p. 141) of a process proponent (this author) who said at the 1985 TESOL Convention that examination writing was not " 'real' " (p. 141) writing. Horowitz is not alone in his complaint. Cited as a major flaw in a process approach is the fact that "the Process Approach fails to give students an accurate picture of university writing" (Johns, 1990b). The issue of what university writing is and what kind of writing ESL students should be doing is a thorny one, and the use of the term *real* relates to this issue in practice as well as in theory.

In practice, I and many of my colleagues teach two types of writing in our classes: writing for learning (with prewriting, drafts, revisions, and editing) and writing for display (i.e., examination writing). Our students are aware of the different purposes and different strategies. They recognize that these are distinct. The use of the term *real* in this context was initiated by Searle (1969), who makes a clear distinction between real questions and exam questions. In real questions, the speaker wants to know the answer; in exam questions, the speaker wants to know if the hearer knows. Similar distinctions can be made with writing. In a writing class, students need to be taught both how to use the process to their advantage as language learners and writers, and also how to produce an acceptable product upon demand. A shortcoming of the debate around these issues is that process and product have been seen as *either/or* rather than *both/and* entities. However, while students certainly need to learn how to pass exams, they also need to perceive writing as a tool for learning, a tool that can be useful to them throughout their professional and personal lives.

As evidence of the difficulty of defining authentic writing, it is interesting to note that even Horowitz (1986b) has used the designation *real* to describe writing. He suggests ways to simulate "the essential characteristics of *real* university writing assignments" (p. 449) and discusses the context of "a *real* academic task" (italics added; p. 459). Here, too, the use of the term *real* could be questioned. However, we should not assume that the implication is necessarily that the topics and tasks that come from ESL teachers' own repertoire are somehow unreal; it is, rather, that Horowitz and others find them less appropriate in certain settings. In any case, the L2 debate provides a great deal of evidence for what Harris (1989) has observed in L1 writing: "One seems asked to defend either the power of the discourse community or the imagination of the individual writer" (p. 2). Obviously, the whole area of the types of writing students are expected to do and the types of writing we should teach is one surrounded by controversy.

The Nature of the Academic Discourse Community

Frequently cited as important in determining the nature of "real" writing and the topics we should assign are the demands of the "academic discourse community." These demands provide a set of standards that readers of academic prose, teachers in academic settings, expect. So some L2 writing teachers look to other disciplines to determine their course content, their readings, their models, and their instruction of rhetorical form. One thorny issue here is whether we should put our trust in this community, or whether we shouldn't rather be attempting to influence and change the academic community for the benefit of our students, while teaching our students how to interpret the community values and transform them (for discussion of similar issues, see Auerbach, 1986, 1990; Peirce, 1989).

According to Johns (1990a), teachers who emphasize the conventions of the discourse community will begin with "the *rules* [italics added] of discourse in the community" (p. 32), since academic faculty "insist that students learn to 'talk like engineers', for example, *surrendering their own language and mode of thought* [italics added] to the requirements of the target community" (p. 33). The language used here—"rules" and "surrender"—reveals perceptions regarding who exercises power in the community and the value of that power. In contrast, Patricia Bizzell (cited in Enos, 1987) sees the academic community as synonymous with "dominant social classes" and has recommended that we not direct our students towards assimilation but rather find ways to give them "critical distance" on academic cultural literacy, so that eventually "elements from students' native discourse communities can be granted legitimacy in the academic community" (p. vi).

Another thorny problem is whether we view the academic discourse community as benign, open, and beneficial to our students or whether we see discourse communities as powerful and controlling, and, as Giroux (cited in Faigley, 1986) puts it, "often more concerned with ways of excluding new members than with ways of admitting them" (p. 537). These opposing views point to the validity of Berlin's (1988) statement that every pedagogy implies "a set of tacit assumptions about what is real, what is good, what is possible, and how power ought to be distributed" (p. 492). Teaching writing is inherently political, and how we perceive the purposes of writing vis-à-vis the academic community will reflect our political stance.

Reflecting our stance, too, is how we interpret the information that comes to us from members of the academic community. In a survey of 200 faculty members' opinions in response to the question, "Which is more important for success in your classes, a general knowledge of English or a knowledge of English specific to the discipline?" (Johns, 1981, p. 57), most faculty members ranked general English above specific purposes English. This result was interpreted in the following way:

> There could be a number of reasons for the general English preferences, the most compelling of which is that most faculty do not understand the nature and breadth of ESP. They tend to think of it as an aspect of the discipline that has to do with vocabulary alone. (p. 54)

The mix of signals perhaps reflects a more generalized ambivalence of TESOL practitioners: Subject-area faculty are viewed as a valuable resource; however, when they do not support what ESL teachers and researchers expect, it is tempting to discount their perceptions.

A focus on the academic discourse community also raises issues as to whether academic writing is good writing, whether academic discourse "often masks a lack of genuine understanding" (Elbow, 1991, p. 137) of how a principle works, and indeed whether there is a fixed and stable construct of academic writing even in one discipline. Elbow goes so far as to say that we can't teach academic discourse "because there's no such thing to teach" (p. 138). This issue of the nature, requirements, even the existence of an academic discourse community is a thicket in which we could be entangled for a long time.

Contrastive Rhetoric

Although it has been twenty-five years since contrastive rhetoric research was introduced (Kaplan, 1966; Leki, 1991) and the concept is frequently mentioned in discussions of theory and research, its applications to classroom instruction have not developed correspondingly. Published research informs teachers about the different ways in which the written products of other languages are structured (e.g., Eggington, 1987; Hinds, 1987; Tsao, 1983), but the nature of transfer in L2 writing remains under debate (see Mohan & Lo, 1985) and transfer has been found not to be significant in certain types of task, such as paraphrase (Connor & McCagg, 1983). The declared intention of contrastive rhetoric research is, however, "not to provide pedagogic method" but rather to provide teachers and students with knowledge about how the links between culture and writing are reflected in written products (Grabe & Kaplan, 1989, p. 271).

Rather than abstracting a principle of the "linear" development of English prose (Kaplan, 1966) as a pedagogic principle, contrastive rhetoric is more useful as a consciousness-raising device for students; teachers can discuss what they have observed about texts in different cultures and have students discover whether research findings hold true in their experience of their L1 texts.

The thicket that contrastive rhetoric presents for teachers as they wander into the woods of theory is the question of the value of prescribing one form of text—English form—not just as an alternative, but as the one privileged form of text, presented as the most logical and desirable, with which other learned systems interfere. Land and Whitley (1989), in discussing how readers read and judge ESL students' essays, found that nonnative speaker readers could "accommodate to more kinds of rhetorical patterns" (p. 287) than could native-speaker readers. If we are to move away from courses that are "as retributive as they are instructive" and away from "composition as colonization," we need, they say, to "recognize, value, and foster the alternative rhetorics that the ESL student brings to our language" (p. 286), not treat them only as features that interfere with language learning. Land and Whitley fear that "in teaching Standard Written English rhetorical conventions, we are teaching students to reproduce in a mechanical fashion our preferred vehicle of understanding" (p. 285).

In the same way that multiple "literacies" (Street, 1984) are posed against the idea of one dominant cultural literacy (Hirsch, 1987), so a broad use of contrastive rhetoric as a classroom consciousness-raising tool can point to linguistic variety and rhetorical choices; a narrow use would emphasize only prescriptions aimed at counteracting L1 interference. An extensive research study (Cumming, 1989) of the factors of writing expertise and second-language proficiency of L2 writers revealed in the qualities of their texts and their writing behaviors warns against such a narrow use of contrastive rhetoric: "Pedagogical prescriptions about the interference of learners' mother tongue in second-language performance—espoused in audiolingual methodologies and theories of linguistic transfer or contrastive rhetoric—appear misdirected" (pp. 127–128) since students' L1 is shown to be an important resource rather than a hindrance in decision making in writing.

Responding to Writing

With a number of approaches to teaching writing to choose from, teachers are faced with a similar variety of ways to respond to students' writing. Since a response on a student's paper is potentially one of the most influential texts in a writing class (Raimes, 1988), teachers are always concerned about the best approach. Some of the options follow, illustrating the variety at our disposal. We can correct errors; code errors; locate errors; indicate the number of errors (see Robb, Ross, & Shortreed, 1986, for a discussion of these); comment on form; make generalized comments about content, e.g., "good description" or "add details" (Fathman & Whalley, 1990, p. 182); make text-specific comments, e.g., "I'm wondering here what Carver tells the readers about the children"; ask questions; make suggestions; emote with comments like "Nice!" or "I'm bored" (Lees, 1979, p. 264); praise; ask students to comment on the source of the error (Raimes, 1990); or ask L1 peers to reformulate the students' texts (Cohen, 1983). Given the range of choices, it's hardly surprising that responding is a thorny issue. It is, in fact, so problematic that much of our written response to students' texts is inconsistent, arbitrary, and often contradictory (Zamel, 1985).

In an effort to understand more about teachers' responses, researchers are looking at students' responses to feedback (Cohen, 1987; Cohen & Cavalcanti, 1990; Radecki & Swales, 1988), finding mainly that students simply "make a mental note" of a teacher's response. The fact that little of the research examines activities that occur after the act of responding seems to get at the heart of the problem. If teachers see their response as the end of the interaction, then students will stop there. If, however, the response includes specific directions on what to do next, an "assignment" (Lees, 1979, p. 265), there is a chance for application of principles.

FALSE TRAILS

The five thorny issues just discussed are ones that trouble teachers and concern theorists and researchers. There are many others, too, rendering our journey into the woods exciting, even hazardous. As teachers read the theories and research and try to figure out what approach to adopt in a writing classroom, they will sometimes confront a false trail that seems to promise a quick way out of the woods, an easy solution. We have seen evidence of false trails in the rise and demise of various methods (Clarke, 1982, 1984; Richards, 1984). Similarly, prescriptions of one approach for our whole profession and all our students can be seen as false trails, too, since they actually lead back to another "explicitly mandated reality" (Clarke & Silberstein, 1988) to replace the mandate of form-focused instruction. Such a prescription in the teaching of writing appears in proposals for the widespread adoption of content-based language teaching as "the dominant approach to teaching ESL at all levels" (Celce-Murcia, 1989, p. 14).

I regard proposals like this as false trails because they perpetuate one of the errors that have been at the heart of many of our thorny problems about writing. That problem, alluded to earlier, is that we tend to discuss ESL/EFL students as if they are one or at the most two groups. Much of the dissension and controversy that has surfaced at conferences and in our literature would, I submit, simply cease to exist if we defined our terms. Our field is too diverse for us to recommend ways of teaching ESL in general. There is no such thing as a generalized ESL student. Before making pedagogical recommendations, we need to determine the following: the type of institution (high school, two-year college, four-year college, research university?) and the ESL student (undergraduate or graduate? freshman or junior? international student [returning to country of origin] or immigrant/refugee? with writing expertise in L1 or not? with what level of language proficiency?). If we are to prescribe content, we need to ask, Whose content? For the nonnative-speaking first-year students in my university, to offer modules of marketing, accounting, and nursing is to depart from the very tradition of a liberal arts education. On the other hand, for very specialized international graduate students, a content approach might be the most appropriate. When Johns and Connor (1989, reported in Leki, 1990) maintain that no such thing as general English exists, they are referring to international students, but immigrant students need general English; that is, they need more than ways to adapt to course requirements for a few years. They need to be able to write in English for the rest of their working and earning lives. They need to learn not only what academia expects but how to forge their place in it, and how to change it. Indeed, on many campuses now, a diverse student body is urging the replacement of the male Eurocentric curriculum model with one emphasizing gender representation and cultural diversity. Adopting a content-based approach for all ESL students would be succumbing to what I have called "the butler's stance" (Raimes, forthcoming), one that overvalues service to other disciplines and prescribes content at the expense of writer, reader, and form.

Being lost in the woods might be uncomfortable, but we have to beware of taking an easy path that might, in fact, lead us back to where we started, to a reliance on form and prescription.

OUT OF THE WOODS: EMERGING TRADITIONS IN THE TEACHING OF WRITING

What is the story now after a twenty-five-year journey, beset by thickets, thorns, and false trails? Are new traditions emerging?

I am reminded of an article I wrote for this journal eight years ago (Raimes, 1983b), in which I argued that in spite of the thrust towards communicative competence, there had been no real revolution in our field. While there were then signs of some shifts in the assumptions about what we do, we were still enmeshed in tradition but were beginning to raise important questions. At that time Kuhn's (1970) description of a paradigm shift seemed apt for the field of ESL/EFL in general: "the proliferation of competing articulations, the willingness to try anything, the expression of explicit discontent, the recourse to philosophy and to debate over fundamentals" (p. 91). That description seems still to be apt for the teaching of writing, where there is certainly evidence of competition, discontent, and debate, and where now, given the plurality of approaches, designs, and procedures, it seems more appropriate to talk of *traditions* rather than of one *tradition*.

If any clear traditions are emerging, they have more to do with recognition of where we are now rather than delineation of exactly where we are going. I see five such emerging traditions of recognition: recognition of the complexity of composing, of student diversity, of learners' processes, of the politics of pedagogy, and of the value of practice as well as theory. I end with a brief discussion of each.

Recognition of the Complexity of Composing

Despite all the false trails and some theorists' desire to offer one approach as the answer to our problems, what seems to be emerging is a recognition that the complexity of the writing process and the writing context means that when we teach writing we have to balance the four elements of form, the writer, content, and the reader. These are not discrete entities. Rather,

> writers are readers as they read their own texts. Readers are writers as they make responses on a written text. Content and subject matter do not exist without language. The form of a text is determined by the interaction of writer, reader, and content. Language inevitably reflects subject matter, the writer, and the writer's view of the reader's background knowledge and expectations. (Raimes, forthcoming)

This complexity may mean no one single theory of writing can be developed (Johns, 1990a) or it may mean that a variety of theories need to be developed to support and inform diverse approaches (Silva, 1990). In either case, recognition of complexity is a necessary basis for principled model building.

Recognition of Student Diversity

While there is still a tendency to discuss our field as if it were the easily definable entity it was twenty-five years ago, there are signs that we are beginning to recognize the diversity of our students and our mission, and to realize that not all approaches and procedures might apply to all ESL/EFL students. Reid (1984) notes this when she reminds Zamel of the differences between advanced students and novice writers, particularly with regard to cognitive development; Horowitz (1990) notes this when he lists the questions that we need to ask about our students before we decide to use literature or any other content. For heterogeneous classes, a "balanced" stance is recommended (Booth, 1963; Raimes, forthcoming), one that presents a governing philosophy but pays attention within that philosophy to all four elements involved in writing: form, writer, content, and reader. The combination of complexity and diversity makes it imperative for us not to seek universal prescriptions, but instead to "strive to validate other, local forms of knowledge about language and teaching" (Pennycook, 1989, p. 613).

Recognition of Learners' Processes

Amidst all the winding and intersecting paths and false trails, one trail seems to be consistently well marked and well traveled. While there is controversy about what a process approach to teaching writing actually comprises and to what extent it can take academic demands into account, there is widespread acceptance of the notion that language teachers need to know about and to take into account the process of how learners learn a language and how writers produce a written product. Such a notion of process underlies a great deal of current communicative, task-based, and collaborative instruction and curriculum development (Nunan, 1989a, 1989b). Even writing theorists who are identified with content-based and reader-based approaches frequently acknowledge the important role that the writer's processes play in the writing class (Johns, 1986b; Shih, 1986; Swales, 1987). The process approach more than any other seems to be providing unifying theoretical and methodological principles.

Recognition of the Politics of Pedagogy

Along with the recognition of the complexity of composing and the diversity of our students and their processes has come a more explicitly political understanding: The approach we take to the academic discourse community and the culturally diverse students in our classrooms will inevitably reflect "interested knowledge," which is likely to be "a positivist, progressivist, and patriarchal" view presented as "a method" (Pennycook, 1989, p. 589). All approaches should, therefore, be examined with a set of questions in mind: Who learns to do what? Why? Who benefits? (See Auerbach, 1986, 1990.) Recognizing the power of literacy, we need to ask "what kind of literacy we want to support: literacy to serve which purposes and on behalf of whose interests" (Lunsford, Moglen, & Slevin, 1990, p. 2) and to keep in mind that "to propose a pedagogy is to propose a political vision" (Simon, 1987, p. 371).

Recognition of the Value of Practice

Both in L1 and in L2 instruction, the power that theory, or method, has held over instruction is being challenged by what Shulman (1987) calls "the wisdom of practice" (p. 11). North (1987) argues that in L1 writing instruction we need to give credit to "practitioners' lore" as well as research; teachers need to use their knowledge "to argue for the value of what they know and how they come to know it" (p. 55). Before we heed our theorists and adopt their views, it will help us if we first discover how often they teach writing to ESL students, where they teach it, how they teach it, and who their students are. We need to establish a context. We need to know the environment in which they have developed what Prabhu (1990, p. 172) calls "a teacher's sense of plausibility about teaching," which is the development of a "concept (or theory, or in a more dormant state, pedagogic intuition), of how learning takes place and how teaching causes and supports it." But better than putting the research into a teaching context is for teachers to become researchers themselves. Classroom-based research and action research is increasingly recommended to decrease teachers' reliance on theorists and researchers (Richards & Nunan, 1990). Teachers can keep sight of the forest as well as the trees.

These recognitions characterize our position at the end of our twenty-five-year journey from "once upon a time," journeying into the woods, facing the tangle of thickets and thorny problems to trying to recognize—and avoid—false trails. Our own telling of the story might also include having taken some false trails or having met and vanquished a few big bad wolves in our travels. The fact that we are beginning to emerge from the woods with new recognitions but not a single new approach is perhaps the happiest 1991 ending that we can expect, given the diversity and complexity of our students and of learning and teaching writing. But by the turn of the century, we could well be reading (and writing) a different story.

ACKNOWLEDGMENTS

Many thanks to Kate Parry, Ruth Spack, and Vivian Zamell, who read earlier drafts of this paper and offered perceptive and helpful advice. Thanks also go to the graduate students in my course, Rhetoric and Composition, who steered me away from the idea of using "Little Red Writing Hood" as a subtitle for this paper.

REFERENCES

Auerbach, E. R. (1986). Competency-based ESL: One step forward or two steps back? *TESOL Quarterly, 20*(3), 411–429.

Auerbach, E. R. (1990). Review of *Alien winds: The reeducation of America's Indochinese refugees. TESOL Quarterly, 24*(1), 85–91.

Benesch, S. (Ed.). (1988). *Ending remediation: ESL and content in higher education.* Washington, DC: TESOL.

Benesch, S., & Rorschach, B. (1989). *Academic writing workshop II.* Belmont, CA: Wadsworth.

Berlin, J. A. (1988). Rhetoric and ideology in the writing class. *College English, 50*(5), 477–494.

Booth, W. C. (1963). The rhetorical stance. *College Composition and Communication, 14*(2), 139–145.

Braine, G. (1988). Comments on Ruth Spack's "Initiating ESL students into the academic discourse community: How far should we go?" *TESOL Quarterly, 22*(4), 700–702.

Bridgeman, B., & Carlson, S. B. (1983). *Survey of academic writing tasks required of graduate and undergraduate foreign students* (TOEFL Research Rep. No. 15). Princeton, NJ: Educational Testing Service.

Brinton, D., Snow, M. A., & Wesche, M. (1989). *Content-based second language instruction.* New York: Newbury House.

Bruffee, K. (1984). Collaborative learning and the "conversation of mankind." *College English, 46*(7), 635–652.

Byrd, D. R. H., & Gallingane, G. (1990) *Write away 2.* New York: Newbury House.

Canseco, G., & Byrd, P. (1989). Writing required in graduate courses in business administration. *TESOL Quarterly, 23*(2), 305–316.

Celce-Murcia, M. (1989). Models for content-based curricula for ESL. *CATESOL Journal, 2*(1), 5–16.

Clarke, M. A. (1982). On bandwagons, tyranny, and common sense. *TESOL Quarterly, 16*(4), 437–448.

Clarke, M. A. (1984). On the nature of technique: What do we owe the gurus? *TESOL Quarterly, 18*(4), 577–594.

Clarke, M. A., & Silberstein, S. (1988). Problems, prescriptions and paradoxes in second language teaching. *TESOL Quarterly, 22*(4), 685–700.

Cohen, A. D. (1983, December). Reformulating compositions. *TESOL Newsletter,* p.1, 4–5.

Cohen, A. D. (1987). Student processing of feedback on their compositions. In A. Wenden & J. Rubin (Eds.), *Learner strategies in language learning* (pp. 57-68). Englewood Cliffs, NJ: Prentice Hall.

Cohen, A. D., & Cavalcanti, M. C. (1990). Feedback on compositions: Teacher and student verbal reports. In B. Kroll (Ed.), *Second language writing: Research insights for the classroom* (pp. 155–177). New York: Cambridge University Press.

Connor, U. (1984). A study of cohesion and coherence in English as a second language students' writing. *Papers in Linguistics: International Journal of Human Communication, 17,* 301–316.

Connor, U. M. (1990). Discourse analysis and writing/reading instruction. *Annual Review of Applied Linguistics, 11,* 164–180.

Connor, U., & McCagg, P. (1983). Cross-cultural differences and perceived quality in written paraphrases of English expository prose. *Applied Linguistics, 4,* 259–268.

Cramer, N. A. (1985). *The writing process: 20 projects for group work.* Rowley, MA: Newbury House.

Cumming, A. (1989). Writing expertise and second language proficiency. *Language Learning, 39*(1), 81–141.

Eggington, W. G. (1987). Written academic discourse in Korean: Implications for effective communication. In U. Connor & R.B. Kaplan (Eds.), *Writing across languages: Analysis of L2 text* (pp. 153–168). Reading, MA: Addison-Wesley.

Elbow, P. (1991). Reflections on academic discourse: How it relates to freshmen and colleagues. *College English, 53*(2), 135–155.

Emig, J. (1971). *The composing processes of twelfth graders.* Urbana, IL: National Council of Teachers of English.

Enos, T. (1987). *A sourcebook for basic writing teachers.* New York: Random House.

Faigley, L. (1986). Competing theories of process: A critique and a proposal. *College English, 48*(6), 527–542.

Fathman, A. K. & Whalley, E. (1990). Teacher response to student writing: Focus on form versus content. In B. Kroll (Ed.), *Second language writing: Research insights for the classroom* (pp. 178–190). New York: Cambridge University Press.

Friedlander, A. (1990). Composing in English: Effects of a first language on writing in English as a second language. In B. Kroll (Ed.), *Second language writing: Research insights for the classroom* (pp. 109–125). New York: Cambridge University Press.

Grabe, W., & Kaplan, R. B. (1989). Writing in a second language: Contrastive rhetoric. In D.M. Johnson & D.H. Roen (Eds.), *Richness in writing: Empowering ESL students* (pp. 263–283). New York: Longman.

Hairston, M. (1991, January 23). Required writing courses should not focus on politically charged social issues. *Chronicle of Higher Education,* pp. B1–B3.

Hall, C. (1990). Managing the complexity of revising across languages. *TESOL Quarterly, 24*(1), 43–60.

Hamp-Lyons, L. (1986). No new lamps for old yet, please. *TESOL Quarterly, 20*(4), 790–796.

Harris, J. (1989). The idea of community in the study of writing. *College Composition and Communication, 40*(1), 11–22.

Hinds, J. (1987). Reader versus writer responsibility: A new typology. In U. Connor & R. B. Kaplan (Eds.), *Writing across languages: Analysis of L2 text* (pp. 141–152). Reading, MA: Addison-Wesley.

Hirsch, E. D., Jr. (1987). *Cultural literacy: What every American needs to know.* Boston: Houghton Mifflin.

Horowitz, D. M. (1986a). Process, not product: Less than meets the eye. *TESOL Quarterly, 20*(1), 141–144.

Horowitz, D. M. (1986b). What professors actually require: Academic tasks for the ESL classroom. *TESOL Quarterly, 20*(3), 445–462.

Horowitz, D. M. (1986c). The author responds to Liebman-Kleine. *TESOL Quarterly, 20*(4), 788–790.

Horowitz, D. M. (1990). Fiction and nonfiction in the ESL/EFL classroom: Does the difference make a difference? *English for Specific Purposes, 9,* 161–168.

Jenkins, S., & Hinds, J. (1987). Business letter writing: English, French, and Japanese. *TESOL Quarterly, 21*(2), 327–349.

Johns, A. M. (1981). Necessary English: A faculty survey. *TESOL Quarterly, 15*(1), 51–57.

Johns, A. M. (1984). Textual cohesion and the Chinese speaker of English. *Language Learning and Communication, 3,* 69–74.

Johns, A .M. (1986a). Coherence and academic writing: Some definitions and suggestions for teaching. *TESOL Quarterly, 20*(2), 247–265.

Johns, A. M. (1986b). The ESL student and the revision process: Some insights from schema theory. *Journal of Basic Writing, 5*(2), 70–80.

Johns, A. M. (1988). The discourse communities dilemma: Identifying transferable skills for the academic milieu. *English for Specific Purposes, 7,* 55–60.

Johns, A. M. (1990a). L1 composition theories: Implications for developing theories of L2 composition. In B. Kroll (Ed.), *Second language writing: Research insights for the classroom* (pp. 24–36). New York: Cambridge University Press.

Johns, A. M. (1990b, March). *Process, literature, and academic realities: Dan Horowitz and beyond.* Handout for paper presented at the 24th Annual TESOL Convention, San Francisco, CA.

Jones, C. S. (1982). Attention to rhetorical form while composing in a second language. In C. Campbell, V. Flashner, T. Hudson, & J. Lubin (Eds.), *Proceedings of the Los Angeles Second Language Research Forum* (Vol. 2, pp. 130–143). Los Angeles: University of California, Los Angeles.

Jones, C. S. (1985). Problems with monitor use in second language composing. In M. Rose (Ed.), *Studies in writer's block and other composing process problems* (pp. 96–118). New York: Guilford Press.

Jones, C. S., & Tetroe, J. (1987). Composing in a second language. In A. Matsuhashi (Ed.), *Writing in real time: Modeling production processes* (pp. 34–57). Norwood, NJ: Ablex.

Kaplan, R. B. (1966). Cultural thought patterns in intercultural education. *Language Learning, 16*(1), 1–20.

Kaplan, R. B. (1987). Cultural thought patterns revisited. In U. Connor & R.B. Kaplan (Eds.), *Writing across languages: Analysis of L2 text* (pp. 9–20). Reading, MA: Addison-Wesley.

Kaplan, R. B., & Shaw, P. A. (1983). *Exploring academic discourse*. Rowley, MA: Newbury House.

Krapels, A. (1990). An overview of second language writing process research. In B. Kroll (Ed.), *Second language writing: Research insights for the classroom* (pp. 37–56). New York: Cambridge University Press.

Kuhn, T. S. (1970). *The structure of scientific revolutions* (2nd ed.). Chicago: University of Chicago Press.

Kunz, L. (1972). *26 steps: A course in controlled composition for intermediate and advanced ESL students*. New York: Language Innovations.

Land, R. E., & Whitley, C. (1989). Evaluating second language essays in regular composition classes: Toward a pluralistic U.S. rhetoric. In D. M. Johnson & D. H. Roen (Eds.), *Richness in writing: Empowering ESL students* (pp. 284–293). New York: Longman.

Lautamatti, L. (1987). Observations in the development of the topic in simplified discourse. In U. Connor & R.B. Kaplan (Eds.), *Writing across languages: Analysis of L2 text* (pp. 87–114). Reading, MA: Addison-Wesley.

Lees, E. O. (1979). Evaluating student writing. *College Composition and Communication, 30*(4), 370–374.

Leki, I. (1990). Potential problems with peer responding in ESL writing classes. *CATESOL Journal, 3*(1), 5–19.

Leki, I. (1991). Twenty-five years of contrastive rhetoric: Text analysis and writing pedagogies. *TESOL Quarterly, 25*(1), 123–143.

Liebman-Kleine, J. (1986). In defense of teaching process in ESL composition. *TESOL Quarterly, 20*(4), 783–788.

Long, M. H., & Porter, P. A. (1985). Group work, interlanguage talk, and second language acquisition. *TESOL Quarterly, 19*(2), 207–228.

Lunsford, A., Moglen, H., & Slevin, J. (Eds.). (1990). *The right to literacy*. New York: Modern Language Association.

Mlynarczyk, R. (forthcoming). Personal and academic writing: A false dichotomy? *TESOL Journal.*

Mohan, B. A. (1979). Relating language teaching and content teaching. *TESOL Quarterly, 13*(2) 171–182.

Mohan, B. A. (1986). *Language and content*. Reading, MA: Addison-Wesley.

Mohan, B. A., & Lo, W. A. (1985). Academic writing and Chinese students: Transfer and developmental factors. *TESOL Quarterly, 19*(3), 515–534.

North, S. M. (1987). *The making of knowledge in composition: Portrait of an emerging field*. Portsmouth, NH: Boynton/Cook, Heinemann.

Nunan, D. (1989a). *Designing tasks for the communicative classroom*. Cambridge: Cambridge University Press.

Nunan, D. (1989b). Toward a collaborative approach to curriculum development: A case study. *TESOL Quarterly, 23*(1), 9–25.

O'Hare, F. (1973). *Sentence combining: Improving student writing without formal grammar instruction*. Urbana, IL: National Council of Teachers of English.

Pack, A. C., & Henrichsen, L. E. (1980). *Sentence combination*. Rowley, MA: Newbury House.

Paulston, C. B., & Dykstra, G. (1973). *Controlled composition in English as a second language*. New York: Regents.

Peirce, B. N. (1989). Toward a pedagogy of possibility in the teaching of English internationally: People's English in South Africa. *TESOL Quarterly, 23*(3), 401–420.

Pennycook, A. (1989). The concept of method, interested knowledge, and the politics of language teaching. *TESOL Quarterly, 23*(4), 589–618.

Peyton, J. K. (Ed.). (1990). *Students and teachers writing together: Perspectives on journal writing*. Alexandria, VA: TESOL.

Prabhu, N. S. (1990). There is no best method—Why? *TESOL Quarterly, 24*(2), 161–176.

Purves, A. C. (Ed.). (1988). *Writing across languages and cultures*. Newbury Park, CA: Sage.

Radecki, P. M., & Swales, J. M. (1988). ESL student reaction to written comments on their written work. *System, 16*, 355–365.

Raimes, A. (1983a). Anguish as a second language? Remedies for composition teachers. In A. Freedman, I. Pringle, & J. Yalden (Eds.), *Learning to write: First language/second language* (pp. 258–272). Harlow, England: Longman.

Raimes, A. (1983b). Tradition and revolution in ESL teaching. *TESOL Quarterly, 17*(4), 535–552.

Raimes, A. (1985). What unskilled ESL students do as they write: A classroom study of composing. *TESOL Quarterly, 19*(2), 229–258.

Raimes, A. (1987). Language proficiency, writing ability, and composing strategies: A study of ESL college student writers. *Language Learning, 37*(3), 439–468.

Raimes, A. (1988). The texts for teaching writing. In B.K. Das (Ed.), *Materials for language learning and teaching* (pp. 41–58). Singapore: SEAMEO Regional Language Centre.

Raimes, A. (1990). *How English works: A grammar handbook with readings.* (Instructor's Manual). New York: St. Martin's Press.

Raimes, A. (forthcoming). Instructional balance: From theories to practices in teaching writing. *Georgetown University Round Table on Languages and Linguistics 1991.*

Reid, J. (1984). Comments on Vivian Zamel's "The composing process of advanced ESL students: Six case studies." *TESOL Quarterly, 18(1),* 149–159.

Reid, J. (1987, April). ESL composition: The expectations of the academic audience. *TESOL Newsletter,* p. 34.

Reid, J. (1989). English as a second language composition in higher education: The expectations of the academic audience. In D. M. Johnson & D. H. Roen (Eds.), *Richness in writing: Empowering ESL students* (pp. 220–234). New York: Longman.

Reid, J. (1990). Responding to different topic types: A quantitative analysis from a contrastive rhetoric perspective. In B. Kroll (Ed.), *Second language writing: Research insights for the classroom* (pp. 191–210). New York: Cambridge University Press.

Reid, J., & Lindstrom, M. (1985). *The process of paragraph writing.* Englewood Cliffs, NJ: Prentice Hall.

Richards, J. C. (1984). The secret life of methods. *TESOL Quarterly, 18*(1), 7–23.

Richards, J. C., & Nunan, D. (Eds.). 1990. *Second language teacher education.* Cambridge: Cambridge University Press.

Robb, T., Ross, S., & Shortreed, I. (1986). Salience of feedback on errors and its effect on EFL writing quality. *TESOL Quarterly, 20*(1), 83–93.

Santos, T. (1988). Professors' reactions to the academic writing of nonnative-speaking students. *TESOL Quarterly, 22*(1), 69–90.

Scarcella, R. C. (1984). How writers orient their readers in expository essays: A comparative study of native and nonnative English writers. *TESOL Quarterly, 18*(4), 671–688.

Searle, J. R. (1969). *Speech acts: An essay in the philosophy of language.* Cambridge: Cambridge University Press.

Selinker, L., Todd-Trimble, M., & Trimble, L. (1978). Rhetorical function shifts in EST discourse. *TESOL Quarterly, 12*(3), 311–320.

Selzer, J. (1983). The composing processes of an engineer. *College Composition and Communication, 34*(2), 178–187.

Shih, M. (1986). Content-based approaches to teaching academic writing. *TESOL Quarterly 20*(4), 617–648.

Shulman, L. S. (1987). Knowledge and teaching: Foundations of the new reform. *Harvard Educational Review, 57*(1), 1–22.

Silva, T. (1990). Second language composition instruction: Developments, issues, and directions in ESL. In B. Kroll (Ed.), *Second language writing: Research insights for the classroom* (pp. 11–23). New York: Cambridge University Press.

Simon, R. (1987). Empowerment as a pedagogy of possibility. *Language Arts, 64*(4), 370–382.

Snow, M. A., & Brinton, D. M. (1988). The adjunct model of language instruction: An ideal EAP framework. In S. Benesch (Ed.), *Ending remediation: ESL and content in higher education* (pp. 33–52). Washington, DC: TESOL.

Spack, R. (1984). Invention strategies and the ESL college composition student. *TESOL Quarterly, 18*(4), 649–670.

Spack, R. (1985). Literature, reading, writing, and ESL: Bridging the gaps. *TESOL Quarterly, 19*(4), 703–725.

Spack, R. (1988). Initiating ESL students into the academic discourse community: How far should we go? *TESOL Quarterly, 22*(1), 29–51.

Spack, R., & Sadow, C. (1983). Student-teacher working journals in ESL freshman composition. *TESOL Quarterly, 17*(4), 575–593.

Street, B. V. (1984). *Literacy in theory and practice.* Cambridge, England: Cambridge University Press.

Swales, J. (1987). Utilizing the literatures in teaching the research paper. *TESOL Quarterly, 21*(1), 41–68.

Swales, J. M. (1990). *Genre analysis: English in academic and research settings.* Cambridge: Cambridge University Press.

Tsao, Fen-Fu. (1983). Linguistics and written discourse in English and Mandarin. In R.B. Kaplan (Ed.), *Annual review of applied linguistics 1982* (pp. 99–117). Rowley, MA: Newbury House.

Weissberg, R. C. (1984). Given and new: Paragraph development models from scientific English. *TESOL Quarterly, 18*(3), 485–499.

Widdowson, H. G. (1978). *Teaching language as communication.* Oxford: Oxford University Press.

Zamel, V. (1976). Teaching composition in the ESL classroom: What we can learn from research in the teaching of English. *TESOL Quarterly, 10*(1), 67–76.

Zamel, V. (1980). Re-evaluating sentence-combining practice. *TESOL Quarterly, 14*(1), 81–90.

Zamel, V. (1982). Writing: The process of discovering meaning. *TESOL Quarterly, 16*(2), 195–210.

Zamel, V. (1983). The composing processes of advanced ESL students: Six case studies. *TESOL Quarterly, 17*(2), 165–187.

Zamel, V. (1985). Responding to student writing. *TESOL Quarterly, 19*(1), 79–101.

L2 Composing: Strategies and Perceptions

ILONA LEKI *University of Tennessee*

ESL students bring with them to writing classes their diverse personal, cultural, political, and educational histories. The one feature which they share and which sets them apart from average native English-speaking students, however, is that they all have another (maybe more than one other) language besides English in which they are able to function. This bilingualism has implications for the cognitive writing processes ESL students bring to composing in an L2, and these implications need to be taken into account in the writing classroom. But when ESL students first began appearing in numbers in English-medium institutions, their writing needs were considered primarily language learning needs. Thus, researchers and teachers interested in determining appropriate pedagogies for these students focused not on their writing processes, but on their language learning processes. Since bilingualism—that is, language—distinguished ESL students from native English-speaking students, it seemed obvious that ESL writing classes needed to focus on language.

In the early 1980s, L2 writing classes were still emphasizing linguistic competence as a prerequisite to learning to write. Difficulties with writing were generally addressed through language practice activities, and actual composing (creating through writing) was often postponed until students had more or less mastered English syntax and morphology.

But when research on L2 composing processes finally began in the early 1980s, they revealed basic similarities between L1 and L2 writers, concluding that as far as composing processes were concerned, the distinction to be made was not between L1 and L2 writers but between experienced and inexperienced writers. Inexperienced L2 writers used generally ineffective processes similar to those used by inexperienced L1 writers, and experienced L2 writers, regardless of their linguistic proficiency (at least among those already fairly advanced in English), used processes similar to those of experienced L1 writers (Zamel, 1983). As a result of these kinds of findings, researchers began endorsing imitation of L1 writing classroom practices in ESL writing classrooms. Research findings which emphasized the similarity between L1 and L2 writing supported the idea that L2 writing classes needed to become less focused on language and more focused on composing, just as L1 classes were doing. Since their writing processes were so similar to those of native speakers, it was assumed that ESL students could and should be taught in the same way as L1 writers were being taught.

Reprinted by permission of Ilona Leki: Understanding ESL Writers: A Guide for Teachers *(Portsmouth, NH: Boynton/Cook Publishers, Inc., 1992).*

SIMILARITIES

An important finding of L2 composing process research has been that when non-native writers write in English, they are able to rely on strategies that they employ in their L1 writing. ESL students who are expert writers in their L1 are able to plan, to hold in mind concerns about gist while considering organizational possibilities, and to compare text with intentions; they have access to those same skills and strategies when composing in L2 (Cumming, 1989; Zamel, 1983). In both their L1 and in English, experienced ESL writers have in mind some idea of what they hope to achieve in their writing, construct plans to achieve those goals, and seem able to discern when the goals have been met to their own satisfaction. Thus, they seem to function in much the same way as expert writers in English function (Cumming, 1989).

Interestingly, the ability to engage these effective strategies appears to be independent of the writers' L2 language proficiency, at least with intermediate and advanced learners of English (Cumming, 1989). In other words, while language proficiency may have an additive effect on the quality of a text, language proficiency in and of itself appears to be an independent factor in the students' ability to write well in L2. Expert L2 writers with less language proficiency are not impeded in their use of global cognitive strategies in writing by their lesser ability in language; by the same token, inexperienced writers with greater fluency in English are not able to tap into more effective writing processes by virtue of their greater proficiency in English. It is not at all unusual for ESL students, particularly immigrant students, who are quite fluent in spoken English to have trouble writing. After all, being a native English speaker does not guarantee an ability to write. But more importantly, this finding implies that to improve their writing, L2 writers do not need more work with language but rather with writing, since *lack* of fluency in English does not appear to impede employment of effective writing strategies—at least not in any fundamental way.[1] It is possible that more attention to language results in less attention to more global writing functions and therefore restricts the amount, though not the quality, of planning that an L2 writer can do (Jones and Tetroe, 1987).[2]

While it might not be obvious how much of their L1 writing ability is available to L2 writers, it does seem intuitively clear that those who never learned effective writing strategies in L1 cannot employ them in L2 despite a great deal of fluency in L2. Like their native English-speaking counterparts, inexperienced ESL writers have more difficulty knowing where their writing is going and keeping larger chunks of meaning in mind as they write. Like basic writers, they appear to use a "what next?" approach to organizing their material (Cumming, 1989; Bereiter and Scardamalia, 1987), stopping at the end of a thought unit and puzzling over what they might add to it. Whether intermediate or advanced users of English, these inexperienced writers seem to attend to details of language use as they compose and, in experimental writing protocols, may refer to learned rules of English grammar or mechanics, relying on Monitor use to push their writing along (Cumming, 1989; Jones, 1985).

For the writing teacher, then, helping inexperienced ESL writers improve their writing should be quite similar to teaching inexperienced native writers. It may be more difficult to determine immediately which ESL writers are proficient writers in their L1s and which are not, but since their writing processes are similar to those of native English speakers, they can probably benefit from many of the same teaching techniques.

DIFFERENCES

The idea that L1 and L2 writing processes are basically similar has now won general acceptance; nevertheless, that important differences also exist seems to be a given among ESL teachers and researchers as well. Thus, as research has evolved in the study of L2 composing processes, the focus is shifting from similarities between L1 and L2 writers to differences. Unfortunately, there is still not very much information on the nature of these differences, and a clear picture of these students' writing processes is only just beginning to emerge.

Studies of cognition as information processing suggest that cognitive resources are limited, and if processing capacity is being used for one function, other functions can only make use of whatever capacity is left over (Bereiter and Scardamalia, 1987). It seems obvious, then, that if students must use part of their cognitive capacity to focus on language because they are not familiar with that language, other functions, perhaps higher functions of organization, cannot be engaged at full capacity. For ESL writers, this may explain research that shows that ESL students who can plan in their L1 can also plan in writing in their L2 but not as extensively or elaborately (Jones and Tetroe, 1987).

Other interesting observations of how L2 writers work and how their strategies differ from those of L1 writers have been uncovered. Bereiter and Scardamalia (1987) noticed that inexperienced writers stopped at the end of sentences to reread what they had written and to puzzle over "What next?" but Raimes (1985) observed some of her inexperienced ESL writers doing something different. They did not stop at the end of sentences but often plunged immediately into the beginning of the next sentence and, once there, ground to a halt, unable either to continue with that sentence or to abandon that beginning. The inflexibility of refusing to abandon a fruitless beginning may be characteristic of basic writers, L1 or L2, but what makes these hesitations different, as Raimes points out, is that they occur at this odd point in the sentence. This suggests that the students have, in fact, decided the direction of the next thought but do not have the means for carrying out their plans. They may be better able to plan than basic writers but less able to put their plans into action.

It is also possible that as these L2 students are writing, their short-term memories are taxed in such a way that they can remember only the first words of their plans for the next sentence, with the gist of the idea slipping away. Commenting on broader concerns of text construction, Freedman, Pringle, and Yalden (1983) assert that "constraints of writing, without full proficiency, in a second language may impose psychological limitations on people's abilities to conceptualize their intended meaning and its organization as discourse" (10).

Another difference observed between ESL students and L1 writers (including ESL students writing in their own L1) is related to word choice. While a teacher looking at a student's writing may see errors in word choice, what is not obvious is the tortured indecision some ESL students display as they try to determine the appropriate word to use in a given context. L1 writers appear to rehearse word choices, listening to how chosen words resonate with the writers' intended meanings and perhaps even developing a different perspective on the intended meaning as a result of what a word brings with it. L2 writers rehearse far less in their L2, even though the very same writers do rehearse in their L1 (Arndt, 1987). Thus, L2 writers are perhaps prevented from using a strategy in L2 which they do use well in L1. No doubt it is the lack of resonance that L2 words have for these writers that precludes rehearsing. Instead, dissatisfied with word choices they have made, yet limited in the alternatives available to them, these students revise their word choices over and over, spending a great deal of time on single words, unable to decide which one of the scant number of choices available to them is the correct or most appropriate one. Clearly, there is no question here of words bringing further, richer possible interpretations of the writers' intentions. Rather, these words stubbornly expose only a fraction of their meanings to L2 writers and force them to struggle in the dark, a struggle that remains hidden from the teacher.

L2 ADVANTAGES

Despite all these added difficulties caused by lack of proficiency in L2, ESL students' proficiency in L1 can also be a resource not available to monolinguals. Many writing protocols have shown ESL students switching to their L1s as they plan and write in English. They may be missing the resonance of words in English, but they can apparently use the resonances which words in their native languages have for them as touchstones to spur their thinking along and to verify the exact meanings they intend. Thus, contrary to popular belief, thinking in the L1 should not necessarily be avoided while composing in L2. Both skilled and unskilled L2 writers have been shown to use this technique to their advantage, even going so far as to write sections of their texts in their L1 and later translate them into English with positive results (Friedlander, 1990; Cumming, 1989; Zamel, 1982).

Yet, regardless of what they may do in practice, some L2 writers, like many language teachers, recommend thinking entirely in English (Zamel, 1982). In fact, the picture appears to be more complicated than simply encouraging or discouraging L1 use in L2 writing. While the use of L1 seems to benefit some writers, the use of L1 by writers more proficient in English may give their writing a foreign sound that they avoid when using only L2 to plan and generate their texts (Lay, 1982). Thus, it simply is not yet clear whether or not writing teachers should recommend a strategy of recourse to L1 for ESL students who are having trouble.

To further complicate the issue of L1 use in L2 writing, research shows that the amount of L1 that ESL students use depends in part on the topic that they are addressing (Burtoff, 1983; Johnson, 1985; Lay, 1982). In these studies, students tended to use L1 more frequently when writing about events that took place during a period when these students were functioning in L1 or when they had originally learned about their topics in L1. Thus, topics which presumably are stored in the students' L1 may be particularly beneficial ones to write on for some students (up to a certain level of English proficiency) and particularly detrimental to write on for other students (more proficient in English).

Inexperienced ESL writers may have other advantages over their native English-speaking counterparts. Early in the study of ESL student composing processes, during the time when researchers were looking for similarities, they expected that one of the great impediments to fluent writing would be, as it is for native writers, a focus primarily on form rather than on meaning. Later studies did reveal that when L2 writers focus on form, they do so at the expense of meaning. However, surprisingly, it soon became clear that many ESL writers did not, in fact, focus on form nearly as much as it had been assumed. The long pauses between stretches of writing typical of ESL writers turned out to reflect, more often than not, a search for meaning rather than for errors in grammar or mechanics. While ESL students often express a desire to write error-free English (Leki, 1991), they apparently do not allow a concern with error to prevent their plugging away at meaning. Clearly, error is simply not as stigmatizing for ESL students writing in an L2 as it is for native English-speaking basic writers writing in L1;

even inexperienced ESL writers are able to focus on meaning. In fact, errors may be so much less stigmatizing for ESL students that they may not bother to edit carefully, simply expecting their teachers to correct their errors (Raimes, 1985; Radecki and Swales, 1988).

Perhaps for this reason, ESL writers feel freer to write, and, as a result, in research situations, have produced more text than might have been expected given what basic writers produce under similar conditions. In one study, although ESL writers typically produced only one draft of a piece of writing under experimental conditions whereas native basic writers produced several, the ESL writers produced more words and spent more time working than their native speaker colleagues (Raimes, 1985). Raimes concludes that ESL students generally exhibit a great deal of commitment to the task of learning to write, and learning English, a conclusion many classroom teachers would attest to as well.

But to produce the numbers of words that they manage, L2 writers need considerably more time than native speakers need. The students in Raimes's study (1985) did not use this time to edit at the micro-text level or to revise at the macro-text level by producing multiple drafts. ESL students seem to be using their time to formulate ideas in their L2, "to marshal the vocabulary they need to make their own background knowledge accessible to them in their L2" (Raimes, 1985, 250), and to allow meanings of words to resonate with meanings they intend. If this is the case, single drafts and long pauses while writing perhaps do not need to be remedied through the fluency exercises used to encourage native English-speakers to write rapidly and continuously, forgetting concerns about textual details for the sake of meaning. ESL students are already attending to meaning. But their single drafts may suggest that their language limitations make it "more problematic to write a lot, to sustain the effort of writing, and to analyze the product in order to make changes" (250). Thus, they need more time; in fact, Raimes (1985) concludes that ESL students need more of everything: more time, more contact with English, more opportunity to read and write (248).

L2 DIVERSITY

Research into the composing processes of ESL students provides one more particularly interesting, and perhaps curious, finding that seems to distinguish these writers from native English-speaking writers whose composing processes have been observed. While researchers into the composing processes of native English writers have been able to differentiate between experienced and inexperienced L1 writers based on patterns of strategies they use to produce text, with L2 writers the picture appears more complex and varied. Unlike Perl's (1979) inexperienced L1 writers, who showed a great deal of similarity in the writing strategies they exhibited, the composing behaviors of Raimes's (1985) inexperienced L2 writers were not consistent. Some wrote recursively, some did not; some reread their texts many times, others did not (one reread her text three times, for example, another fifty-one times) (249). Furthermore, a study of post-graduate Chinese students revealed that while they were all able to use L1 writing strategies in English writing, they employed very different strategies (Arndt, 1987). One created an elaborate plan before beginning to write; another was an emergent planner (Cumming, 1989), thinking through his ideas as they appeared before him on the page; another continuously tested and altered what was appearing on the page to make it conform to intentions which she apparently kept in her head; still another wrote fluently and easily, changing her text while rereading what she had written rather than while writing

(Arndt, 1987, 261). In other words, while it may be possible to make some generalizations about composing patterns of L2 writers, as yet it seems that we do not know enough about them to be able to characterize them with much confidence, exactitude, or completeness.

This inability to characterize L2 writers may well be less a reflection of actual diversity (although they are surely diverse) than a quirk of the research conducted to date on L2 composing processes. Findings are inconclusive and sometimes contradictory because most composing process research has been based on case studies focusing on very few students, probably only a total number of between 100 and 150 (Krapels, 1990, 50). If fairly wide variations are seen in small groups of six to eight students, 100 or 150 subjects are probably not enough to show dominant patterns rather than individual variations. (For a review of composing process studies, see Krapels, 1990; for a critique of L2 composing process studies, see Silva, 1989). In any case, one pattern does emerge fairly clearly from this research: L2 writers are not entirely different from L1 writers at the same level of competence in writing, nor are they exactly the same. In terms of pedagogy, then, it appears that we can and should use successful techniques from L1 writing classes to teach writing to L2 students, *but* we also need to keep in mind that these techniques may need to be adjusted for ESL students. And certainly, notions about how much ESL students can accomplish in a given period of time must remain flexible—how much an L2 writer can produce, how long it will take to produce that amount, and, most importantly, how long it will take L2 writers to show improvement both in language and in writing.

ESL STUDENTS' PERCEPTIONS OF WRITING IN ENGLISH

Another relatively untouched area of L2 writing research is the differences ESL students themselves perceive between writing in their first and second languages, yet this information can potentially help writing teachers make the task of writing in L2 easier. In discussing writing in English, Silva's (forthcoming[3]) ESL students, sophisticated and articulate in their L1s, poignantly voice their frustration at the mismatch between their sense of their writing prowess in their L1s and the inadequacy and inferiority of what they can accomplish in English. Commenting on writing in their L1s, these students say:

> Writing in Chinese is just as easy as talking. (1)
>
> My sentences, just like the ink in my pen, come out naturally. (6)
>
> When I write texts in Chinese, I can choose different words to
> express [the] same meaning, depending on my feeling and mood. (12)

Students say that they can concentrate on the topic, style, and text structure in L1, that they write long, complex sentences. None of this is true for these students writing in English.

Instead, they express disappointment that they must focus on finding the right words, forms, and word orders in English and that they must sometimes resort to writing out complex ideas in their L1 and then translating this text into English. In English, writing is more "time consuming . . . less fluent . . . less sophisticated (with simpler words [and] shorter [, simpler] sentences) and less expressive of the writers' thoughts and intentions" (5).

Lack of vocabulary plagues these students. One avoids unfamiliar words for fear of choosing incorrectly, fully aware that, as a result, "the article becomes wordy and powerless" (5). Others lament that they do not know the connotations of words, their nuances in English, and that their "deeper meanings" are then neglected. They have problems with idioms and exceptions. One student sadly admits: "I have to give up some good ideas for I can not find the available words" (12). This problem of limited vocabularies comes into perspective better when we consider that "the average English native speaker college student has a passive reading and listening vocabulary of around 150,000 words. It would take bilingual learners [i.e., ESL students] four years to acquire such a passive vocabulary *if* they could learn forty words a day 365 days a year! Most researchers claim students can learn around seven new words per day" (Murray, 1989, 77).

Beyond the problem of a generally small vocabulary, these students also face the problem of a limited range of vocabulary. Arndt's students (1987) complained that the only English they had been exposed to was technical textbook English; although they were fairly proficient users of this English, their exposure to English was narrow, resulting in inability to discriminate between and exploit varying registers of language. Murray's bilingual immigrant students (1989) experienced the same problem in the opposite direction. They were quite fluent in the everyday English language use of the street but had had little exposure to academic or technical uses of English. (This fact is yet another reason not to assume that the length of time spent in an English-speaking country correlates well with a student's writing, or even language, abilities.)

Sometimes rather than simply expanding on what they already know about writing by learning more, these ESL students face the chore of unlearning previously successful strategies. For one student (Silva, forthcoming), the first thing that comes to mind when beginning an assignment is an appropriate proverb, yet he knows that proverbs are not typically found in academic English writing; another naturally gravitates towards parables but realizes that these are difficult to translate into English and that even if translation were possible, the parables would not have the same effect.

These students see clearly that their relationship with their audience is transformed by writing in English. One student says she cannot write well for her English readers because she does not know much about them (5); another says she does not feel she shares a common understanding with them (7); still another consistently feels unsure about the level of formality to adopt with her L2 audience (9). Again, often their culturally induced inclinations about how to communicate appropriately with their audience must be resisted. A Chinese audience would expect "citations of historical events" rather than data and rational arguments to support a point (7). A Japanese audience expects diffidence, indirectness:

> For example, when I write an application letter to the scholarship committee as an English assignment, I wrote "I would be a successful student." In Japan I could never say such a thing. To appeal directly has almost an opposite effect. (7)

> [In business letters, Japanese writers] have a tendency to write unnecessarily long and formalized introductory remarks, in which they humble themselves and state as often as they can that they are not able to write their essay and thank as many people as they can. Japanese simply go through the introductory remarks, but this confuses American people because they question why this author is writing this essay if he thinks he is not able to write the essay. (10)

Another student finds English writing crude and complains in frustration:

> The kind of writing the teacher wants . . . is stupid. It is so childish. All he wanted was example example example, concrete, concrete, concrete. . . . . I can't understand why the reader cannot infer? Why do we have to be so obvious? (News letter et al., 1989)

Silva finds that, in general, these students have fewer options, sometimes feeling that their only sense of security comes from what they have learned about grammar.[4] One student remarks: "Grammar is the only tool that I can use in writing English essays"(6). Even understanding an assignment takes more time than it would in L1 (4). These students know that writing in an L2 imposes additional burdens. What they can handle with ease in L1, like ink coming out of a pen, becomes an irritating obstacle in L2, perhaps something like a right-handed person suddenly having to eat, write, and manipulate objects of all kinds with only the left hand.

As a result of this added burden, students often express their frustration at the relationship between the amount of time they require to complete academic tasks and the quality of their final products. They complain that even though they begin academic assignments in plenty of time, they often feel pressed to finish the work by the deadline and may not have time to review it (Jones, 1985). While the students themselves may recognize that the quality of some piece of work is not up to their own normal standards of excellence, they nevertheless experience keen disappointment when their work, which has required so much time and effort, is evaluated by a teacher as weak or inadequate.

CONCLUSION

Hidden behind the texts that ESL students produce is once again the great diversity of the ESL student population. Krapels (1990) points out: "The L2 composition class may represent at least half a dozen strikingly different cultures, very different educational backgrounds, ages ranging from sixteen to sixty, and very different needs for being able to write in a foreign language" (45). Their composing processes differ to some degree from those of L1 writers and apparently from those of other L2 writers as well. We know little about the composing processes of students for whom English may be a third or fourth language and what further complications, benefits, or strategies these additional languages account for.

When ESL students appear in writing classes, it is difficult to know exactly how much training in writing they have received in their L1 or how expert they may be at writing in their L1. Little research has been reported on writing strategies in other languages, and to some degree, composing process researchers have assumed a universal of good writing strategies. Can we count on that universality as we teach our students to write? That is, if students are experienced in writing in their L1s, could this experience itself prove to be a complicating element in their writing in L2?

If ESL students are placed into writing classes based on language proficiency, we may have some picture of their language abilities, but these abilities are not unambiguously correlated to writing abilities. Fluency in language may be obscuring lack of experience with writing and even lack of cognitive academic development, a particular problem for some immigrant students; or, on the other hand, lack of fluency in English may mislead us into underestimating a student's writing abilities and experience.

However diverse these students may be, L2 writing research shows that L2 students share a need for more time to accomplish their writing tasks. If ESL students need more time than native students to accomplish the same task, they are obviously expending more energy than their native English-speaking classmates are. It is probably the need to expend more time and energy on both reading and writing, and probably on listening and speaking as well, which puts ESL students at the greatest disadvantage in English-medium classes with native speakers. If ESL students are going to have any chance at all of surviving in writing classes, writing teachers need to remain sensitive to the excess burden placed on ESL students working in English. What might be a reasonable time limit within which native students can be expected to complete a reading or writing assignment is most likely *unreasonable* for ESL students, whether in or out of class. If it seems reasonable for native speakers to be able to produce five essays or 3,000 words in a semester, the same requirement for ESL students is clearly unfair since the ESL students must expend more time, effort, and energy to accomplish the same tasks. Extending time limits or reducing work loads, far from lowering standards, as some fret, merely creates more equalized working conditions. If no other accommodation to the special needs of L2 writers can be made, at the very least, extension of time limits and reduction of work loads for ESL writers, experienced or inexperienced, are absolutely essential adjustments.

NOTES

1. It should be noted, however, that increased proficiency in L2 benefited average writers more than it did either experienced or basic writers, although the effect was still additive rather than indicative of qualitative changes in students' thinking about writing (Cumming, 1989).

2. Evidence from reading research suggests that there is a threshold of L2 proficiency which a learner must have attained in order to be able to make use of good L1 reading strategies (Clarke, 1979). In other words, beginning learners of English who are good readers in their L1s cannot make use of those good reading strategies until they have advanced in their English proficiency. However, Hudson (1982) points out that, just as L2 proficiency can limit the use of good L1 reading strategies, good L1 reading strategies can limit the restrictive effects of lack of L2 proficiency; these two elements, language proficiency and good reading strategies, share a symbiotic relationship.

   For writing, it is not clear how a linguistic threshold might function, however, since not enough research on writing has addressed beginning language learners. An essential difference between reading and writing, especially for the L2 learner, is that in writing the learner controls the language whereas in reading the learner must deal with whatever language appears in the text. As a result, writing at these beginning stages may actually be easier than reading, however counter-intuitive that may seem.

   The question of L2 reading is beyond the scope of this book. Furthermore, most writing teachers are not also reading teachers and are busy enough simply addressing writing problems. But the connection between reading and writing ability is as pertinent in L2 as it is in L1 (see Carson and Leki, 1994).

3. All page number cites are to the pre-publication manuscript.

4. Campbell (1990) finds this insecurity expressed in another domain. In a summary writing assignment, the L2 writers she studied were more dependent on the original text than were the L1 writers. Her L2 students may have felt they could not presume to write better than what was already written, or they may simply not have known other options for expressing the ideas in the original text.

REFERENCES

Arndt, V. 1987. Six writers in search of texts: A protocol-based study of L1 and L2 writing. *ELT Journal* 41:257–267.

Bereiter, C. and M. Scardamalia. 1987. *The psychology of written composition.* Hillsdale, NJ: Lawrence Erlbaum.

Burtoff, M. 1983. The logical organization of written expository discourse in English: A comparative study of Japanese, Arabic, and native speaker strategies. Unpublished doctoral dissertation, Georgetown Univ.

Campbell, C. 1990. Writing with others' words: Using background reading text in academic compositions. In *Second language writing,* ed. B. Kroll. New York: Cambridge.

Carson, I. and I. Leki. 1994. *Reading in the composition classroom: Second language perspectives.* Boston: Newbury House.

Clarke, M. A. 1979. Reading in Spanish and English: Evidence from adult ESL students. *Language Learning* 29:121–150.

Cumming, A. 1989. Writing expertise and second language proficiency. *Language Learning* 39:81–141.

Freedman, A., I. Pringle, and J. Yalden, eds. 1983. *Learning to write: First language/second language.* New York: Longman.

Friedlander, A. 1990. Composing in English: Effects of a first language on writing in English in a second language. In *Second language writing,* ed. B. Kroll. New York: Cambridge.

Hudson, T. 1982. The effects of induced schemata on the "short circuit" in L2 reading: Non-decoding factors in L2 reading performance. *Language Learning* 32:1–31.

Johnson, C. 1985. The composing process of six ESL students. *Dissertation Abstracts International* 46(5):121A.

Jones, S. 1985. Problems with monitor use in second language composing. In *When a writer can't write,* ed. M. Rose. New York: Guilford Press.

Jones, S. and J. Tetroe. 1987. Composing in a second language. In *Writing in real time,* ed. A. Matsuhashi. New York: Longman.

Krapels, A. R. 1990. An overview of second language writing process research. In *Second language writing,* ed. B. Kroll. New York: Cambridge.

Lay, N. 1982. Composing processes of adult ESL learners: A case study. *TESOL Quarterly* 16:406.

Leki, I. 1991. Preferences of ESL students for error correction in college-level writing classes. *Foreign Language Annals* 24(3):203–218.

Murray, D. E. 1989. Teaching the bilingual writer. In *The writing teacher's manual,* ed. H. P. Guth. Belmont, CA: Wadsworth.

Perl, S. 1979. The composing processes of unskilled college writers. *Research in the Teaching of English* 13:317–336.

Radecki, P. M. and J. Swales. 1988 ESL students' reaction to written comments on their written work. *System* 16:355–365.

Raimes, A. 1985. What unskilled writers do as they write: A classroom study. *TESOL Quarterly* 19:229–258.

Silva, T. Forthcoming. L1 vs L2 writing: Graduate students' perceptions. *TESL Canada.*

———.1989. A critical review of ESL composing process research. Paper presented at TESOL Conference, San Antonio.

Zamel, V. 1983. The composing processes of advanced ESL students: Six case studies. *TESOL Quarterly* 17:165–187.

———.1982. Writing: The process of discovering meaning. *TESOL Quarterly* 16:195–209.

Follow-Up Questions and Activities

1. Analyze and discuss the differences you perceive between writing in your native language and in a second language. What are the implications for teaching? What strategies can the L2 writing teacher learn from the L1 writing teacher?

2. If you are currently teaching writing, keep a journal. Respond to the success or failure of a particular teaching activity and share it with the class.

3. Discuss your main goals in teaching writing.

4. Corbett says, "It is debatable whether the creation of those courses and programs [in rhetoric] encouraged the production and the publication of certain kinds of textbooks or whether the publication of certain kinds of textbooks fostered the development of the courses and programs." Write an essay discussing the relationship between textbooks and courses or programs in rhetoric. You may want to take an historical approach to this topic.

5. In her discussion of writing instruction in the 1970s, Raimes states that "Zamel . . . has recommended that teachers not present instruction in the use of thesis sentences and outlines before the students have begun to explore ideas." Write an essay explaining your stance on this issue.

6. Raimes states, "One thorny issue here is whether we should put our trust in this [the academic] community, or whether we shouldn't rather be attempting to influence and change the academic community for the benefit of our students, while teaching our students how to interpret the community values and transform them." Write an essay discussing your views on this dilemma.

7. Leki states that a "relatively untouched area of L2 writing research is the differences ESL students themselves perceive between writing in their first and second languages." Conduct a study that explores the ways in which ESL students view their L1 and/or L2 writing.

2

WRITING AND READING

EDITOR'S INTRODUCTION

The importance of the relationship between writing and reading is becoming increasingly recognized by first language (L1) and second language (L2) theorists. Patricia L. Carrell discusses this relationship in the first essay of this chapter. She points out the usefulness, for example, of having ESL students learn about the different ways in which expository texts can be rhetorically organized and about how to signal the organization of their texts through appropriate linguistic cues. The significance of the writing/reading relationship is also reflected in the "fluency first" approach. According to this approach, students focus on "fluency" in writing and reading before they concern themselves with grammatical accuracy in their writing. Adele MacGowan-Gilhooly defines fluency as "the ability to generate one's ideas in writing intelligibly and with relative ease." Students at the beginning stages of writing achieve this fluency by engaging in massive amounts of writing and reading. Although students receive help from their peers and teachers, their work is not corrected, nor are they given grammar instruction. It is only in more advanced classes that greater attention is given to matters of organization and clarity.

Prereading Questions

1. What role did reading play in your early life? Do you think that it influenced your ability to write or your interest in writing?

2. Do you think error correction in L2 writing should be postponed until students become fairly fluent in reading and writing? Why or why not?

Text as Interaction: Some Implications of Text Analysis and Reading Research for ESL Composition

PATRICIA L. CARRELL *Southern Illinois University*

TEXT ANALYSIS AS COMMUNICATIVE INTERACTION

A number of different approaches have been taken to the analysis of texts. Many researchers have been hard at work trying to understand the fundamental properties of texts, and some theoretical accounts of text have been proposed. Often these accounts have been in terms of linguistic theories of text—i.e., textual analysis techniques which parallel sentence analysis techniques. These approaches are even sometimes called text "grammars." Among others to attempt a linguistic type of analysis of connecting discourse or text have been the American structuralist Charles Fries (1952), the first American transformationalist Zellig Harris (1970), and the tagmemicists Kenneth Pike (1967) and Robert Longacre (1968, 1972). More recently, the properties of texts have been examined in terms of the linguistic property of cohesion (Halliday and Hasan 1976; Hasan 1978). (For a critique of cohesion as the sole explanation of textuality, see Morgan and Sellner 1980; de Beaugrande and Dressler 1981; Carrell 1982, 1983a, 1984a; Mosenthal and Tierney 1983.)

Other text analysis systems that have emerged have a psychological rather than a linguistic basis; they view texts in terms of the psychological processes involved in producing and comprehending them. For example, Kintsch's (1974) propositional system was the basic tool used in the development of Kintsch and van Dijk's (1978) concept of *macrostructure* and its role in a theory of discourse comprehension and production. The story grammars, especially of Stein and Glenn (1979) and Mandler and Johnson (1977), strongly predict comprehension of narrative text based on a text's adherence to the canonical ordering of story parts. Likewise, Meyer's (1975a) research on the content structure of expository text has shown the importance of the top-level rhetorical organization of a text to the reader's comprehension.

One of the most promising approaches to text analysis is the one taken by de Beaugrande (1980; de Beaugrande and Dressler 1981), which draws heavily on a view of text as communicative interaction. de Beaugrande argues that texts cannot be studied via mere extension of linguistic methodology to the domain of texts. A purely linguistic analysis of texts—a grammar for texts, with texts viewed simply as units larger than sentences, or

From *"Text as Interaction: Some Implications of Text Analysis and Reading Research for ESL Composition"* by P. Carrell, 1987. In U. Connor and R. Kaplan (Eds.), Writing Across Languages: Analysis of L2 Text, pp. 47–56. Reading, MA: Addison-Wesley Publishing Company.

sequences of sentences—is doomed to failure. de Beaugrande argues that in order to understand texts we must study them as they function in human interaction. The central notion of de Beaugrande's work is that *textuality*—what makes a text a unified, meaningful whole rather than just a string of unrelated words and sentences—lies not *in* the text *per se* as some independent artifactual object of study, but rather in the social and psychological activities human beings perform with it. Taking the position that real communicative behavior can be explained only if language is modelled as an interactive system, de Beaugrande proposes a procedural approach to the study of texts in communication. A text is viewed as the *outcome* of procedural operations and, as such, cannot be adequately described and explained in isolation from the procedures humans use to produce and receive it. Those interested in more ideas of text as communicative interaction, text as the outcome of human problem-solving procedures, are referred to the writings of de Beaugrande (1980; de Beaugrande and Dressler 1981) and to a review of de Beaugrande and Dressler (Carrell 1984c).

READING RESEARCH: MORE ON COMMUNICATIVE INTERACTION

Closely related to the research on text analysis in terms of comprehension and production processes (in fact, the other side of the same coin) is the study of reading comprehension. Recent research in reading comprehension has clearly shown its dynamic, interactive nature. What a reader understands from a text is not solely a function of the linguistic or even hierarchical structure of the text. Reading comprehension is not solely an analysis problem, a bottom-up process of constructing meaning from the linguistic cues in the text. Rather, reading comprehension is an interactive process between the content and formal, hierarchical structure of the text and the reader's prior knowledge structures, or schemata, for content and form. Reading comprehension is simultaneously both a top-down and a bottom-up process. It is bottom-up in the sense that readers must take in the linguistic cues of the text and integrate them into their ongoing hypotheses about the content and form of the text; it is top-down in the sense that readers must formulate hypotheses, expectations, anticipations, based on their background knowledge of content and form (Rumelhart 1977, 1980).

Thus, the recent research on text analysis and on reading comprehension has shown the important role played by the mental representation of a text formed in the mind of the reader (Meyer 1982). This representation is not identical to the text itself, but is rather the product of the interactive process between the text and the reader (Rumelhart 1980). A better understanding of what the mental representation of a text is and how it is formed in long-term memory has implications for text production, or composition, as well. For example, these recent insights into text comprehension should help us understand the composition process better and, thence, as Meyer suggests, "should help writers plan texts which will enable their readers to create representations which better match the writer's purpose in communication" (1982, p. 37).

Based on the foregoing theoretical preamble, I should now like to discuss some specific empirical research results on the relationship of text structure and reading comprehension and suggest some implications of those findings for ESL composition, or ESL text production. I shall be drawing these findings most particularly from the research of Meyer and her colleagues and students (Meyer 1975a, 1977; Meyer, Brandt, and Bluth 1982; Meyer and Rice 1982; Meyer and Freedle 1984).

However, before discussing Meyer's research findings and their implications for ESL composition, I would like to mention briefly a related reference in which the application of schema theory to ESL composition is proposed. I will not discuss this paper, but because it falls into the same general area of applying schema-theoretical notions of text processing to ESL composition, I would like to mention it. This is a recent paper by Alptekin and Alptekin (1983) on the role of *content* schemata in ESL composition. My focus here is not content schemata, but rather formal rhetorical schemata (see Carrell 1983b for discussion of content versus formal schemata).

EMPIRICAL READING RESEARCH AND IMPLICATIONS FOR ESL COMPOSITION

In her research on the interaction of the rhetorical structure of a text and reading comprehension, Meyer (1975a, 1982) has gathered empirical evidence that five different types of expository text structures affect reading comprehension. These five basic types are called: *causation, comparison, problem/solution, description,* and *time-order.* She does not claim that these five types are either exhaustive or definitive, but rather that they represent significantly distinctive types. Briefly, the *causation* structure develops a topic as a cause-effect relationship. The *comparison* structure develops a topic in terms of opposing or contrasting viewpoints. The *problem/solution* structure develops a topic as a problem and a solution, a remark and a reply, or a question and an answer. The *description* structure develops a topic by presenting a collection of descriptions—e.g., of its component parts or its attributes. Finally, the *time-order* structure develops a topic in terms of events or ideas in chronological order. Using these five types of text structure, Meyer and her colleagues have studied the effects of rhetorical organization on native English speakers' reading comprehension.

In one study, ninth graders each read two texts, one written with the *comparison* structure, the other with the *problem/solution* structure. In analyzing the recall protocols these students wrote immediately after reading and again a week later, Meyer found that if the students organized their recalls according to the text's structure, they remembered far more content, retaining not only the main ideas especially well, even a week after reading, but also recovering more details. These students also did better on a true/false test on the content of the passage, and they were also the students who had demonstrated good reading comprehension skills on standardized tests. Conversely, those who did not use the text's structure to organize their recalls tended to make disorganized lists of ideas, so that they recovered neither the main ideas nor the details very well. These also were the students who scored poorly on the standardized reading tests. Meyer has conducted similar studies with older readers, including university undergraduates, with the same results.

In a recent ESL study (Carrell 1984a), results similar to Meyer's were obtained. Using expository texts that conveyed the same content, but that structured that content with either a *comparison, problem/solution, causation,* or *description* top-level rhetorical organization, it was found that the ESL readers who organized their recalls according to the structure of the text version they read recalled significantly more ideas from the original text than those who did not use the structure of the original text to organize their recalls.

Meyer and one of her graduate students (Bartlett 1978) went on to show that the relationship between use of the text's structure in organizing one's recall of the text is not only highly correlated with the amount of information recalled, but causative. Bartlett spent a week teaching a group of ninth graders to identify and use four of the five types of top-level text structures (all but the *time-order* type). This group read and was tested for recall of texts on three occasions: before training, a day after training, and three weeks after instruction. A control group did the same tasks but received no instruction about the text types. The trained group remembered nearly twice as much content from the texts after their instruction (both one day after and three weeks after) than they could before. And on the tests after instruction, the trained group did twice as well as the control group. Moreover, the classroom teacher in the experimental group wrote a follow-up letter sometime after the experiment attesting to the lasting effects of the instruction on the reading comprehension and recall behavior of his students.

There are two types of implications of these results. First are the implications of reading instruction—namely, that ESL reading instruction might profitably be geared to the identification of text structure so that readers can effectively learn and remember the materials they study. Carrell (1984b) reviews a number of studies which have shown that teaching various aspects of text structure can facilitate reading comprehension for native English readers. That paper also describes a training study currently in progress designed to address the same question for ESL readers—namely, can we facilitate ESL reading comprehension by teaching text structure? Therefore, no more about Meyer's implications for ESL reading instruction will be said here.

Second, however, are the parallel implications for ESL composition—namely, a need for ESL writing instruction to teach writers the various types of structures so that they learn how to structure the texts they produce to offer readers this support. Meyer's studies all suggest that composition teachers who assign papers that describe, compare, raise problems and suggest solutions, and so forth, are on the right track. However, these studies also suggest that students may need to be explicitly and effectively taught about such rhetorical text structures. Teaching the identification of text structure apart from content, as well as providing practice in using different text structures on a variety of topics, should provide benefits to ESL writers. However, the appropriate pedagogical research on this topic has yet to be conducted.

Beyond the general importance to writers and readers alike of recognizing and utilizing textual structure, Meyer has also found that different text structures may be more or less effective for different communication goals. For example, Meyer (Meyer, Brandt, and Bluth 1980) found that when the same content was processed in one of the four different text structures, the *descriptive* type of organization was the least effective in facilitating recall when people read a text for the purpose of remembering it; readers of the *comparison* and *causation* versions did better on recall (immediately and a week later) and on answering questions. Again, similar results were obtained for both ninth graders and adult native English-speaking readers.

The ESL study previously mentioned (Carrell 1984a) found a pattern similar to Meyer's. Expository texts conveying the same basic content but organized with a *comparison, problem/solution,* or *causation* top-level structure were better recalled by ESL readers than were texts with a *description* type of organization. ESL readers who read versions of the text with one of the first three types of top-level organization recalled significantly more ideas than did ESL readers who read the version with the *description* type of organization. This was true of both their immediate recalls, and of delayed recalls written 48 hours later.

In yet another study, using a text that contained both *comparison* and *time-order* information, but in two versions, one emphasizing the *comparison* structure, and the other emphasizing the *time-order* structure, Meyer (1982) found that although the total amount of information recalled did not differ when readers used one or the other of these text's structures to organize their recall, there was a big difference in the *kinds* of information remembered. Readers who identified and used the *comparison* structure tended to remember causal and comparative relationships and related the content in this manner, but recalled few specific facts—e.g., names and historical events. By contrast, readers who recognized and used the *time-order* structure in their recalls tended to remember the specific facts very well, but recalled less of the information that was closely related to the comparative, causal logic in the text. Thus, Meyer's research shows that different textual structures will yield different effects on readers; a writer may achieve different goals with readers by using different structures. This evidence suggests that giving writers explicit instruction in how to structure texts differentially according to the goals of a particular communication ought to lead to more effective written communication; i.e., writers ought to be able to achieve their goals.

Other aspects of Meyer's research findings on reading which have implications for composition are the effects of (1) the hierarchical structure of a text, and (2) the linguistic signals used to communicate that hierarchy. First, related to the hierarchical structure of a text, Meyer's research (1975a; as well as that of Kintsch and van Dijk 1978; Mandler and Johnson 1977) has shown that the hierarchical content structure of a text plays an important role in reading comprehension and reading recall. Research with various text materials, readers, and tasks has generally indicated that content at the top of the hierarchy—the superordinate information in the text—is better recalled and retained over time than content at lower levels. One explanation of this may be that readers make heavier use of the top-level superordinate content, calling it to mind frequently during reading as they try to tie in the larger amounts of subordinate details coming from the text. Thus, this top-level content gets rehearsed more frequently and is the general frame within which the reader is able to make sense of the entire text.

Recognizing that there is a hierarchy in the content of most texts is obviously what leads many composition teachers to emphasize the use of outlines. An outline can function to keep the writer returning periodically to the high levels of the content hierarchy. Sheetz-Brunetti and Johnson (1983) have proposed the use of simple diagrams (visual outlines, pyramids of boxes with connecting lines) to teach ESL composition skills for one type of English expository prose, the description type. However, directions for outlining are often vague about how various entries lower in the hierarchy are (or should be) related to the top level. Meyer's (1982) reading research has shown that readers often cannot tell whether events are related causally or temporally, and they often cannot tell the difference between the causes and the effects. So writers, especially ESL writers, may need particular help with effective outlining.

Which brings us to the second point previously mentioned—signalling. Meyer's research has found that when writers use express signalling devices to label these hierarchical relationships, there is a facilitating effect on reading comprehension. Signalling—with words like *thus, therefore, consequently, nevertheless, evidence, further details, summary, conclusion*—may aid the reader to detect and use the hierarchical structure. What is particularly interesting about Meyer's empirical findings in this area (Meyer, Brandt, and Bluth, 1980) is that the presence or absence of such signalling devices has apparently little or no effect on the reading recall of ninth grade readers at either end of the proficiency scale—either those who are very good readers or those who are very poor readers. Apparently, very good readers can detect the hierarchical structure and utilize it in recall whether or not overt signalling devices are present. Poor readers, on the other hand, cannot make use of signals, whether they are present or not. However, the presence or absence of signalling expressions does make a difference for middle-ability, average readers. Reading recall for these readers is facilitated when signalling expressions are present in the text. Meyer found a similar effect for readers at the junior college level.

What this research suggests for ESL composition is that if the writer uses one distinct text structure and is aiming for an audience of skilled, well-informed readers, signalling may be dispensed with. Such readers will have no difficulty identifying the proper text structure and using it to organize their comprehension and recall. However, to reach larger audiences of average readers, and in particular audiences of other ESL readers, an ESL writer probably ought to learn to include appropriate uses of signalling expressions to aid readers in organizing their comprehension of the text.

CONCLUSION

In this paper I have described some recent theoretical advances in text analysis from the perspective of text as communicative interaction, and I have taken some empirical research findings from one domain of textual interaction—that is, reading research and the effects of a text's rhetorical structure on reading comprehension—and have suggested some implications of these research findings for a related domain of textual interaction, namely ESL composition. I have briefly reviewed some of the empirical findings of reading research, specifically those of Meyer and her colleagues and students, which appear to have direct implications for ESL composition and instruction in ESL composition. I have suggested that teaching ESL writers about the top-level rhetorical, organizational structures of expository text, teaching them how to choose the appropriate plan to accomplish specific communication goals, and teaching them how to signal a text's organization through appropriate linguistic devices should all function to make their writing more effective.

In suggesting these implications for ESL composition from reading comprehension research, perhaps I have merely stated the obvious. After all, these implications are consonant with related research being conducted directly on the composing process as problem-solving behavior and cognitive planning (Flower and Hayes 1981; de Beaugrande 1982a, 1982b). For those of us who view reading and writing as complementary processes in textual communication, this is to be expected. However, reading research and writing research have often gone in separate directions, and only recently have attempts been made to reunite the two domains within the general framework of cognitive science and from the perspective of text as communicative interaction. Within the general framework of cognitive science, and from the perspective of text as textual communication, findings from the independent investigation of reading and writing—that is, text comprehension and text production—should not only complement and support each other, but, it is hoped, should lead to even more powerful theories of text and textual communication. Within the specific framework of

ESL research and pedagogy, findings from ESL reading comprehension research and ESL composition research should also complement and support each other, leading to more powerful theories of ESL reading and writing, and thence to more effective ESL pedagogy.

Patricia Carrell currently teaches in the Department of Applied Linguistics/ESL at Georgia State University and is the Dean of the College of Public and Urban Affairs.

REFERENCES

Alptekin, C. and M. Alptekin. 1983. The role of content schemata in ESL composition. *TESOL Reporter* 16(4): 63–66.

Bartlett, B. J. 1978. Use of top-level structure as an organizational strategy in prose recall. Arizona State University. Ph.D. diss.

Beaugrande, R. de. 1980. *Text, discourse, and process: Toward a multi-disciplinary science of texts.* Norwood, NJ: Ablex. 45–80.

————. 1982a. Psychology and composition: Past, present, and future. In M. Nystrand (ed.) *What writers know: The language, process, and structure of written discourse.* New York: Academic Press. 211-267.

————. 1982b. *The science of composition: A program for research in theory and method.* Norwood, NJ: Ablex.

———— and W. Dressler. 1981. *Introduction to text linguistics.* London: Longman.

Carrell, P. L. 1982. Cohesion is not coherence. *TESOL Quarterly* 16(4): 479–488.

————. 1983a. Reply to Ghadessy. *TESOL Quarterly* 17(4): 687–691.

————. 1983b. Some issues in studying the role of schemata, or background knowledge, in second language comprehension. *Reading in a Foreign Language* 1(2): 81–92.

————. 1984a. The effects of rhetorical organization on ESL readers. *TESOL Quarterly* 18(3): 441–469.

————. 1984b. Facilitating reading comprehension by teaching text structure: What the research shows. Paper presented at the Eighteenth Annual TESOL Convention, Houston, March.

————. 1984c. Review of Introduction to text linguistics, Robert de Beaugrande and W. Dressler. *Language Learning* 34(1): 111–117.

Flower, L. and J. R. Hayes. 1981. A cognitive process theory of writing. *College Composition and Communication* (32): 365–387.

Fries, C. C. 1952. *The structure of English.* New York: Harcourt.

Halliday, M. A. K. and R. Hasan. 1976. *Cohesion in English.* London: Longman. [English Language Series, No. 9.]

Harris, Z. 1970. *Papers in structural and transformational linguistics.* Dordrecht: D. Reidel.

Hasan, R. 1978. On the notion of a text. In J. S. Petőfi (ed.) *Text vs. sentence.* Hamburg: H. Buske.

Kintsch, W. 1974. *The representation of meaning in memory.* Englewood Cliffs, NJ: Prentice-Hall.

———— and T. A. van Dijk. 1978. Toward a model of text comprehension and production. *Psychological Review* 85: 363–394.

Longacre, R. 1968. *Discourse, paragraph and sentence structure in selected Philippine languages.* Santa Ana, CA: Summer Institute of Linguistics.

————. 1972. *Hierarchy and universality of discourse constituents in New Guinea languages.* Washington, DC: Georgetown University Press.

Mandler, J. M. and N. S. Johnson. 1977. Remembrance of things parsed: Story structure and recall. *Cognitive Psychology* 9: 111–151.

Meyer, B. J. F. 1975a. Identification of the structure of prose and its implications for the study of reading and memory. *Journal of Reading Behavior* 7: 7–47.

————. 1977. The structure of prose: Effects on learning and memory and implications for educational practice. In R. C. Anderson, R.J. Spiro, and W. E. Montague (eds.), *Schooling and the acquisition of knowledge.* Hillsdale, NJ: Erlbaum. 179-200.

————. 1982. Reading research and the composition teacher: The importance of plans. *College Composition and Communication* 33: 37-49.

———— and R. O. Freedle. 1984. The effects of different discourse types on recall. *American Educational Research Journal* 21(1): 121–143.

———— and G. E. Rice. 1982. The interaction of reader strategies and the organization of text. *Text* 2: 155–192.

————, D. M. Brandt, and G. J. Bluth. 1980. Use to top-level structure in text: Key for reading comprehension of ninth grade students. *Reading Research Quarterly* 16: 72–103.

Morgan, J. L. and M. B. Sellner. 1980. Discourse and linguistic theory. In R. J. Spiro, B. C. Bruce, and W. F. Brewer (eds.), *Theoretical issues in reading comprehension*. Hillsdale, NJ: Erlbaum. 165–200.

Mosenthal, J. H. and R. J. Tierney. 1983. Cohesion: *Problems with talking about text: A brief commentary*. Technical report no. 298. Champaign, IL: Center for the Study of Reading, University of Illinois.

Pike, K. L. 1967. *Language in relation to a unified theory of the structure of human behavior*. The Hague: Mouton.

Rumelhart, D. E. 1977. Understanding and summarizing brief stories. In D. La Berge and S. J. Samuels (eds.), *Basic processes in reading*. Hillsdale, NJ: Erlbaum. 265–303.

————. 1980. Schemata: The building blocks of cognition. In R. J. Spiro, B. C. Bruce, and W. F. Brewer (eds.), *Theoretical issues in reading comprehension*. Hillsdale, NJ: Erlbaum. 33–58.

Sheetz-Brunetti, J. and T. Johnson. 1983. Using simple diagrams to teach composition skills. *TECFORS* 6(2): 1–7.

Stein, N. L. and C. G. Glenn. 1979. An analysis of story comprehension in elementary school children. In R. O. Freedle (ed.), *New Directions in discourse processing*. Norwood, NJ: Ablex. 53–120.

Fluency First: Reversing the Traditional ESL Sequence

ADELE MACGOWAN-GILHOOLY *City College, City University of New York*

INTRODUCTION

Too many English as a second language (ESL) students do not achieve their educational goals because they do not meet their colleges' writing standards. Those who evaluate ESL students' writing commonly cite the following problems: (1) lack of fluency or adequate control over the language, including inadequate vocabularies; (2) general lack of knowledge and the consequent inability to write effective pieces; and (3) errors in grammar and the mechanics of writing, despite the fact that most ESL students have had years of instruction in both. One way to address these problems is by reversing the traditional grammar-focused approach to ESL and instead using a whole-language approach, we help ESL students acquire greater fluency and knowledge and thus write more effective, and even more correct pieces.

Freeman and Freeman suggest that the following whole-language principles are important for second language (L2) learning in classrooms: language should be learner-centered; language is best learned when kept whole; language instruction should employ listening, speaking, reading, and writing; language in the classroom should be meaningful and functional; language is learned through social interaction; and language is learned when teachers have faith in learners. This article describes an experimental whole-language approach to ESL writing and reading in an open admissions urban institution serving primarily minority students.

BACKGROUND

The ESL students in question typically have great trouble passing the university's required skills assessment tests (SKAT) in writing and reading, tests which students must pass before taking the bulk of their required courses, even the English composition requirement. Prior to 1988, ESL students' average passing rate on the writing test had been only about 35 percent, and on the reading test, 20 percent.

The ESL faculty had historically taken a traditional instructional approach, stressing grammar and intensive reading and writing (a lot of work on relatively short readings and on writing paragraphs and essays). Yet pass rates had remained low. Then in the fall of 1987, a group of faculty at The City College, CUNY began to use a whole-language approach to literacy. Since then students' writing and reading test scores have improved. We started

From "Fluency First: Reversing the Traditional ESL Sequence" by A. MacGowan-Gilhooly, 1991. Copyright © 1991, Journal of Basic Writing, *Instructional Resource Center, Office of Academic Affairs, The City University of New York. Reprinted from the Spring 1991 issue, Volume 10, Number 1, by permission.*

implementing our approach in ESL 10, our first level ESL reading/writing course for students with a basic knowledge of English but weak reading and writing abilities. The ESL 10 students read several books, responded to them in writing in journals, and wrote 10,000-word, semester-long projects. We ran the classes workshop style, with students helping each other revise their own pieces and understand the books they were reading. We used no ESL textbooks and did not teach grammar in those classes, but students made greater gains than we had ever seen in ESL 10. The approach was so successful that we extended it the following semester into our two upper-level ESL reading/writing courses, ESL 20 and 30. Since then, our SKAT reading test passing rate has doubled and the writing test passing rate has increased by 60 percent, even with only two-thirds of the faculty using the approach.

IMPLICATIONS FROM THEORY AND RESEARCH

First Language (L1) Acquisition

Implications for whole-language approach are plentiful in the research literature. Educators can learn much about how lasting learning occurs from the research on L1 acquisition, not only because it is a language, but because L1 is something which everyone learns by the age of four or five, though it is extraordinarily complex. Macaulay summarizes how children learn L1: by being in the midst of abundant talk, by listening and experimenting with speaking, learning names of things, then phrases, and then the syntax they need to express themselves. They progress in L1 acquisition primarily through massive amounts of interaction with parents or more knowledgeable peers, and they control their own L1 learning. Their knowledge of vocabulary, syntax, and pronunciation expands until they are fluent. The key to L1 acquisition is plentiful interaction with more knowledgeable others. The implication for L2 acquisition in classrooms is to provide similar language input and interaction but, due to time limits, in a far more condensed fashion.

L2 Acquisition

Providing optimal input in the classroom in order to foster the development of L2 fluency does not mean teaching grammar. Krashen (1985) and McLaughlin argue from the research on L2 acquisition that L2 best develops in ways similar to L1: in contexts where the negotiation of meaning, and not the correctness of form, is the central motivating force, and where language exposure is real, extensive, and anxiety free. But in most language classrooms, language exposure is artificial (contrived, practiced, grammatically sequenced), limited, and anxiety arousing.

Krashen (1987) hypothesizes that the best classroom L2 acquisition will occur when the input provided to learners is comprehensible, interesting and/or relevant, not grammatically sequenced, provided in abundant quantity, and in such a way as to promote self-confidence and self-direction while arousing little or no anxiety. After examining popular L2 teaching methods and finding most of them wanting in such input, he concludes that pleasure reading and conversation have the greatest potential for meeting all the requirements for optimal L2 acquisition because they are made up of real input, and not the contrived type of input found in ESL textbooks and tapes. A whole-language approach includes much pleasure reading and real conversation.

Krashen also makes an important distinction between L2 learning and L2 acquisition. L2 learning takes effort, like extensive memorization of rules and practice of forms learned. Then when people try to use these learned forms in real language situations, they often make mistakes and find it difficult to express themselves adequately and even to understand others. L1 is acquired naturalistically through interaction with others, with far less mental effort and with a greater payoff. L2 may be acquired in a similar manner in schools with a whole-language approach. This is true for both children and adults.

McLaughlin explains that early stages of language development involve the same cognitive strategies for adults and children. The difference is that adults have superior memory heuristics that enable longer retention and more facile discovery of meaning. Adults also have more extensive L1 experience, vocabulary, and conceptual knowledge that help them to process information more quickly. And if literate in L1, they have far less work to do in acquiring literacy in L2. They can also learn and apply rules of language more easily, although an overemphasis on correctness can also impede progress in L2 acquisition.

McLaughlin and others who have studied L2 acquisition describe learners' errors in terms of strategies. Thus what seems to be L1 interference or perhaps an inability to master L2 grammar is actually the result of the learner's strategies to discover irregularities and rules in L2. L2 adults make similar mistakes, regardless of what L1 they speak, and these represent unsuccessful attempts to discover L2 rules. They make simplification errors, transfer errors, or overgeneralization errors as they strive to make themselves understood, and they make them for as long a time as it takes for them to develop their competence in L2. This period of development is referred to as the interlanguage stage and needs to be supported by efforts to help the learner communicate intelligibly in L2 before requiring that s/he be correct. To learn to communicate intelligibly requires a great deal of exposure to L2 with the types of input and interaction L1 learners receive.

L1 Literacy Development

The research on the most successful learning of reading and writing in L1 also shows that when learners do abundant reading and writing, talk about both, enjoy both, exercise a good deal of control over both, and are not overly concerned about correctness, literacy development, like L1 acquisition, is enjoyable, successful, and almost effortless. And through an approach such as whole language, learners acquire a good deal of functional language knowledge that otherwise they would have to take great pains to learn: spelling, grammar, vocabulary, appreciation of literature, good composing skills, and good reading skills.

On the elementary level, Holdaway, Graves, Harste, and Smith, among others, have shown how children acquire the skills of literacy when they read and write extensively, talk about language and about what they read and write, have abundant time for independent reading and writing, receive constructive feedback on their writing, ask their own questions, formulate and test their own hypotheses, are not afraid of making mistakes, are encouraged to become serious authors, and are immersed in literate activities across the curriculum. They can control and direct many of these activities themselves.

Branscombe, Atwel, Bartholomae, and Petrosky, and many others on the secondary and postsecondary levels, report similar findings. It appears that students who read extensively and talk about their reading, who become fluent writers before having to focus on correctness (Mayher et al.), and who are writing to learn (Gere; Goswami) become more successful academic readers, writers, and learners.

L2 Literacy Development

As already indicated, research on L2 literacy development also points to the desirability of a whole-language approach, with an emphasis on integrative skills rather than grammar study, memorization, and repetitious exercises. According to Hudelson, language development researchers have concluded that people learn languages by actively participating in an ongoing process of figuring out how language works, and that learners must be in control of this process. Research evidence further suggests that the processes of L1 and L2 acquisition are more similar than different, which in the school setting means that L2 learners are in the process of creative construction of the new language. Errors are a natural part of this process as learners formulate and test hypotheses about the language. There are also significant individual differences in the rate of acquisition; thus a uniformly paced curriculum is of little effectiveness. L2 learners want to use the L2 and work hard to be included in the ongoing activities of the classroom. More knowledgeable others and peers offer important teacher functions in providing comprehensible input and motivation to help L2 learners continue learning English. This is true for both oral and written English (1–3).

Like native speakers, L2 writers creatively construct the written language, develop at their own pace, and control the process. Some will experiment and take risks in creating meaning in writing; others will use familiar patterns for a long time. Investigations have shown that given sufficient encouragement and opportunity, ESL writers will work hard to create meaning, even those without native-like control of English (20–21). ESL learners also construct meaning from print as they read, just as L1 readers do (Carrell et al.).

There have been several studies conducted and hypotheses made about the processes of L2 writing which are very similar to those regarding L1 writing. For example, Edelsky found that the quality of writing is much higher for unassigned topics than for assigned ones in ESL writing. Others have found that personal involvement with a piece also has a positive effect on its quality. Pieces on unassigned topics tend to be better developed and have a personal voice. This is particularly true when there is a real audience, when writers have a stake in the piece, and when it is purposeful. And Urzua found that in writing/reading workshops, as opposed to traditional instruction, L2 writers revise more, develop a personal voice, and become more aware of the power of language. She also found that conferencing influences revising positively.

Hudelson concludes from a review of the research on children's ESL writing that ESL learners, while still learning English, can write. Their texts have many features in common with L1 writers' texts, features indicating that they are making predictions about how the L2 works, and testing and revising their ideas. She recommends a variety of strategies for classrooms, including using diaries and journals to promote fluency in writing and utilizing personal narratives and writing workshop techniques to help learners become comfortable with writing on self-selected topics, and with drafting, sharing, and revising. She also suggests incorporating expressive, literary, and expository writing into meaningful content-area learning.

Likewise, Krashen (1985) recommends using subject matter in L2 as a vehicle of presentation and explanation, but without demands for premature production or full grammatical accuracy. He cites the evidence from the successful language immersion programs in Canada and elsewhere, where teachers incorporate language development into content-area instruction. And in their studies of adult L2 writing, Raimes, Zamel, and others have found that the L2 writing process must begin with abundant opportunities to generate ideas before students focus on editing. They and other researchers in ESL (Krashen 1987; Spolsky) also argue that direct grammar instruction does not generally improve L2 writing or even L2 acquisition. In fact, it probably impedes both processes.

As for L2 reading, Carrell's review of the research shows that L2 reading and L1 reading are currently understood in much the same way: as an active process in which the L2 reader is an active information processor who predicts meaning while sampling only parts of the text. In addition, everything in the reader's prior experience and knowledge plays a significant role in the process of L2 reading (Carrell and Eisterhold). Carrell further explains that L2 reading must involve both the predicting/sampling activities as well as bottom-up processing, or some decoding, to be efficient; thus reading experts now propose an interactive L2 reading model involving both types of processing. And Devine explains that research and experience have shown that reading is a vehicle not only for the development of L2 reading abilities, but for learning L2 as well. Krashen (1989) found that ESL students' vocabulary, writing, and spelling improve through extensive reading, another indication that using the language extensively and for real purposes helps one to acquire more of the language.

Learning theorists like Vygotsky, Britton, and Wells have stressed the interdependence of language and learning, and the fact that lasting learning, intellectual growth, and language are inextricably connected. This too suggests classroom learning contexts where learners learn the language and content through an abundance of language-mediated activities and projects over which they can exert considerable control.

THE NEW ESL APPROACH AT CCNY

Borrowing the terms of Mayher et al., that the ideal sequence in the development of writing would stress fluency first, then clarity, and finally correctness, we made these the respective goals for our three ESL writing/reading courses: ESL 10, 20, and 30.

ESL 10

We defined fluency as the ability to generate one's ideas in writing intelligibly and with relative ease, and to comprehend popular fiction with similar ease. To do this, students were given massive exposure to English. They read 1,000 pages of popular fiction, in books like Ernest Hemingway's *A Farewell to Arms,* Daphne DuMaurier's *Rebecca,* Agatha Christie's *Murder on the Orient Express,* B. B. Hiller's *The Karate Kid,* Daniel Keyes' *Flowers for Algernon,* and Harper Lee's *To Kill a Mockingbird.* They also read autobiographical and biographical works like *Anne Frank: The Diary of a Young Girl,* Russell Baker's *Growing Up,* Louis Fischer's *Gandhi: His Life and*

Message for the World, and William Gibson's *The Miracle Worker.* They had to read about seventy pages a week for homework, copy passages that struck them, and write responses to those passages in their double-entry journals. They then discussed their responses and questions in small groups in class.

The ESL 10 students also worked on a writing project that had to total 10,000 words by semester's end. Most wrote autobiographical pieces consisting of significant chapters or memories in their lives; some wrote family histories. Others wrote of political strife they had lived through and escaped from, or mysteries, love stories, science fiction, or magazines. Each week they drafted a new piece for their "books," as we called them, read them to their partners, and got help from them on making the pieces comprehensible, logical, and interesting. Teachers then gave more of the same kind of feedback for students to consider for final revisions.

Although, at the beginning, many students complained about the amount of work required and the lack of grammar lessons, after a few weeks both students and teachers expressed amazement at how much the students had progressed in such a short time. As students became more involved in their reading and in their writing projects, they also became more engaged in them, often reading beyond assigned pages and writing up to twice as much as required. By semester's end, most were reading and writing fluently and even more correctly than in the beginning, without having received any corrections or grammar instruction. The overall enthusiasm and trust generated by the approach led us to continue with it in ESL 10 and extend it into the second level, ESL 20.

ESL 20

The goal for ESL 20 became clarity, which we defined as the ability to write expository pieces with a clear focus, sufficient support for that focus, logical development of ideas, and effective introductions and conclusions. In ESL 20, students went from narrative and descriptive writing and reading to expository writing and reading, but not in one leap. We wanted to ease them into expository writing, and from reading for pleasure into academic reading, or reading to learn. They began by reading two bestsellers, historical fiction or nonfiction, having to do with the U.S.A., such as Steinbeck's *Grapes of Wrath,* William Styron's *Confessions of Nat Turner, The Autobiography of Malcolm X,* and Studs Terkel's *Working.* As in ESL 10, they responded in writing in double-entry journals and discussed their readings in small groups.

They also wrote a 10,000-word, semester-long project on some aspect of America having to do with its people, history, culture, or problems. The project included letter writing, point-of-view writing, reading and writing about a best-seller on the topic, interviewing an expert and reporting on that, library research, and a term paper. Students reviewed their pieces in a workshop setting, as in ESL 10. And again, by semester's end, most students were writing clearly enough to pass ESL 20.

ESL 30

Those teaching ESL 30, the course at the end of which students have to pass the university's writing exam, reported and continue to report that the students coming out of ESL 20 are now much better writers and readers than those formerly entering ESL 30. Teachers say they now do not have to focus as much on helping their ESL 30 students to compose well, and can concentrate on students' remaining problems with grammar and the mechanics of the language (which are no greater or less than when we used a grammar curriculum) and on getting students ready for the test, which requires them to write a 350-word persuasive piece that is almost error-free in fifty minutes. Thus the two major goals of ESL 30 are correctness and preparation for the test.

In ESL 30, teachers who are committed to the whole-language approach require that students revise their pieces first to be sure they are completely clear, intelligible, and well-written before they focus on correcting them. Once they are sure students can write clear and effective persuasive pieces, they have them begin work on eliminating the largest percentage of their errors by choosing just a few of their most serious and most frequently occurring errors, and looking just for them when they edit. This eliminates the bulk of students' errors without the cognitive overburden of trying to correct every error.

To become strong in argumentative writing, students read newspaper and magazine articles and editorials, write in their journals in response to them, discuss their ideas in small groups, debate the issues both aloud and in silent written debates with partners, and build up a knowledge of current issues and principles involved in them, like civil rights, government policies, domestic and foreign problems, personal values and beliefs, and ethics. Students also freewrite frequently, and write a few essays each week which go through the same process as in ESL 10 and 20: peer review, revising, teacher response, more revising, until the essay is clear and correct enough to satisfy the criteria posed by the writing exam. In the process, students ask many questions in the context of their writing, and then write what they've learned on individualized study lists of spelling words, new vocabulary, useful facts, grammar points they need to focus on, mechanics issues, and style issues.

Some ESL 30 teachers also have students write real letters to newspapers, public agencies, government officials, businesses, and others to complain about an issue and to suggest solutions. We have found that this type of real writing is often the most effective. (For more specifics on classroom activities, materials, and techniques, see MacGowan-Gilhooly "Fluency Before Correctness: A Whole Language Experiment in College ESL." *College ESL* 1.1 (Spring 1991).

Evaluation

Students in ESL 10 and 20 are evaluated at the end of the semester through a timed essay exam with topics relevant to the semester-long projects they have done and the books they have read. But this exam is only one factor in their evaluation. They keep a portfolio with their beginning piece from the first day of the semester, their midterm exam, their final, and three pieces from their projects that they think are their best. The ESL 10 and 20 teachers read each other's students' exams and, if necessary, pieces from students' portfolios, and recommend if the student should pass or repeat the course. Then the teacher bases the grade on the quality of the portfolio pieces, including consideration of the quantity of work completed. ESL 30 students are given the writing exam at the end of the course, and two readers other than the teacher, usually one from the ESL staff and one from the English department, evaluate the essays. Students who do not pass the exam must repeat ESL 30.

ESL 10, 20, and 30 classes utilizing the new approach have these commonalities: a workshop format; peer and teacher help with revisions; massive exposure to real language through extensive reading, writing, and speaking; absence of ESL textbooks; absence of sequenced grammar syllabi or uniform curricula; student control over much of their work; a portfolio system; and teachers helping individuals and small groups rather than leading the whole class.

We follow a uniform approach, or philosophy, but not a static method. Indeed, we are enabled to offer a curriculum that is anything but static. Materials and activities change with new insights; teachers regularly exchange ideas to help students increase their learning; students learn from their interests and work from their strengths; there is a great deal of life in the classroom, as students share their knowledge and expertise with others; and the approach helps students utilize better learning strategies and become more responsible for their own learning.

QUANTITATIVE RESULTS

The quantitative results we have so far have reassured us and the students that we are headed in the right direction. The number of students taking courses using the fluency-first approach is approximately 3,000 so far, with 250 in the fall of 1987 and roughly 600 each semester from spring 1988 through spring 1990. Even though a few teachers of ESL 10 and 20 have stuck to a traditional curriculum, most have used the new approach, and overall, ESL students' reading scores since 1987 have almost doubled. We believe that this rate could be even higher if all were using the approach, and if the test were given after ESL 30 or even later; currently it is given after ESL 21, a reading course students take concurrently with ESL 20.

The writing-test pass rate has gone from 35 percent to 56 percent, which is about the average for native speakers, and there is a much lower course repetition rate for ESL 10 and 20. In addition, more students who start on the ESL 10 level are passing the test. Prior to fall 1987, only 20 percent of those students eventually passed the SKAT. And if the SKAT test were given after some content courses instead of after ESL 30, probably even more students would pass it. But we all know that numbers do not tell the whole story.

QUALITATIVE RESULTS

The most compelling evidence of the success of the approach has been qualitative, with uniformly enthusiastic feedback from teachers, almost universally positive feedback from students, and concrete evidence of improvement in students' written work and reading abilities. On a survey conducted at the end of the second semester in which the new approach was being piloted, teachers reported unprecedented improvement in students' control of English, with growth in fluency occurring very fast. Students typically doubled their production by the fourth week of class. Teachers also reported greater clarity in the way students presented ideas, more daring in their use of new vocabulary, greater ability to write interesting pieces, better reading comprehension and speed, greater enjoyment of reading than in previous ESL courses, and better discussions of readings with students providing insights from their own lives and world views.

Many reported that students' essays had more depth and richness, more fluency, and better grammar, and that all the students progressed more in these courses than in previous ones. Students also showed more growth in the affective domain, specifically more confidence, better ability to work with groups, and more tolerance for divergent views. And cognitively, they were better at analytical thinking, and showed much greater intellectual curiosity. Further, the students who did the most work progressed the most, and students generally were more serious, concentrated, self-reliant, and open to others than in previous semesters when the approach was traditional.

Teachers reported a higher degree of engagement, attention, and time on task. Students were more willing to write and less afraid of it. They also did so much reading and discussion that it gave them a shared experience in which everyone seemed to have an equal footing; this was empowering to students who were less skilled in English. And teachers felt that students gained confidence in themselves as writers and saw themselves as serious writers in this approach; traditional approaches seemed to inhibit experimentation and exaggerate the importance of errors. Before the course, students could not apply rules they had learned to their writing; but after it, it seemed they could. Yet the only grammar instruction they had had was in the context of questions about their own writing as they revised it.

When asked what they would change about the approach, teachers said they needed more time for in-class individual conferences, more lab support in the way of tutors, better techniques for getting the groups to be more independent, and greater evidence that students are learning grammar and mechanics in ESL 10 and 20, even though they can see fewer mistakes as students progress through the courses. Teachers also wanted to do less talking and interfering with students' discussions and their written pieces, because such intervention appeared to lessen students' involvement and creativity. Many ended up not even looking at students' first or second drafts, but responding to the third draft after the student had worked with a peer. However, at that point, teachers said they wanted to give even more helpful responses than they were giving. And they wanted to work more on a one-to-one basis than they had been able to do.

The majority of students believed that they had improved considerably because they could write such long pieces and read so much in such a short time, compared with work done in former courses. They felt the organization of their writing had improved, and said they had greater confidence and control when writing and that they were surprised by how much they could write. They also felt they were better able to develop ideas and liked working on the semester-long writing projects the best. They expressed pride in having read several real novels in English, rather than ones abridged for ESL students, but they felt less sure about their correctness in writing. Many students also said that the course, although focusing on reading and writing, had improved their speaking as well. And a few also commented that their ways of thinking have changed, that they felt Americanized because of the course work and that they liked that feeling.

Students said they wanted more grammar, even though they acknowledged greater growth in this ESL approach than in previous courses in which grammar had received major stress. They also wanted more practice for the final exam. And many students said that the writing demands of the double-entry journals were too great. They also said they were teaching each other too much and maybe the teacher should be teaching them more. In other words, despite their recognition of and satisfaction with their own growth, years of traditional instruction limited their confidence in the approach.

ONGOING RESEARCH

The City College has received a grant from the Fund for the Improvement of Postsecondary Education (FIPSE) to conduct further research on the approach, to train teachers in the theory and techniques used, and to disseminate project findings. The first item on our research agenda is to demonstrate how students' writing improves over time using a whole-language, fluency-first approach, compared with how it develops using a grammar-based approach. And we have many questions to answer, such as whether the pressure to pass the test adversely affects students' development in writing in ESL 30, and how well our students do in later required courses. We also want to experiment with students taking greater control and responsibility in the courses, and with other course themes, activities, projects, and readings.

But what we have already learned is that our students now are acquiring fluency in English along with what Mayher et al. call fluency in the written language, and that this latter fluency is the basis for their becoming competent readers and writers, enough to become successful members of the academy. Thus there are decided implications for such an approach in teaching native speakers of English as well.

REFERENCES

Atwell, Nancie. *In the Middle*. Portsmouth, NH: Heinemann, 1988.

Baker, Russell. *Growing Up*. New York: Penguin, 1982.

Bartholomae, David and Anthony Petrosky. *Facts, Artifacts and Counterfacts*. Upper Montclair, NJ: Boynton/Cook, 1986.

Branscombe, Amanda. "I Gave My Classroom Away." *Reclaiming the Classroom: Teacher Research as an Agency for Change*. Eds. D. Goswami and P. Stillman. Upper Montclair, NJ: Boynton/Cook, 1987.

Britton, James N. *Language and Learning*. London: Penguin, 1970.

Carrell, Patricia. "Introduction: Interactive Approaches to Second Language Reading." *Interactive Approaches to Second Language Reading*. New York: Cambridge UP, 1988.

Carrell, Patricia and J. C. Eisterhold. "Schema Theory and ESL Reading Pedagogy." *TESOL Quarterly 17* (1983): 553–573.

Carrell, Patricia L., Joanne Devine, and David Eskey, eds. *Interactive Approaches to Second Language Reading*. New York: Cambridge UP, 1988.

Christie, Agatha. *Murder on the Orient Express*. New York: Simon, 1934.

Devine, Joanne. "The Relationship between General Language Competence and L2 Reading Proficiency: Implications for Teaching." *Interactive Approaches to Second Language Reading*. Eds. P. Carrell, J. Devine, and D. E. Eskey. New York: Cambridge UP, 1988. 260–277.

DuMaurier, Daphne. *Rebecca*. New York: Doubleday, 1938.

Edelsky, Carole. *Writing in a Bilingual Program: Habia una Vez*. Norwood, NJ: Ablex, 1986.

Fischer, Louis. *Gandhi: His Life and Message for the World*. New York: Penguin, 1954.

Frank, Anne. *The Diary of a Young Girl*. New York: Pocket Books, 1952.

Freeman, Yvonne S. and David E. Freeman. "Whole Language Approaches to Writing with Secondary Students of English as a Second Language." *Richness in Writing: Empowering ESL Students*. Eds. Donna M. Johnson and Duane H. Roen. New York: Longman, 1989.

Gere, Anne Ruggles, ed. *Roots in the Sawdust: Writing to Learn Across the Disciplines*. Urbana, IL: NCTE, 1985.

Gibson, William. *The Miracle Worker*. New York: Bantam, 1959.

Goswami, Dixie. "Writing to Learn." Paper presented at Teaching from Strengths FIPSE Project Workshop, Roxbury Community College, Boston, 1985.

Graves, Donald. *Writing: Teachers and Children at Work.* Portsmouth, NH: Heinemann, 1983.

Harste, Jerome C., Carolyn L. Burke, and Virginia A. Woodward. *Language Stories and Literacy Lessons.* Portsmouth, NH: Heinemann, 1984.

Hemingway, Ernest. *A Farewell to Arms.* New York: Scribners, 1929.

Hiller, B. B. *The Karate Kid.* New York: Scholastic, 1984.

Holdaway, Don. *The Foundations of Literacy.* Sydney: Ashton Scholastic, 1979.

Hudelson, Sarah. *Write On: Children Writing in ESL.* Englewood Cliffs, NJ: Prentice Regents; and Washington, DC: Center for Applied Linguistics, 1989.

Keyes, Daniel. *Flowers for Algernon.* New York: Bantam, 1967.

Krashen, Stephen D. "We Acquire Vocabulary and Spelling by Reading: Additional Evidence for the Input Hypothesis." *The Modern Language Journal* 73 (Winter 1989): 440–464.

———. *Principles and Practice in Second Language Acquisition.* Englewood Cliffs, NJ: Prentice International, 1987.

———. *The Input Hypothesis: Issues and Implications.* New York: Longman, 1985.

Lee, Harper. *To Kill a Mockingbird.* New York: Warner, 1966.

Macaulay, Ronald. *Generally Speaking: How Children Learn Language.* Rowley, MA: Newbury, 1980.

Malcolm X as told to Alex Haley. *The Autobiography of Malcolm X.* New York: Ballantine, 1964.

Mayher, John S., Nancy Lester, and Gordon M. Pradl. *Learning to Write/Writing to Learn.* Upper Montclair, NJ: Boynton/Cook, 1983.

McLaughlin, Barry. *Second Language Acquisition in Childhood: Preschool Children.* Hillsdale, NJ: Erlbaum, 1984.

Raimes, Ann. "What Unskilled ESL Students Do as They Write: A Classroom Study of Composing." *TESOL Quarterly 19* (1985): 229–258.

Smith, Frank. *Joining the Literacy Club.* Portsmouth, NH: Heinemann, 1988.

Spolsky, Bernard. "Bridging the Gap: A General Theory of Second Language Learning." *TESOL Quarterly 22* (1988): 377–396.

Steinbeck, John. *Grapes of Wrath.* New York: Penguin, 1939.

Styron, William. *The Confessions of Nat Turner.* New York: Bantam, 1966.

Terkel, Studs. *Working.* New York: Avon, 1972.

Urzua, Carole. " 'You Stopped too Soon': Second Language Children Composing and Revising." *TESOL Quarterly 21* (1987): 279–304.

Vygotsky, Lev S. *Thought and Language.* Cambridge, MA: MIT P, 1962.

Wells, Gordon. *Learning through Interaction: The Study of Language Development.* United Kingdom: Cambridge UP, 1981.

Zamel, Vivian. "Recent Research on Writing Pedagogy." *TESOL Quarterly 21* (1987): 697–716.

———. "The Composing Processes of Advanced ESL Students: Six Case Studies." *TESOL Quarterly 17* (1983): 165–187.

Follow-Up Questions and Activities

1. Discuss ways in which reading can or should be employed in the writing class. You may want to make this a practical exercise and create a syllabus or lesson plan that includes the use of reading material. Or, you may want to write an essay that justifies from a theoretical point of view the use of reading in the writing class.

2. Do you think instruction in rhetorical form should play a central role in L2 writing instruction? Why or why not?

3. Design a lesson plan or activities in which you teach students the top-level rhetorical structure of expository writing.

4. Design a lesson plan in which you teach students how to incorporate the writing of other people in their own writing, such as for a research paper.

5. Discuss the strengths and/or weaknesses of the "fluency first" approach to writing instruction. Do you agree, for example, that fluency should be achieved in the writing class before giving greater attention to clarity and correctness? You could respond to this with a study of your own, or by citing the relevant literature and/or your personal experience.

6. MacGowan-Gilhooly suggests, following a study by Edelsky, that "the quality of writing is much higher for unassigned topics than for assigned ones in ESL writing." Conduct a study or write an essay in which you explore this hypothesis.

7. According to MacGowan-Gilhooly, teachers should have students "begin work on eliminating the largest percentage of their errors by choosing just a few of their most serious and most frequently occurring errors, and looking just for them when they edit." Conduct a study in which you explore the effectiveness of this approach.

3

WRITING AND READER AWARENESS

EDITOR'S INTRODUCTION

One of the persistent problems that teachers face is how to transform student writing that is "writer-based"—writing that is essentially a record of the student's thought process—into writing that is "reader-based"—writing that fully recognizes the needs of the reader. According to Linda Flower, separating the activity of writing into these two relatively distinct stages can be liberating for both the writing teacher and the student. During the early stages of writing, the writer is free to generate and explore ideas and grapple with the relationships between them; meanwhile, the teacher is free to assist the student in this process without calling the student's attention prematurely to the needs of the reader. The student, and teacher, can then concentrate on transforming this associative, narrative-based prose into writing that takes into account the needs of the reader. Another method that is effective in helping students to overcome or transform writer-based prose is peer group feedback. Through reading, editing, and commenting on the work of their classmates, students get a hands-on lesson in the importance of incorporating reader awareness into their own work. According to Jane Stanley, however, students need training in how to approach the work of their classmates before the full potential of peer group feedback can be realized.

Prereading Questions

1. In your writing, when did you begin to pay more attention to the needs of the reader? Why did this change come about?

2. What experiences have you had with incorporating feedback from your peers in your writing?

Writer-Based Prose: A Cognitive Basis for Problems in Writing

LINDA FLOWER *Carnegie Mellon University*

If writing is simply the act of "expressing what you think" or "saying what you mean," why is writing often such a difficult thing to do? And why do papers that do express what the writer meant (to his or her own satisfaction) often fail to communicate the same meaning to a reader? Although we often equate writing with the straightforward act of "saying what we mean," the mental struggles writers go through and the misinterpretations readers still make suggest that we need a better model of this process. Modern communication theory and practical experience agree; writing prose that actually communicates what we mean to another person demands more than a simple act of self-expression. What communication theory does not tell us is how writers do it.

An alternative to the "think it/say it" model is to say that effective writers do not simply *express* thought but *transform* it in certain complex but describable ways for the needs of a reader. Conversely, we may find that ineffective writers are indeed merely "expressing" themselves by offering up an unretouched and underprocessed version of their own thought. Writer-Based prose, the subject of this paper, is a description of this undertransformed mode of verbal expression.

As both a style of writing and a style of thought, Writer-Based prose is natural and adequate for a writer writing to himself or herself. However, it is the source of some of the most common and pervasive problems in academic and professional writing. The symptoms can range from a mere missing referent or an underdeveloped idea to an unfocused and apparently pointless discussion. The symptoms are diverse but the source can often be traced to the writer's underlying strategy for composing and to his or her failure to transform private thought into a public, reader-based expression.

In *function*, Writer-Based prose is a verbal expression written by a writer to himself and for himself. It is the record and the working of his own verbal thought. In its *structure*, Writer-Based prose reflects the associative, narrative path of the writer's own confrontation with her subject. In its *language*, it reveals her use of privately loaded terms and shifting but unexpressed contexts for her statements.

In contrast, Reader-Based prose is a deliberate attempt to communicate something to a reader. To do that it creates a shared language and shared context between writer and reader. It also offers the reader an issue-centered rhetorical structure rather than a replay of the writer's discovery process. In its language and structure, Reader-Based prose reflects the *purpose* of the writer's thought; Writer-Based prose tends to reflect its *process*. Good writing, therefore, is often the cognitively demanding transformation of the natural but private expressions of Writer-Based thought into a structure and style adapted to a reader.

This analysis of Writer-Based prose style and the transformations that create Reader-Based prose will explore two hypotheses:

1. Writer-Based prose represents a major and familiar mode of expression which we all use from time to time. While no piece of writing is a pure example, Writer-Based prose can be identified by features of structure, function, and style. Furthermore, it shares many of these features with the modes of inner and egocentric speech described by Vygotsky and Piaget. This paper will explore that relationship and look at newer research in an effort to describe Writer-Based prose as a verbal style which in turn reflects an underlying cognitive process.

2. Writer-Based prose is a workable concept which can help us teach writing. As a way to intervene in the thinking process, it taps intuitive communication strategies writers already have, but are not adequately using. As a teaching technique, the notion of transforming one's own Writer-Based style has proved to be a powerful idea with a built-in method. It helps writers attack this demanding cognitive task with some of the thoroughness and confidence that comes from an increased and self-conscious control of the process.

My plan for this paper is to explore Writer-Based prose from a number of perspectives. Therefore, the next section, which considers the psychological theory of egocentrism and inner speech, is followed by a case study of Writer-Based prose. I will then pull these practical and theoretical issues together to define the critical features of Writer-Based prose. The final section will look ahead to the implications of this description of Writer-Based prose for writers and teachers.

INNER SPEECH AND EGOCENTRISM

In studying the developing thought of the child, Jean Piaget and Lev Vygotsky both observed a mode of speech which seemed to have little social or communicative function. Absorbed in play, children would carry on spirited elliptical monologues which they seemed to assume others understood, but which in fact made no concessions to the needs of the listener. According to Piaget, in Vygotsky's synopsis, "In egocentric speech, the child talks only about himself, takes no interest in his interlocutor, does not try to communicate, expects no answers, and often does not even care whether anyone listens to him. It is similar to a monologue in a play: The child is thinking aloud, keeping up a running accompaniment, as it were, to whatever he may be doing."[1] In the seven-year-olds Piaget studied, nearly 50 percent of their recorded talk was egocentric in nature.[2] According to Piaget, the child's "non-communicative" or egocentric speech is a reflection not of selfishness, but of the child's limited ability to "assume the point of view of the listener: [the child] talks of himself, to himself, and by himself."[3] In a sense, the child's cognitive capacity has locked her in her own monologue.

---

[1]Lev Vygotsky, *Thought and Language,* ed. and trans. Eugenia Hanfmann and Gertrude Vakar (Cambridge, Mass.: M.I.T. Press, 1962), p. 15.

[2]Jean Piaget, *The Language and Thought of the Child,* trans. Majorie Gabin (New York: Harcourt, Brace, 1932), p. 49.

[3]Herbert Ginsberg and Sylvia Opper, *Piaget's Theory of Intellectual Development* (Englewood Cliffs, N.J.: Prentice-Hall, 1969), p. 89.

When Vygotsky observed a similiar phenomenon in children he called it "inner speech" because he saw it as a forerunner of the private verbal thought adults carry on. Furthermore, Vygotsky argued, this speech is not simply a by-product of play, it is the tool children use to plan, organize, and control their activities. He put the case quite strongly: "We have seen that egocentric speech is not suspended in a void but is directly related to the child's practical dealings with the real world . . . it enters as a constituent part into the process of rational activity" (*Thought and Language,* p. 22).

The egocentric talk of the child and the mental, inner speech of the adult share three important features in common. First, they are highly elliptical. In talking to oneself the psychological subject of discourse (the old information to which we are adding new predicates) is always known. Therefore, explicit subjects and referents disappear. Five people straining to glimpse the bus need only say, "Coming!" Secondly, inner speech frequently deals in the sense of words, not their more specific or limited public meanings. Words become "saturated with sense" in much the way a key word in a poem can come to represent its entire, complex web of meaning. But unlike the word in the poem, the accrued sense of the word in inner speech may be quite personal, even idiosyncratic; it is, as Vygotsky writes, "the sum of all the psychological events aroused in our consciousness by the word" (*Thought and Language*, p. 146).

Finally, a third feature of egocentric/inner speech is the absence of logical and causal relations. In experiments with children's use of logical-causal connectives such as *because, therefore, and although,* Piaget found that children have difficulty managing such relationships and in spontaneous speech will substitute a non-logical, non-causal connective such as *then.* Piaget described this strategy for relating things as *juxtaposition*: "the cognitive tendency simply to link (juxtapose) one thought element to another, rather than to tie them together by some causal or logical relation."[4]

One way to diagnose this problem with sophisticated relationships is to say, as Vygotsky did, that young children often think in *complexes* instead of concepts.[5] When people think in complexes they unite objects into families that really do share common bonds, but the bonds are concrete and factual rather than abstract or logical. For example, the notion of "college student" would be a complex if it were based, for the thinker, on facts such as college students live in dorms, go to classes, and do homework.

Complexes are very functional formations, and it may be that many people do most of their day-to-day thinking without feeling the need to form more demanding complex concepts. *Complexes* collect related objects; *concepts,* however, must express abstract, logical relations. And it is just this sort of abstract, synthetic thinking that writing typically demands. In a child's early years the ability to form complex concepts may depend mostly on developing cognitive capacity. In adults this ability appears also to be a skill developed by training and a tendency fostered by one's background and intellectual experience. But whatever its source, the ability to move from the complexes of egocentric speech to the more formal relations of conceptual thought is critical to most expository writing.

---

[4]John Flavell, *The Developmental Psychology of Jean Piaget* (New York: D. Van Nostrand, 1963), p. 275. For these studies see the last chapter of Piaget's *Language and Thought of the Child* and *Judgment and Reasoning in the Child*, trans. M. Warden (New York: Harcourt, Brace, 1926).

[5]*Thought and Language*, p. 75. See also the paper by Gary Woditsch which places this question in the context of curriculum design, "Developing Generic Skills: A Model for a Competency-Based General Education," available from CUE Center, Bowling Green State University.

Piaget and Vygotsky disagreed on the source, exact function, and teleology of egocentric speech, but they did agree on the features of this distinctive phenomenon, which they felt revealed the underlying logic of the child's thought. For our case, that may be enough. The hypothesis on which this paper rests is not a developmental one. Egocentric speech, or rather its adult written analogue, Writer-Based prose, is not necessarily a stage through which a writer must develop or one at which some writers are arrested. But for adults it does represent an available mode of expression on which to fall back. If Vygotsky is right, it may even be closely related to normal verbal thought. It is clearly a natural, less cognitively demanding mode of thought and one which explains why people, who can express themselves in complex and highly intelligible modes, are often obscure. Egocentric expression happens to the best of us; it comes naturally.

The work of Piaget and Vygotsky, then, suggests a source for the cognitive patterns that underlie Writer-Based prose, and it points to some of the major features such a prose style would possess. Let us now turn to a more detailed analysis of such writing as a verbal style inadequately suited for the needs of the reader.

WRITER-BASED PROSE: A CASE STUDY OF A TRANSFORMATION

As an introduction to the main features of Writer-Based prose and its transformations, let us look at two drafts of a progress report written by students in an organizational psychology class. Working as consulting analysts to a local organization, the writers needed to show progress to their instructor and to present an analysis with causes and conclusions to the client. Both readers—academic and professional—were less concerned with what the students did or saw than with *why* they did it and *what* they made of their observations.

To gauge the Reader-Based effectiveness of this report, skim quickly over Draft 1 and imagine the response of the instructor of the course, who needed to answer these questions: As analysts, what assumptions and decisions did my students make? Why did they make them? At what stage in the project are they now? Or, play the role of the client-reader who wants to know: How did they define my problem, and what did they conclude? As either reader, can you quickly extract the information the report should be giving you? Next, try the same test on Draft 2.

Draft 1: **GROUP REPORT**

(1) Work began on our project with the initial group decision to evaluate the Oskaloosa Brewing Company. Oskaloosa Brewing Company is a regionally located brewery manufacturing several different types of beer, notably River City and Brough Cream Ale. This beer is marketed under various names in Pennsylvania and other neighboring states. As a group, we decided to analyze this organization because two of our group members had had frequent customer contact with the sales department. Also, we were aware that Oskaloosa Brewing had been losing money for the past five years and we felt we might be able to find some obvious problems in their organizational structure.

(2) Our first meeting, held February 17th, was with the head of the sales department, Jim Tucker. Generally, he gave us an outline of the organization from president to worker, and discussed the various departments that we might ultimately decide to analyze. The two that seemed the most promising and most applicable to the project were the sales and production

departments. After a few group meetings and discussions with the personnel manager, Susan Harris, and our advisor Professor Charns, we felt it best suited our needs and the Oskaloosa Brewing's to evaluate their bottling department.

(3) During the next week we had a discussion with the superintendent of production, Henry Holt, and made plans for interviewing the supervisors and line workers. Also, we had a tour of the bottling departments which gave us a first-hand look into the production process. Before beginning our interviewing, our group met several times to formulate appropriate questions to use in interviewing, for both the supervisors and workers. We also had a meeting with Professor Charns to discuss this matter.

(3a) The next step was the actual interviewing process. During the weeks of March 14–18 and March 21–25, our group met several times at Oskaloosa Brewing and interviewed ten supervisors and twelve workers. Finally during this past week, we have had several group meetings to discuss our findings and the potential problem areas within the bottling department. Also, we have spent time organizing the writing of our progress report.

(4) The bottling and packaging division is located in a separate building, adjacent to the brewery, where the beer is actually manufactured. From the brewery the beer is piped into one of five lines (four bottling lines and one canning line), in the bottling house where the bottles are filled, crowned, pasteurized, labeled, packaged in cases, and either shipped out or stored in the warehouse. The head of this operation, and others, is production manager, Phil Smith. Next in line under him in direct control of the bottling house is the superintendent of bottling and packaging, Henry Holt. In addition, there are a total of ten supervisors who report directly to Henry Holt and who oversee the daily operations and coordinate and direct the twenty to thirty union workers who operate the lines.

(5) During production, each supervisor fills out a data sheet to explain what was actually produced during each hour. This form also includes the exact time when a breakdown occurred, what it was caused by, and when production was resumed. Some supervisors' positions are production staff oriented. One takes care of supplying the raw material (bottles, caps, labels, and boxes) for production. Another is responsible for the union workers assignment each day.

These workers are not all permanently assigned to a production line position. Men called "floaters" are used filling in for a sick worker, or helping out after a breakdown.

(6) The union employees are generally older than 35, some in their late fifties. Most have been with the company many years and are accustomed to having more workers per a slower moving line. They are resentful to what they declare "unnecessary" production changes. Oskaloosa Brewery also employs mechanics who normally work on the production line, and assume a mechanics job only when a breakdown occurs. Most of these men are not skilled.

Draft 2: MEMORANDUM

TO: Professor Martin Charns

FROM: Nancy Lowenberg, Todd Scott, Rosemary Nisson, Larry Vollen

DATE: March 31, 1977

RE: *Progress Report: The Oskaloosa Brewing Company*

WHY OSKALOOSA BREWING?

(1) Oskaloosa Brewing Company is a regionally located brewery manufacturing several different types of beer, notably River City and Brough Cream Ale. As a group, we decided to analyze this organization because two of our group members have frequent contact with the sales

department. Also, we were aware that Oskaloosa Brewing had been losing money for the past five years and we felt we might be able to find some obvious problems in their organizational structure.

INITIAL STEPS: WHERE TO CONCENTRATE?

(2) Through several interviews with top management and group discussion, we felt it best suited our needs, and Oskaloosa Brewing's, to evaluate the production department. Our first meeting, held February 17, was with the head of the sales department, Jim Tucker. He gave us an outline of the organization and described the two major departments, sales and production. He indicated that there were more obvious problems in the production department, a belief also implied by Susan Harris, personnel manager.

NEXT STEP

(3) The next step involved a familiarization of the plant and its employees. First, we toured the plant to gain an understanding of the brewing and bottling process. Next, during the weeks of March 14–18 and March 21–25, we interviewed ten supervisors and twelve workers. Finally, during the past week we had group meetings to exchange information and discuss potential problems.

THE PRODUCTION PROCESS

(4) Knowledge of the actual production process is imperative in understanding the effects of various problems on efficient production; therefore, we have included a brief summary of this process.

The bottling and packaging division is located in a separate building, adjacent to the brewery, where the beer is actually manufactured. From the brewery the beer is piped into one of five lines (four bottling lines and one canning line) in the bottling house where the bottles are filled, crowned, pasteurized, labeled, packaged in cases, and either shipped out or stored in the warehouse.

PEOPLE BEHIND THE PROCESS

(5) The head of this operation is production manager, Phil Smith. Next in line under him ntrol of the bottling house is the superintendent of bottling and packaging, Henry Holt. He has authority over ten supervisors who each have two major responsibilities: (1) to fill out production data sheets that show the amount produced/hour, and information about any breakdowns—time, cause, etc., and (2) to oversee the daily operations and coordinate and direct the twenty to thirty union workers who operate the lines. These workers are not all permanently assigned to a production line position. Men called "floaters" are used to fill in for a sick worker or to help out after a breakdown.

(6) The union employees are highly diversified group in both age and experience. They are generally older than 35, some in their late fifties. Most have been with the company many years and are accustomed to having more workers per a slower moving line. They are resentful to what they feel are unnecessary production changes. Oskaloosa Brewing also employs mechanics who normally work on the production line, and assume a mechanics job only when a breakdown occurs. Most of these men are not skilled.

PROBLEMS

> Through extensive interviews with supervisors and union employees, we have recognized four apparent problems within the bottle house operations. First, the employees' goals do not match those of the company. This is especially apparent in the union employees whose loyalty lies with the union instead of the company. This attitude is well-founded as the union ensures them of job security and benefits. . . .

In its tedious misdirection, Draft 1 is typical of Writer-Based prose in student papers and professional reports. The reader is forced to do most of the thinking, sorting the wheat from the chaff and drawing ideas out of details. And yet, although this presentation fails to fulfill our needs, it does have an inner logic of its own. The logic which organizes Writer-Based prose often rests on three principles: its underlying focus is egocentric, and it uses either a narrative framework or a survey form to order ideas.

The *narrative framework* of this discussion is established by the opening announcement: "Work began. . . ." In paragraphs 1–3 facts and ideas are presented in terms of when they were discovered, rather than in terms of their implications or logical connections. The writers recount what happened when; the reader, on the other hand, asks, "Why?" and "So what?" Whether he or she likes it or not the reader is in for a blow-by-blow account of the writers' discovery process.

Although a rudimentary chronology is reasonable for a progress report, a narrative framework is often a substitute for analytic thinking. By burying ideas within the events that precipitated them, a narrative obscures the more important logical and hierarchical relations between ideas. Of course, such a narrative could read like an intellectual detective story, because, like other forms of drama, it creates interest by withholding closure. Unfortunately, most academic and professional readers seem unwilling to sit through these home movies of the writer's mind at work. Narratives can also operate as a cognitive "frame" which itself generates ideas.[6] The temporal pattern, once invoked, opens up a series of empty slots waiting to be filled with the details of what happened next, even though those details may be irrelevant. As the revision of Draft 2 shows, our writers' initial narrative framework led them to generate a shaggy project story, instead of a streamlined logical analysis.

The second salient feature of this prose is its focus on the discovery process of the writers: the "I did/I thought/I felt" focus. Of the fourteen sentences in the first three paragraphs, ten are grammatically focused on the writers' thoughts and actions rather than on issues: "Work began," "We decided," "Also we were aware . . . and we felt. . . ."

In the fourth paragraph the writers shift attention from their discovery process to the facts discovered. In doing so they illustrate a third feature of Writer-Based prose: its idea structure simply copies the structure of the perceived information. A problem arises when the internal structure of the data is not already adapted to the needs of the reader or the intentions of the writer. Paragraph five, for example, appears to be a free-floating description of "What happens during production." Yet the client-reader already knows this and the instructor probably does

---

[6]The seminal paper on frames is M. Minsky's "A Framework for Representing Knowledge" in P. Winston, ed., *The Psychology of Computer Vision* (New York: McGraw Hill, 1973). For a more recent discussion of how they work see B. Kuipers, "A Frame for Frames" in D. Bowbow and A. Collins, eds., *Representation and Understanding: Studies in Cognitive Science* (New York: Academic Press, 1975), pp. 151-184.

not care. Lured by the fascination of facts, these writer-based writers recite a litany of perceived information under the illusion they have produced a rhetorical structure. The resulting structure could as well be a neat hierarchy as a list. The point is that the writers' organizing principle is dictated by their information, not by their intention.

The second version of this report is not so much a "rewrite" (i.e., a new report) as it is a transformation of the old one. The writers had to step back from their experience and information in order to turn facts into concepts. Pinpointing the telling details was not enough: they had to articulate the meaning they saw in the data. Secondly, the writers had to build a rhetorical structure which acknowledged the function these ideas had for their reader. In the second version, the headings, topic sentences, and even some of the subjects and verbs reflect a new functional structure focused on Process, People, and Problems. The report offers a hierarchical organization of the facts in which the hierarchy itself is based on issues both writer and reader agree are important. I think it likely that such transformations frequently go on in the early stages of the composing process for skilled writers. But for some writers the under-transformed Writer-Based prose of Draft 1 is also the final product and the starting point for our work as teachers.

In the remainder of this paper I will look at the features of Writer-Based prose and the ways it functions for the writer. Clearly, we need to know about Reader-Based prose in order to teach it. But it is also clear that writers already possess a great deal of intuitive knowledge about writing for audiences when they are stimulated to use it. As the case study shows, the concept of trying to transform Writer-Based prose for a reader is by itself a powerful tool. It helps writers identify the lineaments of a problem many can start to solve once they recognize it as a definable problem.

WRITER-BASED PROSE: FUNCTION, STRUCTURE, AND STYLE

While Writer-Based prose may be inadequately structured for a reader, it does possess a logic and structure of its own. Furthermore, that structure serves some important functions for the writer in his or her effort to think about a subject. It represents a practical strategy for dealing with information. If we could see Writer-Based prose as a *functional system*—not a set of random errors known only to English teachers—we would be better able to teach writing as a part of any discipline that asks people to express complex ideas.

According to Vygotsky, "the inner speech of the adult represents his 'thinking for himself' rather than social adaptation [communication to others]: i.e., it has the same function that egocentric speech has in the child" (*Language and Thought,* p. 18). It helps him solve problems. Vygotsky found that when a child who is trying to draw encounters an obstacle (no pencils) or a problem (what shall I call it?), the incidence of egocentric speech can double.

If we look at an analogous situation—an adult caught up in the complex mental process of composing—we can see that much of the adult's output is not well adapted for public consumption either. In studies of cognitive processes of writers as they composed, J. R. Hayes and I observed much of the writer's verbal output to be an attempt to manipulate stored information into some acceptable pattern of meaning.[7] To do that, the writer generates a

---

[7]L. Flower and J. Hayes, "Plans That Guide the Composing Process," in *Writing: The Nature, Development and Teaching of Written Communication,* C. Frederikson, M. Whiteman, and J. Dominic, eds. (Hillsdale, N.J.: Lawrence Erlbaum, 1981.

variety of alternative relationships and trial formulations of the information she has in mind. Many of these trial networks will be discarded; most will be significantly altered through recombination and elaboration during the composing process. In those cases in which the writer's first pass at articulating knowledge was also the final draft—when she wrote it just as she thought it—the result was often a series of semi-independent, juxtaposed networks, each with its own focus.

Whether such expression occurs in an experimental protocol or a written draft, it reflects the working of the writer's mind upon his material. Because dealing with one's material is a formidable enough task in itself, a writer may allow himself to ignore the additional problem of accommodating a reader. Writer-Based prose, then, functions as a medium for thinking. It offers the writer the luxury of one less constraint. As we shall see, its typical structure and style are simply paths left by the movement of the writer's mind.

The *structure* of Writer-Based prose reflects an economical strategy we have for coping with information. Readers generally expect writers to produce complex concepts—to collect data and details under larger guiding ideas and place those ideas in an integrated network. But as both Vygotsky and Piaget observed, forming such complex concepts is a demanding cognitive task; if no one minds, it is a lot easier to just list the parts. Nor is it surprising that in children two of the hallmarks of egocentric speech are the absence of expressed causal relations and the tendency to express ideas without proof or development. Adults too avoid the task of building complex concepts buttressed by development and proof, by structuring their information in two distinctive ways: as a narrative of their own discovery process or as a survey of the data before them.

As we saw in the Oskaloosa Brewing case study, a *narrative* structured around one's own discovery process may seem the most natural way to write. For this reason it can sometimes be the best way as well, if a writer is trying to express a complex network of information but is not yet sure how all the parts are related. For example, my notes show that early fragments of this paper started out with a narrative, list-like structure focused on my own experience: "Writer-Based prose is a working hypothesis because it works in the classroom. In fact, when I first started teaching the concept. . . . In fact, it was my students' intuitive recognition of the difference between Writer-Based and Reader-Based style in their own thought and writing. . . . It was their ability to use even a sketchy version of the distinction to transform their own writing that led me to pursue the idea more thoroughly."

The final version of this sketch (the paragraph numbered 2 on p. 63) keeps the reference to teaching experience, but subordinates it to the more central issue of why the concept works. This transformation illustrates how a writer's major propositions can, on first appearance, emerge embedded in a narrative of the events or thoughts which spawned the proposition. In this example, the Writer-Based early version recorded the raw material of observations; the final draft formed them into concepts and conclusions.

This transformation process may take place regularly when a writer is trying to express complicated information which is not yet fully conceptualized. Although much of this mental work normally precedes actual writing, a first draft may simply reflect the writer's current place in the process. When this happens rewriting and editing are vital operations. Far from being a simple matter of correcting errors, editing a first draft is often the act of transforming a narrative network of information into a more fully hierarchical set of propositions.

A second source of prefabricated structure for writers is the internal structure of the information itself. Writers use a *survey* strategy to compose because it is a powerful procedure for retrieving and organizing information. Unfortunately, the original organization of the data itself (e.g., the production process at Oskaloosa Brewing) rarely fits the most effective plan for any given piece of focused analytical writing.

The prose that results from such a survey can, of course, take as many forms as the data. It can range from a highly structured piece of discourse (the writer repeats a textbook exposition) to an unfocused printout of the writer's memories and thoughts on the subject. The form is merely a symptom, because the governing force is the writer's mental strategy: namely, to compose by surveying the available contents of memory without adapting them to a current purpose. The internal structure of the data dictates the rhetorical structure of the discourse, much as the proceedings of Congress organize the *Congressional Record*. As an information processor, the writer is performing what computer scientists would call a "memory dump": dutifully printing out memory in exactly the form in which it is stored.

A survey strategy offers the writer a useful way into the composing process in two ways. First, it eliminates many of the constraints normally imposed by a speech act, particularly the contract between reader and writer for mutually useful discourse. Secondly, a survey of one's own stored knowledge, marching along like a textbook or flowing with the tide of association, is far easier to write than a fresh or refocused conceptualization would be.

But clearly most of the advantages here accrue to the writer. One of the tacit assumptions of the Writer-Based writer is that, once the relevant information is presented, the reader will then do the work of abstracting the essential features, building a conceptual hierarchy, and transforming the whole discussion into a functional network of ideas.

Although Writer-Based prose often fails for readers and tends to preclude further concept formation, it may be a useful road into the creative process for some writers. The structures which fail to work for readers may be powerful strategies for retrieving information from memory and for exploring one's own knowledge network. This is illustrated in Linde and Labov's well-known New York apartment tour experiment.[8] Interested in the strategies people use for retrieving information from memory and planning a discourse, Linde and Labov asked one hundred New Yorkers to "tell me the layout of your apartment" as a part of a "sociological survey." Only 3% of the subjects responded with a map which gave an overview and then filled in the details; for example, "I'd say it's laid out in a huge square pattern, broken down into 4 units." The overwhelming majority (97%) all solved the problem by describing a tour: "You walk in the front door. There was a narrow hallway. To the left, etc." Furthermore, they had a common set of rules for how to conduct the tour (e.g., you don't "walk into" a small room with no outlet, such as a pantry; you just say, "on the left is . . ."). Clearly the tour structure is so widely used because it is a remarkably efficient strategy for recovering all of the relevant information about one's apartment, yet without repeating any of it. For example, one rule for "touring" is that when you dead-end after walking through two rooms, you don't "walk" back but suddenly appear back in the hall.

For us, the revealing sidenote to this experiment is that although the tour strategy was intuitively selected by the overwhelming majority of the speakers, the resulting description was generally very difficult for the listener to follow and almost impossible to reproduce. The

---

[8]C. Linde and W. Labov, "Spatial Networks as a Site for the Study of Language and Thought," *Language*, 51(1975), 924–939.

tour strategy—like the narrative and textbook structure in prose—is a masterful method for searching memory but a dud for communicating that information to anyone else.

Finally, the *style* of Writer-Based prose also has its own logic. Its two main stylistic features grow out of the private nature of interior monologue, that is, of writing which is primarily a record or expression of the writer's flow of thought. The first feature is that in such monologues the organization of sentences and paragraphs reflects the shifting focus of the writer's attention. However, the psychological subject on which the writer is focused may not be reflected in the grammatical subject of the sentence or made explicit in the discussion at all. Secondly, the writer may depend on code words to carry his or her meaning. That is, the language may be "saturated with sense" and able to evoke—for the writer—a complex but unexpressed context.

Writers of formal written discourse have two goals for style which we can usefully distinguish from one another. One goal might be described as stylistic control, that is, the ability to choose a more embedded or more elegant transformation from variations which are roughly equivalent in meaning. The second goal is to create a completely autonomous text, that is, a text that does not need context, gestures, or audible effects to convey its meaning.

It is easy to see how the limits of short-term memory can affect a writer's stylistic control. For an inexperienced writer, the complex transformation of a periodic sentence—which would require remembering and relating a variety of elements and optional structures such as this sentence contains—can be a difficult juggling act. After all, the ability to form parallel constructions is not innate. Yet with practice many of these skills can become more automatic and require less conscious attention.

The second goal of formal written discourse—the complete autonomy of the text—leads to even more complex problems. According to David Olson the history of written language has been the progressive creation of an instrument which would convey complete and explicit meanings in a text. The history of writing is the transformation of language from utterance to text—from oral meaning created within a shared context of a speaker and listener to a written meaning fully represented in an autonomous text.[9]

In contrast to this goal of autonomy, Writer-Based prose is writing whose meaning is still to an important degree in the writer's head. The culprit here is often the unstated psychological subject. The work of the "remedial" student is a good place to examine the phenomenon because it often reveals first thoughts more clearly than the reworked prose of a more experienced writer who edits as he or she writes. In the most imaginative, comprehensive and practical book to be written on the basic writer, Mina Shaughnessy has studied the linguistic strategies which lie behind the "errors" of many otherwise able young adults who have failed to master the written code. As we might predict, the ambiguous referent is ubiquitous in basic writing: *he's*, *she's* and *it's* are sprinkled through the prose without visible means of support. *It* frequently works as a code word for the subject the writer had in mind but not on the page. As Professor Shaughnessy says, *it* "frequently becomes a free-floating substitute for thoughts that the writer neglects to articulate and that the reader must usually strain to reach if he can."[10]

---

[9]David R. Olson, "From Utterance to Text: The Bias of Language in Speech and Writing," *Harvard Educational Review,* 47 (1977), 257–281.

[10]Mina Shaughnessy, *Errors and Expectations* (New York: Oxford University Press, 1977), p. 69.

> With all the jobs available, he will have to know more of *it* because there is a great demand for *it*.

For the writer of the above sentence, the pronoun was probably not ambiguous at all; *it* no doubt referred to the psychological subject of his sentence. Psychologically, the subject of an utterance is the old information, the object you are looking at, the idea on which your attention has been focused. The predicate is the new information you are adding. This means that the psychological subject and grammatical subject of a sentence may not be the same at all. In our example, "college knowledge" was the writer's psychological subject—the topic he had been thinking about. The sentence itself is simply a psychological predicate. The pronoun *it* refers quite reasonably to the unstated but obvious subject in the writer's mind.

The subject is even more likely to be missing when a sentence refers to the writer herself or to "one" in her position. In the following examples, again from *Errors and Expectations,* the "unnecessary" subject is a person (like the writer) who has a chance to go to college:

> Even if a person graduated from high school who is going on to college to obtain a specific position in his career [ ] should first know how much in demand his possible future job really is.
>
> [he]

> If he doesn't because the U.S. Labor Department says there wouldn't be enough jobs opened, [ ] is a waste to society and a "cop-out" to humanity.
>
> [he]

Unstated subjects can produce a variety of minor problems from ambiguous referents to amusing dangling modifiers (e.g., "driving around the mountain, a bear came into view"). Although prescriptive stylists are quite hard on such "errors," they are often cleared up by context or common sense. However, the controlling but unstated presence of a psychological subject can lead to some stylistic "errors" that do seriously disrupt communication. Sentence fragments are a good example.

One feature of an explicit, fully autonomous text is that the grammatical subject is usually a precise entity, often a word. By contrast, the psychological subject to which a writer wished to refer may be a complex event or entire network of information. Here written language is often rather intransigent; it is hard to refer to an entire clause or discussion unless one can produce a summary noun. Grammar, for example, normally forces us to select a specific referent for a pronoun or modifier: it wants referents and relations spelled out.[11] This specificity is, of course, its strength as a vehicle for precise reasoning and abstract thought. Errors arise when a writer uses one clause to announce his topic or psychological subject and a second clause to record a psychological predicate, a response to that old information. For example:

> The jobs that are listed in the paper, I feel you need a college degree.
>
> The job that my mother has, I know I could never be satisfied with it.

The preceding sentences are in error because they have failed to specify the grammatical relationship between their two elements. However, for anyone from the Bronx, each statement would be perfectly effective because it fits a familiar formula. It is an example of topicalization

---

[11]"Pronouns like *this, that, which* and *it* should not vaguely refer to an entire sentence or clause," and "Make a pronoun refer clearly to one antecedent, not uncertainly to two." Floyd Watkins, et al., *Practical English Handbook* (Boston: Houghton Mifflin, 1974), p. 30.

or Y-movement and fits a conventionalized, Yiddish influenced, intonation pattern much like the one in "Spinach—you can have it!" The sentences depend heavily on certain conventions of oral speech, and insofar as they invoke those patterns for the reader, they communicate effectively.[12]

However, most fragments do not succeed for the reader. And they fail, ironically enough, for the same reason—they too invoke intonation patterns in the reader which turn out to be misleading. The lack of punctuation gives off incorrect cues about how to segment the sentence. Set off on an incorrect intonation pattern, the thwarted reader must stop, reread and reinterpret the sentence. The following examples are from Maxine Hairston's *A Contemporary Rhetoric* (Boston: Houghton Mifflin, 1974):

> The authorities did not approve of their acts. These acts being considered detrimental to society. (society, they . . .)

> Young people need to be on their own. To show their parents that they are reliable. (reliable, young people . . .)

(p. 322)

Fragments are easy to avoid; they require only minimal tinkering to correct. Then why is the error so persistent? One possible reason is that for the writer the fragment is a fresh predicate intended to modify the entire preceding psychological subject. The writer wants to carry out a verbal trick easily managed in speech. For the reader, however, this minor grammatical oversight is significant. It sets up and violates both intonation patterns and strong structural expectations, such as those in the last example where we expect a pause and a noun phrase to follow "reliable." The fragment, which actually refers backward, is posing as an introductory clause.

The problem with fragments is that they are perfectly adequate for the writer. In speech they may even be an effective way to express a new idea which is predicated on the entire preceding unit thought. But in a written text, fragments are errors because they do not take the needs of the reader into consideration. Looked at this way, the "goodness" of a stylistic technique or grammatical rule such as parallelism, clear antecedents, or agreement is that it is geared to the habits, expectations, and needs of the reader as well as to the demands of textual autonomy.

Vygotsky noticed how the language of children and inner speech was often "saturated with sense." Similarly, the words a writer chooses can also operate as code words, condensing a wealth of meaning in an apparently innocuous word. The following examples come from an exercise which asks writers to identify and transform some of their own pieces of mental shorthand.

The students were asked to circle any code words or loaded expressions they found in their first drafts of a summer internship application. That is, they tried to identify those expressions that might convey only a general or vague meaning to a reader, but which represented a large body of facts, experiences, or ideas for them. They then treated this code word as one would any intuition—pushing it for its buried connections and turning those into a communicable idea. The results are not unlike those brilliant explications one often hears

---

[12]I am greatly indebted here to Thomas Huckin for his insightful comments on style and to his work in linguistics on how intonation patterns affect writers and readers.

from students who tell you what their paper really meant. This example also shows how much detailed and perceptive thought can be lying behind a vague and conventional word:

First Draft: "By having these two jobs, I was able to see the business in an entirely (different perspective)" (Circle indicates a loaded expression marked by the writer.)

Second Draft with explanation of what she actually had in mind in using the circled phrase: "By having these two jobs, I was able to see the true relationship and relative importance of the various departments in the company. I could see their mutual dependence and how an event in one part of the firm can have an important effect on another."

The tendency to think in code words is a fact of life for the writer. Yet the following example shows how much work can go into exploring our own saturated language. Like any intuition, such language is only a source of potential meanings, much as Aristotle's topics are places for finding potential arguments. In this extended example, the writer first explores her expression itself, laying out all the thoughts which were loosely connected under its name. This process of pushing our own language to give up its buried meanings forces us to make these loose connections explicit and, in the process, allows us to examine them critically. For the writer in our example, pushing her own key words leads to an important set of new ideas in the paper.

Excerpt from an application for the
National Institute of Health Internship Program

First Draft: "I want a career that will help other people while at the same time be challenging scientifically. I had the opportunity to do a biochemical assay for a neuropsychopharmacologist at X— Clinic in Chicago. Besides learning the scientific procedures and techniques that are used, I realized some of the (organizational, financial and people problems) which are encountered in research. This internship program would let me pursue further my interest in research, while concurrently exposing me (to relevant and diverse) areas of bioengineering."

Excerpt from Writer's Notes Working on the Circled Phrases

Brainstorm

How did research of Sleep Center tie into overall program of X— Clinic? Not everyone within dept. knew what the others were doing, could not see overall picture of efforts.

Dr O.—dept. head—trained for lab yet did 38–40 hrs. paperwork. Couldn't set up test assay in Sleep Center because needed equip. from biochem.

Difficulties in getting equipment

1. Politics between administrators
   Photometer at U . of — even though Clinic had bought it.
2. Ordering time, not sufficient inventory, had to hunt through boxes for chemicals.
3. Had to schedule use by personal contact on borrowing equipment—done at time of use and no previous planning.

No definite guidelines had been given to biochem. people as to what was "going on" with assay. Partner who was supposed to learn assay was on vacation. Two people were learning, one was on vac.

1. No money from state for equipment or research grants.
2. Departments stealing from each other.
3. Lobbying, politics, included.

My supervisor from India, felt prejudices on job. Couldn't advance, told me life story and difficulties in obtaining jobs at Univ. Not interested in research at Clinic per se, looking for better opportunities, studying for Vet boards.

Revision (additions in italics)

"As a biomedical researcher, I would fulfill my goal of a career that will help other people while at the same time be challenging scientifically. I had exposure to research while doing a biochemical assay for a neuropsychopharmacologist at X— Clinic in Chicago. Besides learning the scientific procedures and techniques that are used, I realized some of the organizational, financial and people problems which are encountered in research. *These problems included a lack of funds and equipment, disagreements among research staff, and the extensive amounts of time, paperwork and steps required for testing a hypothesis which was only one very small but necessary part of the overall project.* But besides knowing some of the frustrations, I also know that many medical advancements, such as the cardiac pacemaker, artificial limbs and cures for diseases, exist and benefit many people because of the efforts of researchers. Therefore I would like to pursue my interest in research by participating in the NIH Internship Program. The exposure to many *diverse projects, designed to better understand and improve the body's functioning,* would help me to decide which areas of biomedical engineering to pursue."

We could sum up this analysis of style by noting two points. At times a Writer-Based prose style is simply an interior monologue in which some necessary information (such as intonation pattern or a psychological subject) is not expressed in the text. The solution to the reader's problem is relatively trivial in that it involves adding information that the writer already possesses. At other times, a style may be Writer-Based because the writer is thinking in code words at the level of intuited but unarticulated connections. Turning such saturated language into communicable ideas can require the writer to bring the entire composing process into play.

IMPLICATIONS FOR WRITERS AND TEACHERS

From an educational perspective, Writer-Based prose is one of the "problems" composition courses are designed to correct. It is a major cause of that notorious "breakdown" of communication between writer and reader. However, if we step back and look at it in the broader context of cognitive operations involved, we see that it represents a major, functional stage in the composing process and a powerful strategy well fitted to a part of the job of writing.

In the best of all possible worlds, good writers strive for Reader-Based prose from the very beginning: they retrieve and organize information within the framework of a reader/writer contract. Their top goal or initial question is not, "What do I know about physics, and in particularly the physics of wind resistance?" but, "What does a model plane builder need to know?" Many times a writer can do this. For a physics teacher this particular writing problem would be a trivial one. However, for a person ten years out of Physics 101, simply retrieving any relevant information would be a full-time processing job. The reader would simply have to wait. For the inexperienced writer, trying to put complex thought into written language may also be task enough. In that case, the reader is an extra constraint that must wait its turn. A Reader-Based strategy which includes the reader in the entire thinking process is clearly the best way to write, but it is not always possible. When it is very difficult or impossible to write for a reader from the beginning, writing and then transforming Writer-Based prose is a practical alternative which breaks this complex process down into manageable parts. When transforming is a practiced skill, it enters naturally into the pulse of the composing process as a writer's constant, steady effort to test and adapt his or her thought to a reader's needs. Transforming Writer-Based prose is, then, not only a necessary procedure for all writers at times, but a useful place to start teaching intellectually significant writing skills.

In this final section I will try to account for the peculiar virtues of Writer-Based prose and suggest ways that teachers of writing—in any field—can take advantage of them. Seen in the context of memory retrieval, Writer-Based thinking appears to be a tapline to the rich sources of episodic memory. In the context of the composing process, Writer-Based prose is a way to deal with the overload that writing often imposes on short-term memory. By teaching writers to use this transformation process we can foster the peculiar strengths of Writer-Based thought and still alert writers to the next transformation that many may simply fail to attempt.

One way to account for why Writer-Based prose seems to "come naturally" to most of us from time to time is to recognize its ties to our episodic as opposed to semantic memory. As Tulving describes it, "episodic memory is a more or less faithful record of a person's experiences." A statement drawn from episodic memory "refers to a personal experience that is remembered in its temporal-spatial relation to other such experiences. The remembered episodes are . . . autobiographical events, describable in terms of their perceptible dimensions or attributes."[13]

Semantic memory, by contrast, "is the memory necessary for the use of language. It is a mental thesaurus, organized knowledge a person possesses about words and other verbal symbols, their meaning and referents, about relations among them, and about rules, formulas, and algorithms for the manipulation of these symbols, concepts, and relations." Although we know that table salt is NaCl and that motivation is a mental state, we probably do not remember learning the fact or the first time we thought of that concept. In semantic memory facts and concepts stand as the nexus for other words and symbols, but shorn of their temporal

---

[13]Edel Tulving, "Episodic and Semantic Memory," in Edel Tulving and Wayne Donaldson, eds., *Organization of Memory* (New York: Academic Press, 1972), p. 387.

and autobiographical roots. If we explored the notion of "writing" in the semantic memory of someone we might produce a network such as this (Fig.1):

Figure 1

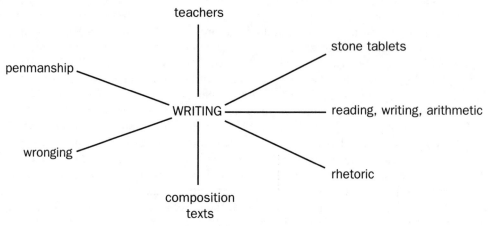

In an effort to retrieve what she or he knew about stone tablets, for example, this same person might turn to episodic memory: "I once heard a lecture on the Rosetta stone, over in Maynard Hall. The woman, as I recall, said that . . . and I remember wondering if. . . ."

Writers obviously use both kinds of memory. The problem only arises when they confuse a fertile source of ideas in episodic memory with a final product. In fact, a study by Russo and Wisher argues that we sometimes store our ideas or images (the symbols of thought) with the mental operations we performed to produce these symbols.[14] Furthermore, it is easier to recall the symbols (that fleeting idea, perhaps) when we bring back the original operation. In other words, our own thinking acts can serve as memory cues, and the easiest way to recover some item from memory may be to *reprocess* it, to reconstruct the original thought process in which it appeared. Much Writer-Based prose appears to be doing just this—reprocessing an earlier thinking experience as a way to recover what one knows.

Writing is one of those activities that places an enormous burden on short-term or working memory. As George Miller put it, "The most glaring result [of numerous experiments] has been to highlight man's inadequacy as a communication channel. As the amount of input information is increased, the amount of information that the man transmits increases at first but then runs into a ceiling. . . . That ceiling is always very low. Indeed, it is an act of charity to call man a channel at all. Compared to telephone or television channels, man is better characterized as a bottleneck."[15]

The short-term memory is the active central processor of the mind, that is, it is the sum of all the information we can hold in conscious attention at one time. We notice its capacity most acutely when we try to learn a new task, such as driving a car or playing bridge. Its

---

[14]J. Russo and R. Wisher, "Reprocessing as a Recognition Cue," *Memory and Cognition,* 4 (1976), 683–689.

[15]George Miller, *The Psychology of Communication* (New York: Basic Books, 1967), p. 48.

limited capacity means that when faced with a complex problem—such as writing a college paper—we can hold and compare only a few alternative relationships in mind at once.

Trying to evaluate, elaborate, and relate all that we know on a given topic can easily overload the capacity of our working memory. Trying to compose even a single sentence can have the same effect, as we try to juggle grammatical and syntactic alternatives plus all the possibilities of tone, nuance, and rhythm even a simple sentence offers. Composing, then, is a cognitive activity that constantly threatens to overload short-term memory. For two reasons Writer-Based prose is a highly effective strategy for dealing with this problem.

1. Because the characteristic structure of Writer-Based prose is often a list (either of mental events or the features of the topic) it temporarily suspends the additional problem of forming complex concepts. If that task is suspended indefinitely, the result will fail to be good analytical writing or serious thought, but as a first stage in the process the list-structure has real value. It allows the writer freedom to generate a breadth of information and a variety of alternative relationships before locking himself or herself into a premature formulation. Furthermore, by allowing the writer to temporarily separate the two complex but somewhat different tasks of generating information and forming networks, each task may be performed more consciously and effectively.

2. Taking the perspective of another mind is also a demanding cognitive operation. It means holding not only your own knowledge network but someone else's in conscious attention and comparing them. Young children simply can't do it.[16] Adults choose not to do it when their central processing is already overloaded with the effort to generate and structure their own ideas. Writer-Based prose simply eliminates this constraint by temporarily dropping the reader out of the writer's deliberations.[17]

My own research suggests that good writers take advantage of these strategies in their composing process. They use scenarios, generate lists, and ignore the reader, but only for a while. Their composing process, unlike that of less effective writers, is marked by constant re-examination of their growing product and an attempt to refine, elaborate, or test its relationships, plus an attempt to anticipate the response of a reader. Everyone uses the strategies of Writer-Based prose; good writers go a step further to transform the writing these strategies produce.

But what about the writers who fail to make this transformation or (like all of us) fail to do it adequately in places? This is the problem faced by all teachers who assign papers. I think this study has two main and quite happy implications for us as teachers and writers.

The first is that Writer-Based prose is not a composite of errors or a mistake that should be scrapped. Instead, it is a half-way place for many writers and often represents the results of an extensive search and selection process. As a stage in the composing process it may be a rich compilation of significant thoughts which cohere *for the writer* into a network she or he has not yet fully articulated. Writer-Based prose is the writer's homework, and so long as the writer is also the audience, it may even be a well-thought-out communication.

---

[16]Marlene Scardamalia, "How Children Cope with the Cognitive Demands of Writing," in *Writing: The Nature, Development and Teaching of Written Communication,* C. Frederikson, M. Whiteman, and J. Dominic, eds.

[17]Linda Flower and John R. Hayes, "The Dynamics of Composing: Making Plans and Juggling Constraints," in *Cognitive Processes in Writing: An Interdisciplinary Approach,* Lee Gregg and Irwin Steinberg, eds. (Hillsdale, N.J.: Lawrence Erlbaum, 1979).

The second happy implication is that writing Reader-Based prose is often simply the task of transforming the groundwork laid in the first stage of the process.[18] Good analytical writing is not different in kind from the writer-based thought that seems to come naturally. It is an extension of our communication with ourselves transformed in certain predictable ways to meet the needs of the reader. The most general transformation is simply to try to take into account the reader's purpose in reading. Most people have well-developed strategies for doing this when they talk. For a variety of reasons—from cognitive effort to the illusion of the omniscient teacher/reader—many people simply do not consider the reader when they write.

More specifically, the transformations that produce Reader-Based writing include these:

• Selecting a focus of mutual interest to both reader and writer (e.g., moving from the Writer-Based focus of "How did I go about my research or reading of the assignment and what did I see?" to a focus on "What significant conclusions can be drawn and why?").

• Moving from facts, scenarios, and details to concepts.

• Transforming a narrative or textbook structure into a rhetorical structure built on the logical and hierarchical relationships between ideas and organized around the purpose for writing, rather than the writer's process.

Teaching writers to recognize their own Writer-Based writing and transform it has a number of advantages. It places a strong positive value on writing that represents an effort and achievement for the writer even though it fails to communicate to the reader. This legitimate recognition of the uncommunicated content of Writer-Based prose can give anyone, but especially inexperienced writers, the confidence and motivation to go on. By defining writing as a multistage process (instead of a holistic act of "expression") we provide a rationale for editing and alert many writers to a problem they could handle once it is set apart from other problems and they deliberately set out to tackle it. By recognizing transformation as a special skill and task, we give writers a greater degree of self-conscious control over the abilities they already have and a more precise introduction to some skills they may yet develop.

---

[18]For a study of heuristics and teaching techniques for this transformation process, see L. Flower and J. Hayes, "Problem-Solving Strategies and the Writing Process," *College English, 39* (1977)), 449–461.

Coaching Student Writers to Be Effective Peer Evaluators

JANE STANLEY *International University of Japan*

Peer-evaluation groups have long been widely accepted pedagogy in the L1 English composition classroom. More recently, many ESL composition teachers have responded to the persuasion of L1 composition theorists and have included peer-evaluation sessions in their course outlines. In fact, some empirical evidence has accumulated to justify this inclusion. Studies of both native and nonnative English composition classrooms suggest that peer evaluation can provide student writers with a wide range of benefits, including reduced writing anxiety, improved sense of audience, and increased fluency. Elbow (1973, 1981) contended that student writers derive great benefit from recognizing an audience in their peer group members. He noted that as student writers see confusion or incomprehension in their group partners' responses or in their faces, writing becomes a task of communicating, rather than merely an exercise to be completed for the teacher. Kroll and Vann (1981) endorsed Elbow's stance and claim that peer-evaluation groups enable the writer to recognize egocentrism in his or her writing. In addition to its facilitating the transition from what Flower and Hayes (1981) term "writer-based prose" to "reader-based prose," Beaven (1977) credited peer-evaluation groups with promoting the development of interpersonal skills. The concomitant increase in confidence, according to Beaven, results in a willingness to take risks in writing and an improvement of writing abilities. King (1979) argued that peer-evaluation sessions resulted in better attitudes toward writing. Kastra (1987) tested King's contention in a study of ninth-grade writers. She found that students who participated in peer evaluation demonstrated a more positive attitude toward writing than did the students who had received teacher response alone. She also found a significant increase in writing fluency in the group that had participated in peer-evaluation sessions. Clifford (1981) found that students whose classwork included participation in peer-evaluation sessions showed significant improvement on holistically scored writing samples. Bruffee (1984) contended that the collaborative environment created in peer groups encourages writers to address high-order composition concerns, such as focus and idea development. Bruffee's claim was empirically supported by Danis (1980), who found that the majority of peer-group participants in her study of college-level writers identified both superficial and substantive problems in each other's essays. Gere and Stevens (1985) studied peer-evaluation groups in grades 5, 8, and 12 and found that these writers addressed questions of meaning and content in their interactions, rather than merely serving as proofreaders for each other.

From "Coaching Student Writers to be Effective Peer Evaluators" by J. Stanley, 1992, Journal of Second Language Writing, 1, pp. 217–233. Reprinted with permission.

Other studies have considered whether peer evaluation surpasses teacher response. Ford (1973) and Karengianes, Pascarella, and Pflaum (1980) found peer evaluation to be more beneficial than teacher response in producing improved drafts. Partridge (1981) found the opposite: Teacher response resulted in more improvement. Finally, a group of studies was unable to ascertain the superiority of either treatment. Pfeiffer (1981) and Putz (1970) found that peer evaluation produced neither better nor worse final drafts than did teacher response. In a study of L2 students, Chaudron (1984) found no overall difference between those revisions resulting from peer evaluation and those resulting from teacher response. Chaudron recommended that peer-evaluation groups should thus be considered by teachers as a means of cutting their paper overload without sacrificing quality of instruction.

Notwithstanding the high marks peer evaluation has received in the research literature, some dissenting views of the efficacy of this practice have surfaced in recent years. A national survey of 560 composition teachers has revealed a substantial level of doubt regarding the helpfulness of peer evaluation (Freedman, 1985). Increasingly, composition teachers have begun to articulate their reservations in print. Danis (1982) noted that students are not always sure of their group role. Writers in the freshman composition classes she studied were commonly unable to elicit necessary information regarding their essays from group members and were hesitant to ask for clarification. Danis further observed that students often do not regard their peers as the real audience, merely as interim arbitrators. Flynn's (1982) findings support Danis's observations. In her study of freshman composition classes, she found that students offered unhelpful and unfocused responses to their peer-group partners. Significantly, she noted that students tended to supply meaning to essays they read, to close coherence gaps that the writer had left open. Flynn attributed this willingness of students to "overinterpret" their partners' essays to their unfamiliarity with the genre of student writing. She argues that students are experienced readers of professionally crafted prose; this leads them to expect that all writing is coherent and well-focused. Thus, student evaluators commonly bring to peer evaluation the skills that they bring to the task of reading professionally authored materials. That is, they read for global meaning, use their schemata to fill in cohesive gaps, and infer information even where the writer has failed to provide the necessary background to authorize such an inference. As a result, student readers are insufficiently critical of student writing, presuming that the comprehensibility shortcomings lie with them as readers, rather than with the writer. Finally, Flynn suggests that students' skills as evaluators would be sharpened if they were introduced to the genre of the student essay.

Leki (1990) identified a broad range of problems with peer evaluation in the ESL classroom. Primary among these is students' tendency to address surface errors of grammar and mechanics while failing to respond to more problematic issues of meaning. Another concern is that students sometimes resort to inappropriate rubber stamp advice (e.g., "be specific") when at a loss to comment. Leki reported a further disincentive for using peer evaluation, originally described by Acton (1984), as the possibility that peer comments may lack tact or a constructive spirit. Finally, she noted that the experienced ESL writers sometimes find it difficult to judge when their peers' advice is valid.

Allaei and Connor (1990) agreed that ESL writers may suspect the validity of their peer evaluators' advice, but they attributed some of this unsureness to cultural differences. They suggested that students from diverse language backgrounds may impose differing rhetorical expectations on a classmate's text. They also argued that the differing communication styles of students from different cultures may complicate group work considerably.

In summary, then, while peer evaluation has been accorded a place in many ESL composition classrooms, productive group work has not always resulted. Flynn (1982), Leki (1990), and Allaei and Connor (1990) all urge teachers to consider the ways in which they prepare students to become peer evaluators. Gere (1987) points to inadequate student preparation for group work as a major cause of unsuccessful peer-evaluation sessions: "When I meet teachers who say, 'Oh, I tried writing groups and they didn't work,' I begin by asking about preparation" (p. 103).

This study begins at the same point. A writing class of fifteen students is given lengthy preparation for peer evaluation, during which time they consider the genre of the student essay and discover rules for effective communication within the group. These students are then followed through numerous peer-evaluation sessions. Their peer-group conversations, recorded on audiotape, are then examined in some detail. From these tapes a picture emerges of the quality and type of interactional work that students are willing to undertake, given adequate preparation.

As a backdrop to this class, the group work of another class is also studied. The second class has been prepared for peer evaluation in a less time-intensive way: Their teacher has demonstrated a peer-evaluation session and has provided worksheets and checklists to guide the sessions.

The goal in this study is to examine the types of peer-group interactions that can occur in the ESL writing classroom and to consider whether more elaborate preparation results in more fruitful conversations about writing. Finally, the study looks at the drafts produced after each session. The focus here is not on the quality of the writing, but on the extent to which students' peer-group discussions motivated them to rework their writing.

METHOD

The Students

The students who participated in this study were enrolled in one of two sections of a freshman composition course at the University of Hawaii, Manoa's English Language Institute. The mean Test of English as a Foreign Language (TOEFL) score in one section was 547; in the other, 549. Placement in this course was based on students' performance on a writing sample as evaluated by the ESL Composition Profile (Jacobs, Zinkgraf, Wormuth, Hartfiel, & Hughey, 1981); their scores ranged from 75 to 84. Mean length of U.S. residency in one section was 5.2 years; in the other, 5.8. The age range for students in each section was 18 to 22 years. The first languages of students in one section were as follows: Korean (4 students), Mandarin (3), Cantonese (2), Japanese (1), Tagalog (1), and Vietnamese (1). In the other section, first languages were Korean (4), Mandarin (4), Cantonese (4), Japanese (4), French (1), Spanish (1), and Samoan (1). Students chose their sections to fit their schedules. One section met in the late morning; the other, in the early afternoon. Instructors' names were not announced prior to registration. Each section was taught by a different teacher, but both used the same text and made an effort to match their pace and delivery of instruction. The central difference between the two sections was their preparation for peer-evaluation group work.

Preparation for Group Work

To prepare the students for participation in group work, Section 1 was offered extensive coaching (approximately seven hours during the first four weeks of a fifteen-week semester). As the instructor of this section, I conducted the coaching sessions. Coaching focused on two important aspects of peer-group-evaluation sessions: familiarizing students with the genre of the student essay and introducing students to the task of making effective responses to each other.

The genre of the student essay was introduced through a series of drafts written by previous students of this course. (The writers' names were, of course, masked.) Students followed several writers through successive stages of readiness, from rough first draft to polished fourth. With every draft, students were asked to challenge their preconceptions about the writing task. They were asked to comment on, not bridge, cohesive gaps. They were asked not to supply meaning where the writer had been inexplicit, but to pinpoint vague or unclear sections of text. They were urged to judge the writer's claims and assumptions against their own knowledge and to report their judgment. By looking at a succession of drafts, they saw each essay as a work in progress. As they read later drafts, they searched for evidence of reworkings and repairs. In short, they were pressed to read student essays with an uncommonly close eye.

Of course, the ultimate success of a peer-evaluation session lies not in how carefully students read each other's drafts, but in how well they communicate their perceptions to the writer. Accordingly, the coaching addressed what Collins (1982) identifies as the "how-to-say-it" aspect of evaluation. Students were asked to do a two-step evaluation of each sample essay. First, they reported what they noticed as the strengths and shortcomings of the essay. Second, they described how they might best communicate these thoughts to the writer.

The students worked with each draft in small groups. In the initial sessions, I offered them specific advice about the types of issues that would be appropriate to raise at each stage of writing. That is, the first draft was seen as a point at which to address issues of content; later drafts, issues of structure, and so on. Responses were elicited from the groups, and a whole-class discussion of the draft followed. After the essay's problems and strengths had been set forth, students were asked to describe how they would tell the writer about their responses to the essay. This process was repeated with a number of sample drafts at different stages of development.

As a way of sensitizing students to the difficulties of responding, I asked them to role play in pairs, one student reading and responding, the other student reporting what he or she had "gotten" from the evaluation. (Fujimoto, 1987, outlines a model of this procedure.) As each group's successful and unsuccessful communications were discussed by the whole class, there emerged an agreed-upon strategy for successful response. The strategy that evolved was simple: The more specific the comment the better, the shorter the comment the better. It was agreed that commenters who did confirmation checks with the writer were more likely to be understood. Writers who asked for clarification made evaluation easier. These strategies for effective communication during peer evaluation were discussed at some length.

Eventually, a class consensus on evaluator tact developed. Students agreed to blame the anonymous "reader" for many problems (e.g., "The general reader might think this paragraph is really boring."). Perhaps most importantly, the students realized that the noncommittal "this is fine" is an inappropriate expression of disinterest in a fellow writer's work.

During the seven hours, students worked through several sample essays of differing levels of sophistication. In role plays, attention was paid both to the evaluator's perception of the essay and to his or her presentation of these perceptions to the surrogate writer. Individual strategies for accomplishing both tasks were discussed and became shared class knowledge.

At every step in the coaching, students were encouraged to believe that they could trust their peer group's responses and that they should actively solicit their group's assistance. During the seven hours, much effort was made to convince students that peer-evaluation sessions were an important way to improve their writing skills.

In contrast, Section 2 was prepared for peer evaluation in a far more economical manner. One hour of class time was devoted to a discussion of peer evaluation. Within that hour, students were offered what Lunsford (1986) calls a "fishbowl" demonstration of a peer-evaluation session. The instructor of this section and I role played a peer-evaluation session for twenty-five minutes. The draft upon which the session was based was the work of a student from a previous semester. As the students watched the demonstration, they referred to their own copies of the draft. After the modeled session, the instructor initiated a class discussion of the draft, as well as of the importance of peer evaluation. Students began peer evaluation at the next class meeting, with the support of checklists. Throughout the semester, the instructor made considerable effort to communicate to the students his enthusiasm for peer evaluation.

A fishbowl demonstration of this type was used as a backdrop in this study because a number of composition instructors who were consulted agreed that such an activity typically constituted preparation for group work in their classes and in other composition classes that they had observed. Because the preparation done in Section 2 occupied only one hour in contrast to the first section's seven hours, the students in Section 2 had a surplus of six hours. This time was used throughout the semester in whole-class discussions and activities on issues of rhetoric, conventions of style, and so forth.

Collection of Data

Students in each section wrote six essays during the semester. Peer evaluations of all the drafts for all six essays were audiotaped. For some essays, three drafts were evaluated by peer groups and taped; for other essays, only two drafts were evaluated and taped. The sessions averaged about forty minutes in length. The points of analysis were type of response, mean number of turns per speaker per session, and mean length of turn. Each of these points of analysis is described at length in the analysis portion of this article. Finally, the drafts that were written after each peer-evaluation session were examined. The goal of this step was not to establish relative quality of the writings, but to determine the extent to which students responded to their peers' efforts by making changes in their work.

ANALYSIS: THE PEER-EVALUATION SESSIONS

The focus of the analysis was to consider whether the coaching had influenced the students' interactions. Thus, I was curious to see the extent to which the "rules" for peer evaluation ultimately found their way into group work. For example, do students who had discovered that specific is better actually make specific comments within their group?

In order to make the conversations accessible for analysis, I developed a code. For each transcript, the evaluators' responses during group work were assigned into seven categories: pointing, advising, collaborating, announcing, reacting, eliciting, and questioning. The writers' responses were assigned into four categories: responding, eliciting, announcing, and clarifying. Each transcript was coded according to these response types. Another teacher and I coded the sessions independently. Our intercoder reliability was 92 percent. A sample of the coding sheet that was used can be found at the end of this chapter. A full explanation of the coding system and examples from the transcripts follow.

Evaluator Response Code

Pointing, as described by Brady and Jacobs (1988), occurs when an evaluator verbally points to particular words or phrases from the text and responds to them. Three types of pointing responses were identified in this data:

1. Pointing to specific phrases or sentences, for example, "Where you say, 'These European cars have better advantages for people who like elegancy but not sportiness and high performance,' what do you mean?"
2. Pointing to particular word choices, for example, "Where you say 'violence,' it sounds like it's a negative thing. Is that what you mean?"
3. Pointing to cohesive gaps, for example, "You say, 'Therefore many Asian athletes have prefer soccer.' How does this sentence connect to the one before it?"

Advising is more directive than pointing. In this case, evaluators outline changes that they think the writer should make. The advice can be either specific or general.

1. A specific advising example is "You need to give an example to explain that idea."
2. General advising takes two forms: (a) a blanket remark, such as, "You need more ideas in this paper"; or (b) a representation of the audience, such as, "You have to write this to people who are not using journals, so you can convince them."

Collaborating goes beyond advising. When they collaborate, group members paraphrase the writer's words or compose their own sentences for the writer, for example, "Say something like 'Soccer was popular in Asia before, but now more and more Americans. . . .' "

Announcing occurs when the evaluator "walks through" the essay. Typical announcing remarks are, "OK, the first paragraph talks about how high school and college are different. Then the second paragraph talks about schedule differences. Next. . . ." Within the announcing category, four types were identified:

1. Announcing text sections (as in the example just given).
2. Announcing thesis statements or topic sentences, as in, "Your thesis statement is X."
3. Announcing missing elements, as in, "There's no conclusion in your essay."
4. Announcing a "rule," as in, "A thesis statement needs to give an opinion."

Reacting is the label that is given to purely evaluative remarks that neither point nor advise. Evaluative remarks can be general or specific.

1. Reacting generally, for example, "This is really good."
2. Reacting specifically, for example, "Pretty good introduction. It covers your main point and has a thesis."

Eliciting is the term borrowed from Gere and Stevens (1985) to describe situations when an evaluator attempts to "draw out" the writer and encourage his or her participation, for example, "Yumi, what do you really want to say about people who follow these diets?" A second type of eliciting occurs when one evaluator calls on the other evaluators for opinions, for example, "Jae, do you think her conclusion is OK?"

Questioning is a mild sort of challenge put to the writer. Two types of questioning responses were identified:

1. Questioning elements of the text, such as, "What's the topic of your second paragraph about, anyway?"
2. Questioning the logic of an argument, such as, "If people don't know about the reading you do, how can reading be a social advantage?"

Writer Response Code

Responding occurs when the writer answers the evaluator. Four types of responses were identified:

1. Responding by accepting the evaluator's remark, for example, "OK, so that's not clear to you." Only those remarks that could be construed as a meaningful acknowledgement to the writer were accepted in this category. Thus, a minimal response of "Mmhh" or "Yes" was not coded as a response.
2. Responding by restating or interpreting the evaluator's remark, for example, "OK, so what you're saying is. . . ."
3. Responding by requesting clarification, for example, "What do you mean?"
4. Responding by justifying a draft, for example, "No, I already discussed that in the third paragraph."

Eliciting occurs when the writer asks for some specific advice, for example, "Are my examples clear enough?" or for some information regarding "rules," such as, "Is it OK to state only the advantages, or do we have to give both sides?"

Announcing for the writer is much the same as for the evaluator. Two types of announcing responses were identified in the writers' conversations:

1. The writer "tells" the essay, as in, "Next, my conclusions."
2. The writer announces a problem, as in, "My problem is I don't give much description." This remark was not categorized as an elicitation because evaluators did not respond to it as a direct request.

Clarifying occurs when the writer attempts to clarify the evaluators' understanding. Two types of clarification were offered—original and reiterative.

Original clarifications are as follows:

1. Clarifying by elaborating on text, such as, "See, it's easy for everybody because snorkelers don't have to know how to swim very well."
2. Clarifying by describing intentions, such as, "What I wanted to say was. . . ."
3. Clarifying by describing scope of text, such as, "This essay is not only about skill—faster—it's also about understanding—better thinking—too.
4. Clarifying by describing the writing process, such as, "I decided this was two different ideas, so I separated it into two paragraphs."

Reiterative clarifications include the following:

5. Clarifying by quoting from text, for example, "Everyone should daydream, because, like I say, 'Think of the great inventions that come from daydreams. . . .'"
6. Clarifying by reiterating major points, for example, "I said each student should have a personal computer because, first, you can do your math homework better, second, if you need word processing in your English, last. . . ."

In addition to type of response, turn-taking patterns were also of interest. These are significant because, during coaching, the students had agreed that frequent clarification requests and restatements of issues improved group communication. Thus, a transcript which shows an even distribution of turns would likely indicate an evaluation session to which all members were actively contributing. At the other end of the participation spectrum would be a transcript with an uneven distribution of turns per participant. Such a distribution would suggest a session during which one group member "lectured" the relatively passive other group members.

Thus, the mean number of turns per participant per session was calculated. For this analysis, a speaker was said to hold a turn until interrupted, or until another speaker claimed the floor after a pause. At some points in the tapes, it seemed evident that a speaker had yielded the floor, only to resume speaking after a long pause. This was counted as a single turn because speakers were sometimes observed to use their silent scanning of the draft as a floor-holding technique.

A further point of analysis was mean length of turn. Calculation of the length of turn is relevant in assessing the effectiveness of coaching which stressed that "shorter is better." Length of turn was calculated by T-unit, defined as one independent clause and whatever dependent clauses are attached to it (Hunt, 1965).

FINDINGS: THE PEER-EVALUATION SESSIONS

The most readily apparent evidence that coaching resulted in improved group interaction was that the coached groups simply produced far more conversation about their drafts than did the groups who had not received coaching. Coached groups made substantially more comments in every response category. The total number of responses coded for the coached group was 623; for the uncoached group, 137. Table 1 shows the frequency of occurrence of

Table 1
Frequency of Response Types Among Coached and Uncoached Students and Percentage of Total Number of Responses

	Coached Students		Uncoached Students	
	n	%	*n*	%
Evaluator Response Type				
Pointing	101	16	23	17
Advising	70	11	17	12
Collaborating	56	8	1	0.7
Announcing	79	13	20	15
Reacting	66	10	35	25
Eliciting	9	1	0	0
Questioning	40	6	1	0.7
Writer Response Type				
Responding to evaluator	88	14	17	12
Eliciting	31	5	11	8
Announcing	17	3	6	4
Clarifying	66	10	6	4
Total Responses	623		137	

each response type, as well as its percentage of the total number of responses. Because the number of peer-evaluation sessions analyzed in this study is too small to yield reliable statistical evidence, simple counts of response types are presented.

During coaching, students continually had been urged to be specific in their responses. Coached students carried that message to their group work, as can be seen in the high incidence of specific response types such as pointing, advising, and collaborating. Students who had received coaching offered their partners substantially more specific responses to their writing. They pointed to problematic portions of text, alerted writers to lapses in coherence, offered specific advice for solving these problems, and collaborated with the writer on more suitable phrases far more often than did the uncoached students.

One justification of the hours spent in coaching was the expectation that students who felt "trained" would be more secure in their roles as evaluators and thus would demonstrate a higher level of engagement in the peer-evaluation task. Evidence of engagement can be seen in tallies of two response categories: announcing elements of their partners' texts as they move through the essay, and reacting to text elements by offering judgments on the quality of the writing. Instances of both response categories appeared far more frequently among the coached students. Another indicator of increased engagement among the coached students is their higher incidence of eliciting remarks where they attempt to draw out the writer. Thus, the coaching paid off in that students showed more commitment to the task of understanding their partners' drafts and to making sure that their partners understood theirs.

Teachers who choose not to use peer evaluation in their classrooms sometimes feel that their students are reluctant to challenge a classmate's work even though they can see problems in the writing. For this reason some coaching time was spent in encouraging students to set aside this reluctance during peer-evaluation sessions. In this respect coaching met with considerable success, as can be shown in the far greater frequency of questions among the coached groups. Although it was difficult even for coached students to direct a strong challenge to their partners, they were able to question writers about the logic of their arguments.

A major element of the role playing part of coaching was debriefing, during which one of the group members recapped what he or she "got" from the others' comments. It was hoped that this would encourage writers to make clarification checks, request restatements, and generally to make more than the minimal "I see" response to their partners' comments. This aspect of coaching seemed to work well for the coached writers who made substantially more effort to understand their group members' comments. A further indicator of writers trying to draw upon their evaluators' knowledge can be seen in the eliciting category, where writers pressed their evaluators for comments about specific sections of text.

One of the goals of peer-evaluation groups is to facilitate students' shift from writer-based prose to reader-based prose. Evidence of this shift can be seen in the writers' efforts to announce their intentions or to clarify their meanings during group sessions. Although the coaching did not specifically encourage this sort of writer comment, the coached students showed a higher frequency of announcing and clarifying responses than did the uncoached students.

In order to consider how "evenhanded" the peer-evaluation sessions were, the ratio of writers (W) turns to evaluator (Ev) turns was calculated, as was the length of each turn. In the coached groups, the writers took, on average, more turns per session than did their evaluators (W = 8.8; Ev = 6.8), in contrast to the uncoached groups (W = 5.6; Ev = 6.8). That the coached writers took more turns is not surprising in view of their higher incidence of clarification checks and requests for restatements. As for floor-holding, average T-units per session suggest that members of uncoached groups had a stronger tendency to monopolize the discussion (W = 14.3; Ev = 40.1), whereas coached groups showed a somewhat more balanced conversational pattern (W = 16.3; Ev = 18.8). Again, it must be noted that because of small sample size, these figures have not been submitted to statistical analysis.

ANALYSIS: THE DRAFTS

A second focus of the analysis was on the extent to which comments exchanged during peer-evaluation sessions led students to revise their drafts. To investigate the relationship between the peer evaluators' comments and the writers' revisions, the following method was used: Nine drafts were collected from each student in both the coached and uncoached sections during the semester. The transcript of the evaluation of each draft was matched with the draft that immediately followed it. For example, a transcribed evaluation of Draft 2 was read against the text of Draft 3. The drafts were analyzed for evidence of response to evaluators' comments. An illustration will make this process clearer.

A transcript contained the following comment: "Instead of 'Many young people use dangerous drugs,' you could say something like 'Using dangerous drugs is now a serious problem among young people in US.'" This was coded as a collaboration. The draft that followed this session contained the following revision: "Today, many people find that using dangerous drugs is now a serious problem for young people in US." This was judged to be a revision in response to the collaboration.

All transcripts and their drafts were analyzed in this way. I read and rated the entire corpus, and a second teacher read and rated 16 percent of the total. Our reliability figure was 90 percent.

FINDINGS: THE DRAFTS

The drafts of the coached groups evidenced more responses to peer evaluation than did the uncoached groups' drafts. The four response categories that most often produced revision among the coached groups are pointing remarks (26 revisions), advising remarks (21), collaborating (11), and questioning (10). Among the uncoached groups, the level of revision in response to evaluators' comments was quite a bit lower, but four response categories did produce revisions: pointing remarks (10), collaborating (2), advising (2), and reacting (2).

It is clear that the pointing remarks were most powerful in calling the writer to account and were most likely to be responded to in revisions. The coached groups' higher number of revisions in response to peer evaluation again suggests a greater level of engagement in the sessions.

CONCLUSIONS

It seems apparent from this study that the quality of peer interactions can be improved substantially by preparing students more thoroughly for group work. Students who received coaching were seen to look at each other's writing more closely and to offer the writers more specific guidelines for revision than did the uncoached students. Evidence for these claims lies in the higher incidence within coached groups of specific response types such as pointing, advising, and collaborating. Further evidence of this deeper engagement in the evaluation process can be seen in the more frequent occurrences of announcing and clarifying responses within the coached groups. Additionally, the writers in the coached groups were more assertive in getting advice from their evaluators. This assertiveness was evidenced in the more frequent incidence of coached writers responding to evaluators through restatements and comprehension checks. The coached groups dealt more often in concrete, specific issues and more often gave the writer a blueprint for revision. This is shown in their higher number of revisions in response to evaluations.

The quality and the quantity of the responses produced by the coached groups in the study suggest that peer-evaluation groups were worth the effort with these students. However, it must be conceded that the investment of coaching time was substantial. For teachers who would like to promote quality peer interactions, but who worry that such a large expenditure of time is not cost-effective, it may be helpful to reflect on the considerable social and intellectual challenge that a peer-evaluation group presents. Students needs to be socialized to the microculture of the peer-evaluation group. They need to learn rules of effective group interaction, etiquette, and tact. They need to arrive at a classroom consensus of appropriate styles of discussing a classmate's writing and of questioning his or her ideas. Development of this awareness takes time.

It takes even more time for students to learn how to evaluate their classmates' writing. In peer-evaluation groups, teachers ask students to consider the quality of their partners' ideas, to gauge the soundness of their logic, to track the coherence of their arguments. These are essential skills for writers, and they are not easily attained. It is not fair to expect that students will be able to perform these demanding tasks without first having been offered organized practice with and discussion of the skills involved. This takes time.

Peer-evaluation groups can be very productive, but this study shows that the productivity does not come without a considerable investment of time and effort in preparing students for group work.

I am indebted to Suzanne Jacobs, University of Hawaii, Manoa, for her helpful comments on an earlier draft of this article

RESPONSE TYPES CODE SHEET

Peer Evaluator Responses

Announces

_____ thesis statement, topic sentences ("Your thesis statement is 'X.' ")

_____ a "rule" ("A thesis statement needs to have an opinion.")

_____ missing elements ("There is no conclusion here.")

_____ text sections ("The second paragraph talks about. . . .")

Points to

_____ specific phrases or sentences ("Where you say 'XXXXX,' what do you mean?") ("Is 'XXXXX' your thesis statement?")

_____ word choice ("When you say 'X,' do you mean . . . ?")

_____ cohesive gaps ("How does this sentence relate to the first one?")

Advises

Specifically:

_____ solutions to specific problems ("You need to give an example to explain this idea.")

Generally:

_____ by representing the audience ("You have to write this to people who are not using journals, so you can convince them.")

Reacts

_____ evaluatively (general) ("This is really good.")

_____ evaluatively (specific) ("Pretty good introduction. It covers the main points of your essay and has a good thesis.")

Collaborates

_____ by offering a paraphrase/quote

_____ by calling for opinions from other PEs ("Jae, do you think her conclusion is OK?")

Elicits

_____ writer's opinion about essay

Questions

_____ elements of text ("What is the topic of your second paragraph?")

_____ the logic of an argument ("If you don't tell people about your reading, how can reading be a social advantage?")

Writer Responses

Announces

_____ text part ("My conclusion is next.")

_____ problem ("My problem is I didn't describe a lot.")

Clarifies text

_____ quotes from text

_____ paraphrases text

_____ recapitulates major points

_____ describes intentions ("What I wanted to say was. . . .")

_____ describes scope of text ("This is not only about skill; it's about understanding too.")

_____ describes writing process ("I decided this was too long, so I separated it into another paragraph.")

Responds

_____ accepts PE remark ("OK, so that's not clear to you.")

_____ restates/interprets PE remark ("OK, what you're saying is. . . .")

_____ requests clarification ("What do you mean?")

_____ justifies ("I already said that in the second paragraph.")

Questions

_____ "rules" ("Is it OK to only state the advantages, or do we have to give both?")

Elicits

_____ ("Are my examples going too far?") ("Do you think that it is too strong?")

Essay No. _____   Student No. _____

REFERENCES

Acton, W. (1984). Some pragmatic dimensions of ESL writing tutorials. *TECFORS, 7,* 107.

Allaei, S., & Connor, U. (1990). Exploring the dynamics of cross-cultural collaboration. *The Writing Instructor, 10,* 19–28.

Beaven, M. (1977). Individualized goal-setting, self-evaluation, and peer evaluation. In C. Cooper & L. Odell (Eds.), *Evaluating writing: Describing, measuring, judging* (pp. 135–156). Urbana, IL: National Council of Teachers of English.

Brady, S., & Jacobs, S. (1988). Children responding to children. In T. Newkirk & N. Atwell (Eds.), *Understanding writing: Ways of observing learning and teaching* (pp. 142–149). Portsmouth, NH: Heinemann.

Bruffee, K. (1984). Collaborative learning and the "conversation of mankind." *College English, 46,* 635–652.

Chaudron, C. (1984). The effects of feedback on student's composition revisions. *RELC Journal, 15,* 1–14.

Clifford, J. (1981). Composing in stages: The effects of a collaborative pedagogy. *Research in the Teaching of English, 15,* 37–53.

Collins, J. (1982). Training teachers of basic writing in the writing laboratory. *College Composition and Communication, 33,* 426–433.

Danis, M. (1980). Peer-response groups in a college writing workshop: Students' suggestions for revising compositions. *Dissertation Abstracts International, 41,* 5008A–5009A.

Danis, M. (1982, March). *Weaving the web of meaning: Interactional patterns in peer response groups.* Paper presented at the Conference on College Composition and Communication, San Francisco. (ERIC Document Reproduction Service No. ED 214 202)

Elbow, P. (1973). *Writing without teachers.* New York: Oxford University Press.

Elbow, P. (1981). *Writing with power.* New York: Oxford University Press.

Flower, L., & Hayes, J. (1981). A cognitive process theory of writing. *College Composition and Communication, 32,* 365–388.

Flynn, E. (1982, November). *Effects of peer critiquing and model analysis on the quality of biology student laboratory reports.* Paper presented at the annual meeting of the National Council of Teachers of English, Washington, DC. (ERIC Document Reproduction Service No. ED 234 403)

Ford, B. (1973). The effects of peer editing/grading on the grammar-usage and theme-composition of college freshmen. *Dissertation Abstracts International, 34,* 1532A.

Freedman, S. (1985). Response to and evaluation of writing: A review. *Resources in Education.* (ERIC Document Reproduction Service No. ED 247 605)

Fujimoto, D. (1987). *Training peer tutors for the writing lab.* Unpublished master's thesis, University of Hawaii, Manoa.

Gere, A. (1987). *Writing groups: History, theory and implications.* Carbondale, IL: Southern Illinois University Press.

Gere, A., & Stevens, R. (1985). The language of writing groups: How oral response shapes revision. In S. Freedman (Ed.), *The acquisition of written language: Response and revision* (pp. 85–105). Norwood, NJ: Ablex.

Hunt, K. (1965). *Grammatical structures written at three grade levels.* Champaign, IL: National Council of Teachers of English.

Jacobs, H., Zinkgraf, S., Wormuth, D., Hartfiel, V., & Hughey, J. (1981). *Testing ESL composition: A practical approach.* Rowley, MA: Newbury House.

Karengianes, M., Pascarella, E., & Pflaum, S. (1980). The effects of peer editing on the writing proficiency of low-achieving tenth grade students. *The Journal of Educational Research, 73,* 203–207.

Kastra, J. (1987). Effects of peer evaluation on attitudes toward writing fluency of ninth graders. *Journal of Educational Research, 80,* 168–172.

King, J. (1979, March). *Measuring attitudes toward writing: The King construct scale.* Paper presented at the Conference on College Composition and Communication, Minneapolis, MN.

Kroll, B., & Vann, R. (1981). *Exploring speaking-writing relationships: Connections and contrasts.* Urbana, IL: National Council of Teachers of English.

Leki, I. (1990). Potential problems with peer responding in ESL writing classes. *CATESOL Journal, 3,* 5–17.

Lunsford, R. (1986). Planning for spontaneity in the writing classroom and a passel of other paradoxes. In C. Bridges (Ed.), *Training the new teacher of college composition* (pp. 95–108). Urbana, IL: National Council of Teachers of English.

Partridge, K. (1981). *A comparison of the effectiveness of peer vs. teacher evaluation for helping students of English as a second language to improve the quality of their written compositions.* Unpublished master's thesis, University of Hawaii, Manoa.

Pfeiffer, J. (1981). *The effects of peer evaluation and personality on writing anxiety and writing performance in college freshmen.* Unpublished doctoral dissertation, Texas Tech University, Lubbock.

Putz, J. (1970). When the teacher stops teaching—An experiment with freshman English. *College English, 34,* 50–57.

Follow-Up Questions and Activities

1. Do you agree with Flower's distinction between writer-based and reader-based prose? What are the implications for teaching?

2. At what point in the writing process should students begin to pay attention to the reader, and what are the implications for writing instruction?

3. Do several minutes of nonstop freewriting in class. Then use that prose as the basis for a more reader-based essay. What results do you or your classmates find that might be useful for teaching?

4. Flower writes that the results of having students work with code words is not unlike "those brilliant explications one often hears from students who tell you what their paper really meant." Conduct a study in which you observe or tape record a teacher-student conference and discuss the instances in which the student was able to express himself or herself better orally than in writing. In your write-up of the study, be certain to include the implications for writing instruction.

5. Flower states, "When it is very difficult or impossible to write for a reader from the beginning, writing and then transforming Writer-Based prose is a practical alternative which breaks this complex process down into manageable parts." Create a lesson plan in which you have your students break the writing process "into manageable parts," and then write an essay that explains the effectiveness of this approach.

6. According to Stanley, "the ultimate success of a peer-evaluation session lies not in how carefully students read each other's drafts, but in how well they communicate their perceptions to the writer." Write a brief essay in which you report your opinion of this statement.

7. Observe or tape-record a peer group feedback session. Discuss it with the class and report your findings and their implications in an essay.

8. Devise a lesson plan and rationale for the use of peer group feedback in the writing class.

4

COMPOSING

EDITOR'S INTRODUCTION

Recognition by the teacher and student that writing can best be viewed as a process does not automatically solve many of the problems that students encounter as they write. Students sometimes need help in generating ideas both before and during the writing process, and the best of writers sometimes become blocked. Ruth Spack discusses the art of invention and offers strategies to help students generate topics and ideas for writing. Some students, however, experience writing blocks during the composition stage. According to Mike Rose, writers often apply overly rigid rules to the complex process of composition. Rather than adhering to the "rule," for example, that every composition should have at least three main ideas, students should pay attention, he suggests, to exploring their own insights into an issue.

Prereading Questions

1. What are some of the strategies you employ to generate ideas for your own writing? Do you employ these strategies before or during your writing, or both? How could your students benefit from these strategies?

2. Have you ever experienced a writing block? What did you do to overcome it?

Invention Strategies and the ESL College Composition Student

RUTH SPACK *Tufts University and Boston University*

INTRODUCTION

Most composition textbooks for native English speakers and ESL students present a straightforward, mechanical view of writing which does not acknowledge the complexity of the composing process. These texts have not shown students how meticulous and even painful writing can be, especially for nonnative speakers. In short, they exhibit a lack of understanding of what students must go through to write.

Such composition texts are steeped in what Richard E. Young calls the "current-traditional paradigm" (1978:30). The term *paradigm,* borrowed from Thomas Kuhn's *The Structure of Scientific Revolutions* (1970), signifies a system of shared beliefs and assumptions, a conceptual model in intellectual disciplines which determines "the problems that need to be solved, the rules that govern research and . . . the standards by which performance is to be measured" (Hairston 1982:76). The conceptual model for teaching writing has, since the beginning of the century, emphasized the composed product rather than the composing process; analyzed discourse into words, sentences, and paragraphs; classified discourse into description, narration, exposition, and argument; and focused on style and usage (Young 1978). According to Hairston (1982), practitioners of this traditional paradigm assume that writers know what they are going to say before they begin to write and that the primary task of writers is to predetermine the form by which to organize their ideas. Furthermore, practitioners see the composing process as a linear movement and equate teaching editing with teaching writing. Young contends that current-traditional rhetoric is based on "vitalist assumptions, inherited from the Romantics," that "creative processes, which include the composing process, are not susceptible to conscious control by formal procedures" (1978:31–32); thus, current-traditional rhetoric repudiates the possibility of teaching anyone how a written product comes into being.

In the 1960s, the conventional paradigm was challenged precisely because it had not been tested against the actual composing processes of writers, and a demand for new directions in research and pedagogy—for a major paradigm revision—arose (Young 1978). In the first-language composition field, several theories accelerated what Kuhn (1970) calls the "paradigm change," or "shift." Referring to thinking as an activity of the mind which generates and develops ideas, Rohman (1965), for example, urged writing researchers to determine what kind of thinking precedes writing and to teach students that structure of thinking. Christensen's articles on generative rhetoric argued for a "rhetoric of the sentence that . . . will *generate* ideas" (1967b:191) and for a teacher-student writing relationship in which the teacher intervenes to show students how to put themselves "imaginatively in the reader's place" (1967a:206). Murray (1968) recommended that we shift our focus from written product to writing process—that we ask not, What does the writer write? but, How does the writer write?—and that we take the mystery out of the creative process of composing by teaching our students that the act of writing itself can generate meaning.

Recent empirical studies of the composing processes of unskilled and skilled native English-speaking writers (Perl 1979, Pianko 1979, Flower and Hays 1980, Sommers 1980) have corroborated Emig's (1971) finding that the writing process is a series of overlapping and interacting processes. Drawing on theories of cognitive psychology, Flower and Hayes (1977) characterized writing as a form of problem solving, the study of which explores the mental procedures writers use to process information to communicate intentions and ideas to others. Poor writers have been identified as those who have not effectively assimilated these procedures. Perl (1979), for example, found that unskilled writers interfere with their thinking by editing their writing prematurely. Rose (1980) concluded that students with writer's block operate with rigid rules rather than with the flexibility necessary to reflect on what they have written. Too many students think of writing as a test of their ability to utilize mechanical skills (Britton, Burgess, Martin, McLeod, and Rosen 1975). Finding that poor writers are concerned primarily with surface features, while good writers are concerned also with "the rhetorical situation"—that is, the audience, the circumstance which elicits the discourse, and the constraints of the writer (Bitzer 1968) as well as the writer's own goals—Flower and Hayes have determined that the ability to explore a rhetorical problem is "eminently teachable" (1980:31). Case studies reveal that students need time to be taught and to practice the stage of discovery in the writing process during which writers initially contemplate and assimilate their subjects (Emig 1971, Mischel 1974, Stallard 1974).

From this work and from linguistic research, a new paradigm for the teaching of writing to native English speakers is emerging (Young 1978, Hairston 1982). Its principal features are 1) a view of writing as a recursive process which can be taught, 2) an emphasis on writing as a way of learning as well as communicating, 3) a willingness to draw on other disciplines, notably cognitive psychology and linguistics, 4) the incorporation of a rhetorical context, a view that writing assignments include a sense of audience, purpose, and occasion, 5) a procedure for feedback which encourages the instructor to intervene during the process, 6) a method of evaluation which determines how well a written product adapts the goals of the writer to the needs of the reader, and 7) the principle that writing teachers should be people who write (Hairston 1982).

Some ESL writing teachers and researchers who have become aware of the paradigm shift in the first-language writing instruction field have described how an ESL writing course can benefit from this research by shifting its focus from the written product to the writing process (Zamel 1976, Raimes 1979, Taylor 1981, Clark 1982, Watson 1982). The findings of Zamel's case studies of advanced ESL college students (1982, 1983) indicate that these ESL writers employ composing strategies similar to those of their native-speaker counterparts. Such research alerts us to the need for writing instruction which teaches ESL students that they can experience writing as a creative process for exploring and communicating meaning.

THE ART OF INVENTION

The current-traditional paradigm is based on three arts of the classical rhetorical model of oral discourse: invention, arrangement, and style (Hairston 1982). Yet the teaching of the art of invention is, for the most part, excluded from the conventional paradigm because proponents of the current-traditional model believe invention skills are innate and therefore cannot be taught (Young 1978). They see rhetoric as "the art of presenting ideas," not as original inquiry or as the development of new knowledge (Young 1978:32). The development of effective procedures for finding ideas, therefore, has low priority for the current-traditionalists, and their handbooks and rhetoric texts emphasize instead organization and correctness (Harrington 1968).

Concurrent with the formulation of a new paradigm is a renewed interest in the art of invention. To Young, this comes as no surprise:

> Invention requires a process view of rhetoric; and if the composing process is to be taught, rather than left to the student to be learned, arts associated with the various stages of the process are necessary (1978:35).

To the classical rhetoricians, invention meant the disclosure of valid arguments to further one's cause. As a method of inquiry to discover these arguments, Aristotle introduced the notion of *topics,* which represent different ways to view a subject. For example, an orator could investigate and collect information about a subject by arguing from similarities and differences (comparison), from the meanings of words (definition), from causes and effects (relationship), and so on. In the classical approach, invention was thought of as a means of putting the speaker in contact with knowledge and relationships that already existed (Young and Becker 1967).

The use of the topics of classical invention has been revived in the past decade, although they have been changed to meet the needs of modern times. The communication theory of the humanist psychologist Carl Rogers, for example, has played a role in influencing the way rhetoricians look at invention (see Young, Becker, and Pike 1970). Rogerian-based rhetoric questions the efficacy in today's heterogeneous world of the logical, argumentative strategies of classical rhetoric, which were designed primarily to control a homogeneous society by persuading its members to accept the rhetor's point of view. In a modern rhetorical situation, where mutual communication, acceptance, and understanding between writer and audience are the goals, these authoritative strategies may block that goal and therefore be ineffective (Bator 1980). Because the classical art of rhetoric stresses "authoritative confirmation of present beliefs" at the expense of "the imaginative discovery of new facts and relationships," includes only patterns of persuasion at the expense of other patterns of discourse, treats form as independent of both the subject matter and the writer, and limits style primarily to the technique of forming effective sentences, classical invention has recently been expanded to include a variety of ways to view a subject or problem (Young and Becker 1967:132).

Topics are now defined as "probes or a series of questions that one might ask about a subject in order to discover things to say about that subject" (Winterowd 1973:702). Since the purpose of topics is to generate ideas about a subject, not to fill up a page with words, topics can be considered problem-solving devices, or heuristics (Winterowd 1973). According to the *Oxford English Dictionary, heuristics* is a fairly recent term, dating from about 1860, and meaning only "serving to find out or discover"; however, the term has come to serve as a label for systematic procedures of discovery in several disciplines, including mathematics and psychology, and was brought to the attention of rhetoricians by Lauer (1970).

Kenneth Burke's dramatistic analyses, centered on motivation in language behavior, led to a new art of invention in the field of rhetoric (Young 1978). According to Burke, "any complete statement about motives will offer *some kind* of answers to these five questions: what was done (act), when or where it was done (scene), who did it (agent), how he did it (agency), and why (purpose)" (1945:x). When two of these five aspects ("the pentad") of a subject are combined—agent and purpose, for example, or purpose and act—new insights and human dramas arise.

Young, Becker, and Pike (1970) developed a complex discovery procedure based on the linguistic theory of tagmemics, which argues that to know an object or concept, we must know how it differs from others in its class, how much it can change and still be itself, and how it fits into a larger system. Each concept or object can also be viewed as a static entity, a dynamic process, or a system of interrelated parts. Young, Becker, and Pike constructed a chart to organize these characteristics and perspectives into a set of operations and questions designed to lead students to shift categories systematically to aid the process of inquiry and to move toward the solution of a rhetorical problem.

Rohman's prewriting strategies serve to "introduce students to the dynamics of creation" by teaching them to experience a subject in a new way and to see writing as one important form of self-actualization (1965:107). Rohman's method, based on the premise that the prewriting stage is hidden in the mind, employs three approaches: the keeping of a daily journal, the practice of principles derived from religious meditation, and the use of analogy as a mechanism for looking at an event in several different ways.

While Rohman's influence on the paradigm shift has been significant in its emphasis on imitating a creative process rather than on imitating a written product, some of his underlying assumptions have been called into question. Yarnoff (1980) specifically takes issue with Rohman's statement that "writers set out in apparent ignorance of what they are groping for . . . When it is 'out,' they have discovered their subject; all that's left is the writing of it" (1965:107), on the grounds that it engenders complacency, fails to acknowledge the complexity of the writing process, and leaves no room for a critical examination of ideas. Likewise, Sommers (1980) points out that Rohman's view of the composing process is essentially a linear one, proceeding from prewriting to writing, and does not incorporate the concept that thinking occurs in every stage of the process. Similarly, Flower and Hayes warn against a "myth of discovery" which might lead writers to self-defeating strategies if they believe that hidden reserves of insight and preformed ideas exist. Discovery is hard work: "Writers don't *find* meanings; they *make* them" (1980:21).

Nevertheless, Rohman's theory, along with those of Burke (1945) and Young, Becker, and Pike (1970), set the stage for the development of other invention strategies for composition. Larson (1968), for example, has proposed a plan of systematic questioning. Macrorie (1968) has recommended free writing, and Elbow (1973) has expanded the activity of free writing to include a summing-up procedure. Odell (1973) has designed a problem-solving strategy for a literature and composition course. Detailed descriptions and examples of a variety of invention techniques can be found in many recent first-language composition textbooks (see, for example, Maimon, Belcher, Hearn, Nodine, and O'Connor 1981, Winterowd 1981, Cowan 1982).

Experimental research has been conducted to test the effectiveness of specific methods of invention: studies by Rohman and Wlecke (1964) and Burhans (1968) of prewriting procedures; by Young and Koen (1973) and Odell (1974) of tagmemic heuristics; and by Hilgers (1980) of Elbow's free-writing heuristics and of problem-solving heuristics. It has been impossible, though, to determine which invention strategy is more suited to our times, not only because of design flaws in these studies but also because our conception of the composing process, which influences our criteria for judgment, is still evolving (Young 1978). The process may not be the same for all kinds of discourse, and different theories of invention may be suitable for different kinds of processes (Young 1978). Kinney, classifying heuristics into *empirical* modes (interviews, visits, observations), *rational* modes (classical topics; Burke's pentad; Larson's questions; Young, Becker, and Pike's procedure; problem-solving formulas), and *intuitive* modes (brainstorming; free-association lists; Rohman's journal, meditation, and analogy; Elbow's free writing), argues for "a balance in our heuristics" (1979:354). To teach students that inventing depends solely on one mode, to the exclusion of others, claims Kinney, would limit their potential as writers.

The ESL writing field has not yet fully embraced this trend. Although individual ESL teachers have begun to recognize the importance of invention as an art that can be taught as part of a creative process of discovery and communication (Raimes 1979, Taylor 1981, Daubney-Davis 1982a, 1982b, 1982c, McKay 1982, Zamel 1982, 1983), ESL composition textbooks still treat writing as a linear movement toward the final product and emphasize form and correctness (Raimes 1983, Zamel 1983). Published research on invention in ESL composition is, to this author's knowledge, non-existent.

INVENTION TECHNIQUES IN AN ESL FRESHMAN WRITING COURSE

The art of invention has a prominent place in my ESL freshman composition class, a two-semester course which fulfills the college's writing requirement. The class consists primarily of freshman students from every academic field at the university and from a variety of national backgrounds. All these students carry a full academic load. Although their English proficiency varies, they have studied formal grammar, have satisfactory listening and reading skills, can communicate orally with some ease, and have done some writing in English. Their TOEFL scores are at least 550. All need strong writing skills to compete academically with their native English-speaking counterparts.

During the first semester, the students write a variety of essays, ranging from personal to global topics, which grow out of discussions on readings in the humanities and social sciences; write a longer research paper; and keep working journals which focus on issues related to writing and which are sometimes used to generate ideas for other class-related writing assignments (Spack and Sadow 1983). During the second semester, the students write several literary analyses based on assigned works of fiction; the topics of these papers grow out of class discussion, notes, journals, and research.

The course has two goals: 1) to provide the students with the necessary tools to meet the university's standard of written academic work and 2) to make them aware that the act of writing is a complex process of using language to discover and clarify meaning (Murray 1968). To those ends, class time is spent on analyzing readings and on sharing writing. After students are given a writing assignment, they are provided time in and out of class to use invention techniques to generate ideas for their papers; their discoveries are often shared in the classroom. Students subsequently write a trial draft and bring that to class. They read their drafts and, following a set of guidelines, discuss with each other how ideas can be developed and clarified. Students may use invention techniques again to generate more material and then bring back another draft to share.

One of the texts I have used, Cowan and Cowan's *Writing* (1980), contains examples of a number of invention techniques, six of which I present to my students: 1) oral group brainstorming, 2) list making, 3) looping (write nonstop, with no self-censorship, on anything that comes to mind on a specific topic; then stop, read, reflect, and sum up in a single sentence what has just been written; repeat this procedure twice), 4) dialogue writing (carry on a conversation with yourself in writing about a specific topic), 5) cubing (swiftly consider a subject from six points of view: describe it, compare it, associate it, analyze it, apply it, argue for or against it), and 6) classical invention (write brief answers to several questions about a subject, which are grouped according to Aristotle's common topics: definition, comparison, relationship, circumstance, and testimony). Samples showing how one student used five of these techniques are included later in this article.

I teach each of these techniques on successive days at the beginning of the semester to show the students some procedures for getting started on a writing assignment. I write with my students to give credibility to the art of invention, to experience what invention accomplishes, and to learn about the writing process by writing (Emig 1971). We share many of our ideas aloud. Although some of the ideas generated may not lead to a successful essay, students come to see that some of what they write down is meaningful, entertaining, or instructive in some way.

One advantage of introducing the invention techniques is that they can teach students to begin, not by trying to write a polished essay, but by writing down their ideas quickly in raw form, ignoring at this stage any concern about surface error. When inexperienced writers attempt to write a perfect essay from the outset, they slow down, trying to put down exactly the right word, to put the right word into the right phrase, to put the right phrase into the right sentence, and so on (Shaughnessy 1977). They think, and then they write. Invention techniques allow students to think and write at the same time. Editing errors and revising for better organization should be attended to at a later stage in writing to prevent a breakdown of what Perl calls "the rhythms generated by thinking and writing" (1979:333). Students are encouraged to use their native language or to coin words when a vocabulary word in English does not immediately come to mind so that they can keep their pens moving.

Invention is taught as a stage in the composing process at which it is appropriate to take risks, to employ whatever intellectual, cognitive, and linguistic skills students can muster. They are told to write down words and ideas rather than to write down grammar (Raimes 1979). Many need to be reassured that not all writing needs to be flawless and that even native speakers make mistakes when their primary goal is discovery. Usually, though, if students continue to practice a given technique, they become more proficient at it and gain confidence in their ability to use it. In addition, when they have the opportunity to listen in class to other students' and the teacher's invention notes, they can learn to value this loosely structured use of language and become more accepting of their own informal writing.

While students should not give up on invention techniques too early, neither should they have specific techniques imposed on them when they actually begin an assignment. As Maimon, Belcher, Hearn, Nodine, and O'Connor write, "a heuristic is a strategy, not a rule" (1981:8). Invention can be systematized, but not every system will work for every writer. Just as some writers need yellow legal pads, a library cubicle, or the sound of music to get themselves started on their writing, so do writers differ in their need for heuristic structures. I do agree with Winterowd (1973), however, that some work with systematized heuristics will introduce students to techniques they can use to develop their own problem-solving devices, once they have grasped the principles underlying the art of invention. The idea is to dislodge the misconception that writing can be produced only by talent or by sudden inspiration. The techniques should not be viewed as restrictive but should enable students to "gain the *freedom* to express themselves" (Winterowd 1973:708).

Telling students about this stage of the writing process cannot be as valuable as guiding them through it. Invention techniques need to be practiced in the classroom first if students are to be expected to use them outside of class in their writing assignments. I have observed, for example, that none of my students uses the techniques which I do not specifically teach but which are described in the Cowans' textbook—Burke's pentad; a variation of Young, Becker, and Pike's procedure; and the reporter's formula (who? what? where? when? how?)—even though they are assigned to read about them. Unless students are taught how to use specific techniques, they are unlikely to do so. This is not to say, however, that students cannot or will not devise their own invention strategies. They can, and they do, and they should. The point is that students can learn the value of systematic exploration when it is carefully explained and shared, is closely tied to a writing assignment, and leads toward focused and well-developed writing.

THE INVENTION NOTES OF ONE ESL COLLEGE STUDENT

Rolando, a Paraguayan student whose invention writings follow, was a first-semester freshman who had studied English conversation and grammar in his teens in his native country. He had also spent six months as an exchange student in a U.S. junior high school and a semester in an American Language Academy program just prior to entering college. Rolando had never been taught invention techniques before he enrolled in freshman English. He and his classmates were asked to use at least one of the techniques which they had learned during the early days of our course—or to use a technique of their own—to get started on a writing assignment. Because Rolando used five of the techniques taught, I have chosen his work as a unique illustration of how an ESL student can successfully employ these invention strategies.

The general assignment for this essay was to discuss a college-related problem and/or solution which the students had experienced, knew of, or could research. To aid them in their search for a specific topic, the students read and discussed in class examples of professional and student essays on related themes such as the problems of procrastination, communication, and learning to write. In addition, they were given a selection of real-life writing contexts, which contained a purpose and an intended audience.[1] They could adapt these contexts to provide themselves with a real need to communicate and a real problem to solve.

For Rolando to produce his paper was no easy task. It was a prodigious struggle with language and ideas which required hours of writing and thought. Rolando had to take risks with writing that he had never taken before, beginning with ignoring errors in the early stages of writing. The early goals of composing are to find a suitable subject for an essay, to determine what directions the topic can take, to generate content, and to discover something to say. These were Rolando's goals when he used invention techniques. The lack of attention to error on Rolando's part will at first appear flagrant, but it should be remembered that at this stage his invention was purely private, exploratory, and experimental writing.

Rolando began by using the technique of looping, which he had practiced in class. He wrote nonstop, making no corrections, for five to ten minutes on the topic of "Problem/Solution." He then stopped, reread what he had written, reflected on it, and wrote down a "center of gravity" sentence (Elbow 1973) which expressed the essence of what he had just written. That sentence became the topic for his second five-minute loop, after which he completed the procedure yet another time, for a total of three loops. His first loop, and the directions for the technique, are given below:

> *Write quickly all that comes to your mind about Problem/Solution for 5–10 minutes. Keep your pen moving on the page. If you get distracted, return to your topic as soon as you can. Make no corrections as you write.*
>
> I have obscourse many problems in my life like everybody has but right now I am feeling new problems like the cultural schock. I got out of my country and came to study in the U.S.A. On of the bigest problems is to make friends, to make or have the good oll friends I have back home. Is so hard here you don't know how to act, whether you should ask them their telephone number or wait for them to do it, whether you should call them very often or not. Are they bodered by my language problem, can't they carrie on conversation with me because they always talk about local or national subject of which I not inform. This is really hard and some time make me feel like an estranger in a group were everybody is lauphin and talking and they sopposly were my friends.
>
> *Now read over your notes to see what the "center of gravity" idea is. Express in a single sentence a statement that catches the essence of what you said.*
>
> Some times I feel like an stranger.
>
> *Repeat this procedure twice, starting each time with your newest "center of gravity" sentence.*

Because he felt that the problem which most preoccupied him—making friends in a foreign country—was too "confusing" to be a suitable subject for the assignment, Rolando went on to have a dialogue with himself. Like Flower and Hayes' (1981) good writers, Rolando was looking at many aspects of the rhetorical problem; he was not just looking for information about the topic but was asking himself questions to better define it. Rolando used the

---

[1]For example: Context: You are running for a student government position. Prepare a position paper in which you discuss some problem (for example, library hours, quality of food, lack of sports facilities) you would solve if you won the election. Audience: The student body.

technique of dialogue as he struggled to find a subject other than the problem which had dominated his looping. The first few lines, and the directions for the technique, are given below:

Write as though you were talking out loud to yourself. When you get stuck or reach a dead end, use the second voice to get the conversation moving.

Other problems I have.

[First voice:] I have to start writting I just thought I don't have other problems. There must be some other problems of which I'am aware of, but I can't think, I think is becouse there is one problem that takes so much time and space in my head.

[Second voice:] Well that's a problem, to have a problem that goes around your head night and day and wares your brain away.

[First voice:] What to do I don't know . . .

As it turned out, dialogue writing did not help Rolando come up with a new subject. Like many students who use invention techniques, he discovered instead that such writing can help eliminate subjects which are not appropriate or which are not worth the time necessary to produce an essay.

Rolando began to use classical invention on the problem which refused to go away, which he now called, "To Reach Integration with American Students." He followed the Cowans' method of grouping his thoughts according to Aristotle's common topics and quickly writing down brief answers to the questions listed within each category. Rolando went through all 39 questions. The answers to some questions in the first two categories are included below.[2] (The questions appear in italics.)

To Reach Integration with American Students

Definition

1. *How does the dictionary define* integration? Act or process of integrating, specif act or process of making whole or entire—The unificatio of the increasingly and multiple elements—internal unificatio characteristic of an organism, as the combination of elementary sensation in perceptio

2. *What earlier words did* integration *come from?* Early word Latin intergratio renewing restoring

3. *What do I mean by* integration? What I mean: Being part of a group, become friends . . .

Comparison

1. *What is integration similar to? Why?* When you get a new job and you get along with your work mates. When you enter a sport team and you become and operational and useful part of the team—In that you are not only part but participant, active in the group as a whole. You understand the way they do their things so that you can do it.

2. *What is integration different from? In what ways?* Is different from accepting or recognize because is more than that is making him an active part—working, active . . .

---

[2]Categories not included here: relationship (questions about cause and effect); testimony (questions about primary and secondary sources); circumstance (questions about feasibility).

In the first question of the Comparison section of his classical invention notes, Rolando discovered a similarity between achieving integration with American students and becoming part of a sports team. This comparison would be developed in subsequent invention techniques and would ultimately become the focus of his essay.

After filling out the classical invention questionnaire, Rolando began to cube on his topic, which he now called "The Language Barrier." He quickly wrote about the subject from six perspectives, spending a few minutes on each perspective. Three of the six sections of this exercise, as well as directions, are presented below.[3] Note that in the Associate section, he returns to his sports comparison, which becomes more specific.

The Language Barrier

1. *Describe it (look closely and tell what you see).*
   The language barrier is the idealistic or imaginary barrier that you feel in contry or groups of people that speak a different language than you do. You feel that barrier because even thoug you can speak the language, and you can make yorself understand you can't get your ideas across, you are speaking but you fell your words desintegrate before reaching their effect. You fell continuously that you have to think in every word you are seing when the natural is just to let your spirit expres with out thinking. You doubt of yourself. You feel unsensire, you fell unsecure, you feel false, becouse your choosing so much your words. But when you use them just like that you are misunderstood.

2. *Compare it (what is it similar to? different from?).*
   Is hard to compare but is like you reach to a point where you feel you are in a theather rehersing where every body is talking something that deep inside is not natural, that all talking doesnt belong to reality. I like when seing a poem but you don't know its meaning. I like when you have to write a letter and you don't have the paper to write on, or even you write but you don't know the zip-code so you just don't send your, is like talking to yourself.

3. *Associate it (what does it remind you of? and what other associations come to mind?).*
   It reminds me of reading a very hard book and no understand the meaning but yes the words, is like being a band and no sing with the group. Every time I feel the barrier of language I feel who far I'm from home and how necessarly are cultures. Feeling the language barrier is like when I play tennis I can't get a "serving" and some time I can even answer the ball. You don't know how to say what you say . . .

After he finished cubing, Rolando used the technique of list making, culling main ideas from his invention notes, to prepare for his initial draft. (The list is not included here.) The subject of integration into a new culture—discovered in his looping exercise, compared to sports in his classical invention exercise, and narrowed down to an analogy between tennis and language learning in his cubing exercise—was then shaped into a thesis for an essay:

Thesis

Integration to a new culture

Learning ~~how to use~~ a foreign language as a mean of integration to a ~~new~~ new culture is like ~~a tennis~~ learning how to play tennis ~~when you are a beginner~~.

---

[3] Perspectives not included here: analyze it (tell how it's made; make it up if you aren't sure); apply it (tell what you can do with it; how can it be used?); argue for or against it (take a stand; give any reason—silly, serious, or in-between).

Rolando wrote several drafts before he handed in his finished composition. The process of invention did not end with his development of a thesis. As he wrote successive drafts, new ideas occurred to him and were included, illustrating Flower and Hayes' assertion that "new knowledge . . . can interrupt the process at any time" (1981:380). But the time spent using invention techniques early in the assignment was profitable. According to Lauer, writing contexts should be ones in which students find "*personal* exigencies" (1980:56) so that they can "explore questions that *they* deem compelling" (1980:54). Rolando's invention strategies provided him with a real need to express and communicate his ideas to others. Furthermore, exploring and defining his own rhetorical problem helped him "to create inspiration instead of wait for it" (Flower and Hayes 1980:32). The writing context which he created looked like this:

Context

I am a Tufts student and I have to write an article for the *Tufts Daily*. The paper should discus any problem that foreing student have when they come to study in this country.

Audience

The Tufts community in general.

Through invention, Rolando discovered an organic relationship between the content of his subject and its ultimate form (Judy 1980, Taylor 1981). Beginning with his initial draft, Rolando made an effort to synthesize and further clarify his ideas, to put them down in an organized fashion, to include examples relevant to his audience, and to construct well-developed sentences. A concern for organization and correctness gained priority in his writing after ideas came to life in invention. His finished composition was a carefully constructed essay which shed light on the problems which the language barrier poses for international students studying abroad (see Appendix).

IMPLICATIONS FOR ESL RESEARCH AND PEDAGOGY

We should test the hypothesis that ESL students' writing performance will improve if they are taught invention skills. While empirical studies can be undertaken to determine the efficacy of invention techniques, we can also carry out less rigorous investigations in our own classrooms. First, since a certain procedure might actually interfere with some writers' natural and unique thinking and writing processes, we should offer a repertoire of invention techniques from which our students can choose. Because of the nature of our field, it is important that we learn how students of different backgrounds experience different invention techniques. In my own classroom experience, for example, some Japanese students initially have difficulty with and become agitated by the practice of looping because they have been trained to believe it is wrong to write whatever comes to mind without regard to error. They are much more comfortable with what they perceive to be the more structured technique of cubing, which allows them to relax more, to analyze many aspects of a subject, and to get their thoughts down in a more organized way. These same students, however, usually recognize the value of uncensored, nonstop writing by the end of the semester and are willing to use it. In an ESL writing program, we may need to devise a variety of invention techniques which meet the unique needs of our students. We may also need to present different techniques at different points in the semester to accommodate changes in our students' writing abilities and attitudes.

We should also determine when ESL students are ready to be taught and to use the art of invention. A study by Witte and Faigley (1981) of native English-speaking writers suggests that poorer writers are deficient in invention skills because they lack the working vocabulary necessary to explore and expand on the ideas they discover; practice in invention can therefore have only a limited effect on writing quality. Raimes reminds us that "our students have been telling us for many years, 'What we need is vocabulary,' " and her response is, "They are probably right. They certainly do need vocabulary to engage with content" (1983:549). Therefore, if ESL students are to become immersed in the writing process from inception to completion, they need rich vocabularies. The students I have taught have come to college with a lexical background in English which enables them to benefit from instruction in invention. Nevertheless, non-native speakers such as my students, who are still in the process of gaining control over a new language, have a problem using English words that native speakers do not share. Since English words are not tied to their experiences, ESL students sometimes have difficulty making images and thoughts concrete. On the other hand, they do have their native language to draw on when expressions in English elude them. Students should therefore be allowed to use their first language freely when they invent so that they can meaningfully link image to word. Lay's (1982) investigation of the composing processes of four Chinese college students suggests that recourse to the native language is both helpful and effective.

When students practice invention, they can learn that writing, in addition to being a powerful tool for communicating ideas, is an intellectual thinking process, a creative craft, a way to use language to discover meaning, and a mode of learning. They can gain something lasting from the writing course if the discovery stage helps them recognize the principle that underlies all writing:

> The fundamental structure is *not* one of content but of method. Students must learn the structure of thinking that leads to writing since there is no other "content" to writing apart from the dynamic of conceptualizing (Rohman 1965:107).

This thinking/writing process does not occur passively; it is the result of diligent effort on the part of each writer to self-define a rhetorical problem, even within the limitations of an assignment:

> A writer in the act of discovery is hard at work searching memory, forming concepts, and forging a new structure of ideas, while at the same time trying to juggle all the constraints imposed by . . . purpose, audience, and language itself (Flower and Hayes 1980:21).

The process is all the more challenging for students who are not writing in their native language.

We cannot depend solely on research with and techniques for native English-speaking students for insight into the invention strategies of our ESL students; we need to undertake studies and develop teaching practices which are uniquely suited to ESL composition instruction. Clearly, though, our students can benefit from instruction in and practice of the art of invention, and we can benefit from sharing it with them.

ACKNOWLEDGMENTS

This paper expands on a workshop presented with Catherine Sadow at the 18th Annual TESOL Conference in Houston, Texas, March 1984.

ROLANDO'S FINISHED COMPOSITION*

A few months ago I decided that I wanted to learn how to play tennis. Today after much practice and a few classes, I know how to hold the raquet and basically how to hit the ball, however I still can't say that I actually play tennis. It is taking me so long to learn and it is so difficult! It didn't look that hard when I saw my friends playing it so gracefully. Even so, I am still giving it a try. But to play a sport that I can not master is becoming a pain. I feel so frustrated some times, that I consider forgetting all about tennis. It is hurting my pride.

Today, tennis is not the main source of my frustrations. I have another problem that generates feelings and put[s] me in moods very similar to those that I experience when I play it. This is daily conversation with people. It may sound bizarre, but it is not. I am a foreign student, and, in playing tennis as in speaking English, I am still in the learning process. That is why the best way I can explain this complex feeling created by my communication problem is by associatting it with tennis.

On[e] of the most common situations I find myelf in, when I play tennis, is that people, either concious or unconcious of my level will start the game with a strong service or will answer my weak service with a fast ball which I can not possibly hit back. Comparable examples are the ladies at the cafeteria telling me about the menu, while speaking at an incredible speed. This is often worsened by their personal style, the Somerville accent. I also encounter the same problem when my roommate speaks with his heavy Massachusetts accent. He is from Peabody or "peebady".

Experiences like these are likely to happen when I speak to someone for the first time. Usually, however, once they realize my level, most of them will not "serve for the ace." But with those who still do it is a different story. If, after asking them to repeat their serves many times and, after repeatedly failling to return their balls I don't give up, they will find an excuse to leave the court immediately, or they will simply tell me to "forget it." In daily conversation, even my friends will use this phrase when they give up trying to make thier point, or to understand my point. I do not blame them sometimes, but this little phrase is on[e] of the most frustrating ones I have heard. It can take away my desires to talk, and discourage me in my efforts to get my ideas across—making me leave the court frustrated and angry. I then isolate myself or look for a friend with whom I can speak a language I don't have to concentrate on, and at which I am very good. Spanish. In like manner, when I am tired of tennis and still want to do some sport, I jog alone or play soccer.

Once a person is aware of my level and trys to go at my pace, I still confront some problems. First, in tennis, if you are a fairly experienced player you should be familiar with some basic game plans. The way your opponent is sending the balls may lead you to realize which plan is he using to score upon you. In the same way, if in a language you have

---

*Letters in brackets have been inserted for the sake of clarity. In all other respects, the essay is reproduced exactly as it was written.

experience with the cultural patterns of expressing feelings and moods, and you distinguish the different connotation of words, you may understand the point he is trying to make to you. In tennis I am not very good in predicting what plan my opponent is trying to use; and when I do it is usually too late. Likewise, in conversation, I usually don't react to a joke until it is too late. I also have a hard time realizing how annoyed my roommate gets, because he selects words to make his point, but the connotation[s] of some of them sometimes don't reach me because of my inexperience. I don't know exactly which is worse to him, "mad," "angry," "disturbed" or "pissed of[f]."

Second, in tennis, by observing your opponent's movements you improve your chances to return the ball and prolong the volley. The swing of his raquet, the way he hits the balls, and his possition in relation with the net are good hints for predicting the direction and the power of the ball. I still can't tell precisely how fast the ball is coming, or if I have to return it with a forehand or a backhand shot just by watching my opponent. It is not only that I am unfamiliar with these movements, but I also am too busy analyzing the movements I have done, and the ones I am about to do. At the same time, my opponent can tell very little about my next shot by observing me, because my style is very awkward. When talking to people I also feel the necesity to be familiar with the non-verbal language of Americans. Yesterday, for example, the guy across the hall asked me to turn down my stereo. By the time I had understood what he said, he was gone. I wasn't sure what his talking from the doorway, and the tone of his voice meant. Everything happened so fast, just like a crosscourt backhand. I didn't feel happy with my vague answer and I am sure he didn't either.

Playing tennis, for me, in general is a[n] uncomfortable situation. I waste too much energy and attention on every single movement of my hand, my raquet, my feet etc., and besides I also have to watch the player at the other side of the net; then I don't enjoy the game. In every day conversation, it is also very annoying to pay so much attention to things that should be automatic and to give as much thought to almos[t] every word me and the other person are using.

Exposed to so many unfamiliar rules and ways, I easily lose the train of thought in my conversation; I feel that I am not being natural and start questioning the way I communicate and relate with people. I worry so much about the "how to" that conversation is not always as relaxing as it should be. This is a problem from which the only way to [e]scape is by fully experiencing it. Like in any sport if you want to enjoy it you have to practice much until you master it.

So, if you happen to be talking to a foreigner, be aware of this problem. If you are a foreign student yourself, do not feel depressed; I believe, that on the long run there will be a reward, a better understanding of ourselves and the vital phenomenun of communicasion.

Ruth Spack is currently director of ESL Composition at Tufts University.

REFERENCES

Bator, Paul. 1980. Aristotelian and Rogerian rhetoric. *College Composition and Communication* 31(4):427–432.

Bitzer, Lloyd F. 1968. The rhetorical situation. In *Contemporary theories of rhetoric: Selected readings,* Richard J. Johannsen (Ed.), 381–393. New York: Harper and Row, 1971.

Britton, James, Tony Burgess, Nancy Martin, Alex McLeod, and Harold Rosen. 1975. *The development of writing abilities (11–18).* London: Macmillan.

Burhans, Clinton S., Jr. 1968. *Extended testing of a unified experimental course in composition in a variety of materials and formats.* United States Department of Health, Education, and Welfare (Cooperative Research Project No. 7–1149). East Lansing, Michigan: Michigan State University.

Burke, Kenneth. 1945. *A grammar of motives.* New York: Prentice-Hall.

Christensen, Francis. 1967a. A generative rhetoric of the paragraph. In *Teaching Freshman Composition,* Gary Tate and Edward P. J. Corbett (Eds.), 200–216. New York: Oxford University Press.

Christensen, Francis. 1967b. A generative rhetoric of the sentence. In *Teaching Freshman Composition,* Gary Tate and Edward P. J. Corbett (Eds.), 190–199. New York: Oxford University Press.

Clark, Gregory. 1982. Making the need to write seem real. *TECFORS Newsletter* 5(4):1–3.

Cowan, Elizabeth. 1982. *Writing.* Brief Edition. Glenview, Illinois: Scott, Foresman.

Cowan, Gregory, and Elizabeth Cowan. 1980. *Writing.* New York: John Wiley & Sons.

Daubney-Davis, Ann E. 1982a. Using invention heuristics to teach writing. Part I: An introduction to heuristics. *TECFORS Newsletter* 5(2):1–3.

Daubney-Davis, Ann E. 1982b. Using invention heuristics to teach writing. Part II: A look at methods. *TECFORS Newsletter* 5(3):1–3.

Daubney-Davis, Ann E. 1982c. Using invention heuristics to teach writing. Part III: More methods to try. *TECFORS Newsletter* 5(4):5–7.

Elbow, Peter. 1973. *Writing without teachers.* London: Oxford University Press.

Emig, Janet. 1971. *The composing processes of twelfth graders.* Urbana, Illinois: National Council of Teachers of English.

Flower, Linda S., and John R. Hayes. 1977. Problem-solving strategies and the writing process. *College English* 39(4):449–461.

Flower, Linda, and John R. Hayes. 1980. The cognition of discovery: defining a rhetorical problem. *College Composition and Communication* 31(1):21–32.

Flower, Linda, and John R. Hayes. 1981. A cognitive process theory of writing. *College Composition and Communication* 32(4):365–387.

Hairston, Maxine. 1982. The winds of change: Thomas Kuhn and the revolution in the teaching of writing. *College Composition and Communication* 33(1):76–88.

Harrington, David V. 1968. Teaching students the art of discovery. *College Composition and Communication* 19(1):7–14.

Hilgers, Thomas Lee. 1980. Training college composition students in the use of freewriting and problem-solving heuristics for rhetorical invention. *Research in the Teaching of English* 14(4):293–307.

Judy, Stephen. 1980. The experiential approach: Inner worlds to outer worlds. In *Eight approaches to teaching composition,* Timothy R. Donovan and Ben W. McClelland (Eds.), 37–51. Urbana, Illinois: National Council of Teachers of English.

Kinney, James. 1979. Classifying heuristics. *College Composition and Communication* 30(4):351–355.

Kuhn, Thomas S. 1970. *The structure of scientific revolutions.* Second Edition. Chicago: University of Chicago Press.

Larson, Richard L. 1968. Discovery through questioning: A plan for teaching rhetorical invention. *College English* 30(2):126–134.

Lauer, Sister Janice. 1970. Heuristics and composition. *College Composition and Communication* 21(5):396–404.

Lauer, Janice M. 1980. The rhetorical approach: Stages of writing and strategies for writers. In *Eight approaches to teaching composition,* Timothy R. Donovan and Ben W. McClelland (Eds.), 53–64. Urbana, Illinois: National Council of Teachers of English.

Lay, Nancy Duke S. 1982. Composing processes of adult ESL learners: A case study. *TESOL Quarterly* 16(3):406.

Macrorie, Ken. 1968. *Writing to be read.* Rochelle Park, New Jersey: Hayden.

Maimon, Elaine P., Gerald L. Belcher, Gail W. Hearn, Barbara F. Nodine, and Finbarr W. O'Connor. 1981. *Writing in the arts and sciences.* Cambridge, Massachusetts: Winthrop.

McKay, Sandra. 1982. A focus on prewriting strategies. In *On TESOL '81,* Mary Hines and William Rutherford (Eds.), 89–95. Washington, D.C.: TESOL.

Mischel, Terry. 1974. A case study of a twelfth-grade writer. *Research in the Teaching of English* 8(3):303–314.

Murray, Donald M. 1968. *A writer teaches writing.* Boston: Houghton Mifflin.

Odell, Lee. 1973. Piaget, problem-solving, and composition. *College Composition and Communication* 24(1):36–42.

Odell, Lee. 1974. Measuring the effect of instruction in pre-writing. *Research in the Teaching of English* 8(2):228–240.

Perl, Sondra. 1979. The composing processes of unskilled college writers. *Research in the Teaching of English* 13(4):317–336.

Pianko, Sharon. 1979. A description of the composing processes of college freshman writers. *Research in the Teaching of English* 13(1):5–22.

Raimes, Ann. 1979. *Problems and teaching strategies in ESL composition. Language in Education: Theory and Practice* 14. Arlington, Virginia: Center for Applied Linguistics.

Raimes, Ann. 1983. Tradition and revolution in ESL teaching. *TESOL Quarterly* 17(4):535–552.

Rohman, D. Gordon. 1965. Pre-writing: The stage of discovery in the writing process. *College Composition and Communication* 16(2):106–112.

Rohman, D. Gordon, and Albert O. Wlecke, 1964. Pre-writing: The construction and application of models for concept formulation in writing (ERIC Document Reproduction Service ED 001 273).

Rose, Mike. 1980. Rigid rules, inflexible plans, and the stifling of language: A cognitivist analysis of writer's block. *College Composition and Communication* 31(4):389–401.

Shaughnessy, Mina P. 1977. *Errors and expectations.* New York: Oxford University Press.

Sommers, Nancy. 1980. Revision strategies of student writers and experienced adult writers. *College Composition and Communication* 31(4):378–388.

Spack, Ruth, and Catherine Sadow. 1983. Student-teacher working journals in ESL freshman composition. *TESOL Quarterly* 17(4):575–593.

Stallard, Charles K. 1974. An analysis of the writing behavior of good student writers. *Research in the Teaching of English* 8(2):206–218.

Taylor, Barry P. 1981. Content and written form: a two-way street. *TESOL Quarterly* 15(1):5–13.

Watson, Cynthia B. 1982. The use and abuse of models in the ESL writing class. *TESOL Quarterly* 16(1):5–14.

Winterowd, W. Ross. 1973. "Topics" and levels in the composing process. *College English* 34(5):701–709.

Winterowd, W. Ross. 1981. *The contemporary writer.* Second Edition. New York: Harcourt Brace Jovanovich.

Witte, Stephen P., and Lester Faigley. 1981. Coherence, cohesion, and writing quality. *College Composition and Communication* 32(2):189–204.

Yarnoff, Charles. 1980. Contemporary theories of invention in the rhetorical tradition. *College English* 41(5):552–560.

Young, Richard E., 1978. Paradigms and problems: Needed research in rhetorical invention. In *Research on composing: Points of departure,* Charles Cooper and Lee Odell (Eds.), 29–47. Urbana, Illinois: National Council of Teachers of English.

Young, Richard E., and Alton L. Becker. 1967. Toward a modern theory of rhetoric: A tagmemic contribution. In *Teaching Freshman Composition,* Gary Tate and Edward P.J. Corbett (Eds.), 128–146. New York: Oxford University Press.

Young, Richard E., Alton L. Becker, and Kenneth L. Pike. 1970. *Rhetoric: Discovery and change.* New York: Harcourt Brace Jovanovich.

Young, Richard E., and Frank M. Koen. 1973. Tagmemic discovery procedure: An evaluation of its uses in the teaching of rhetoric. (ERIC Document Reproduction Service ED 084 517).

Zamel, Vivian. 1976. Teaching composition in the ESL classroom: What we can learn from research in the teaching of English. *TESOL Quarterly* 10(1):67–76.

Zamel, Vivian. 1982. Writing: the process of discovering meaning. *TESOL Quarterly* 16(2):195–209.

Zamel, Vivian. 1983. The composing processes of advanced ESL students: Six case studies. *TESOL Quarterly* 17(2):165–187.

Rigid Rules, Inflexible Plans, and the Stifling of Language: A Cognitivist Analysis of Writer's Block

MIKE ROSE *University of California, Los Angeles*

Ruth will labor over the first paragraph of an essay for hours. She'll write a sentence, then erase it. Try another, then scratch part of it out. Finally, as the evening winds on toward ten o'clock and Ruth, anxious about tomorrow's deadline, begins to wind into herself, she'll compose that first paragraph only to sit back and level her favorite exasperated interdiction at herself and her page: "No. You can't say that. You'll bore them to death."

Ruth is one of ten UCLA undergraduates with whom I discussed writer's block, that frustrating, self-defeating inability to generate the next line, the right phrase, the sentence that will release the flow of words once again. These ten people represented a fair cross-section of the UCLA student community: lower-middle-class to upper-middle-class backgrounds and high schools, third-world and Caucasian origins, biology to fine arts majors, C+ to A- grade point averages, enthusiastic to blasé attitudes toward school. They were set off from the community by the twin facts that all ten could write competently, and all were currently enrolled in at least one course that required a significant amount of writing. They were set off among themselves by the fact that five of them wrote with relative to enviable ease while the other five experienced moderate to nearly immobilizing writer's block. This blocking usually resulted in rushed, often late papers and resultant grades that did not truly reflect these students' writing ability. And then, of course, there were other less measurable but probably more serious results: a growing distrust of their abilities and an aversion toward the composing process itself.

What separated the five students who blocked from those who didn't? It wasn't skill; that was held fairly constant. The answer could have rested in the emotional realm—anxiety, fear of evaluation, insecurity, etc. Or perhaps blocking in some way resulted from variation in cognitive style. Perhaps, too, blocking originated in and typified a melding of emotion and cognition not unlike the relationship posited by Shapiro between neurotic feeling and neurotic thinking.[1] Each of these was possible. Extended clinical interviews and testing could have teased out the answer. But there was one answer that surfaced readily in brief explorations of

---

[1]David Shapiro, *Neurotic Styles* (New York: Basic Books, 1965).

these students' writing processes. It was not profoundly emotional, nor was it embedded in that still unclear construct of cognitive style. It was constant, surprising, almost amusing if its results weren't so troublesome, and, in the final analysis, obvious: the five students who experienced blocking were all operating either with writing rules or with planning strategies that impeded rather than enhanced the composing process. The five students who were not hampered by writer's block also utilized rules, but they were less rigid ones, and thus more appropriate to a complex process like writing. Also, the plans these non-blockers brought to the writing process were more functional, more flexible, more open to information from the outside.

These observations are the result of one to three interviews with each student. I used recent notes, drafts, and finished compositions to direct and hone my questions. This procedure is admittedly non-experimental, certainly more clinical than scientific; still, it did lead to several inferences that lay the foundation for future, more rigorous investigation: (a) composing is a highly complex problem-solving process[2] and (b) certain disruptions of that process can be explained with cognitive psychology's problem-solving framework. Such investigation might include a study using "stimulated recall" techniques to validate or disconfirm these hunches. In such a study, blockers and non-blockers would write essays. Their activity would be videotaped and, immediately after writing, they would be shown their respective tapes and questioned about the rules, plans, and beliefs operating in their writing behavior. This procedure would bring us close to the composing process (the writers' recall is stimulated by their viewing the tape), yet would not interfere with actual composing.

In the next section I will introduce several key concepts in the problem-solving literature. In section three I will let the students speak for themselves. Fourth, I will offer a cognitivist analysis of blockers' and non-blockers' grace or torpor. I will close with a brief note on treatment.

SELECTED CONCEPTS IN PROBLEM SOLVING: RULES AND PLANS

As diverse as theories of problem solving are, they share certain basic assumptions and characteristics. Each posits an *introductory period* during which a problem is presented, and all theorists, from Behaviorist to Gestalt to Information Processing, admit that certain aspects, stimuli, or "functions" of the problem must become or be made salient and attended to in certain ways if successful problem-solving processes are to be engaged. Theorists also believe that some conflict, some stress, some gap in information in these perceived "aspects" seems to trigger problem-solving behavior. Next comes a *processing period,* and for all the variance of opinion about this critical stage, theorists recognize the necessity of its existence—recognize that man, at the least, somehow "weighs" possible solutions as they are stumbled upon and, at the most, goes through an elaborate and sophisticated information-processing routine to achieve problem solution. Furthermore, theorists believe—to varying degrees—that past learning and the particular "set," direction, or orientation that the problem solver takes in

---

[2]Barbara Hayes-Ruth, a Rand cognitive psychologist, and I are currently developing an information-processing model of the composing process. A good deal of work has already been done by Linda Flower and John Hayes (see p. 118 of this article). I have just received—and recommend—their "Writing as Problem Solving" (paper presented at American Educational Research Association, April, 1979).

dealing with past experience and present stimuli have critical bearing on the efficacy of solution. Finally, all theorists admit to a *solution period,* an end-state of the process where "stress" and "search" terminate, an answer is attained, and a sense of completion or "closure" is experienced.

These are the gross similarities, and the framework they offer will be useful in understanding the problem-solving behavior of the students discussed in this paper. But since this paper is primarily concerned with the second stage of problem-solving operations, it would be most useful to focus this introduction on two critical constructs in the processing period: rules and plans.

Rules

Robert M. Gagné defines "rule" as "an inferred capability that enables the individual to respond to a class of stimulus situations with a class of performances."[3] Rules can be learned directly[4] or by inference through experience.[5] But, in either case, most problem-solving theorists would affirm Gagné's dictum that "rules are probably the major organizing factor, and quite possibly the primary one, in intellectual functioning."[6] As Gagné implies, we wouldn't be able to function without rules; they guide response to the myriad stimuli that confront us daily, and might even be the central element in complex problem-solving behavior.

Dunker, Polya, and Miller, Galanter, and Pribram offer a very useful distinction between two general kinds of rules: algorithms and heuristics.[7] Algorithms are precise rules that will always result in a specific answer if applied to an appropriate problem. Most mathematical rules, for example, are algorithms. Functions are constant (e.g., pi), procedures are routine (squaring the radius), and outcomes are completely predictable. However, few day-to-day situations are mathematically circumscribed enough to warrant the application of algorithms. Most often we function with the aid of fairly general heuristics or "rules of thumb," guidelines that allow varying degrees of flexibility when approaching problems. Rather than operating with algorithmic precision and certainty, we search, critically, through alternatives, using our heuristic as a divining rod—"if a math problem stumps you, try working backwards to solution"; "if the car won't start, check x, y, or z," and so forth. Heuristics won't allow the precision or the certitude afforded by algorithmic operations; heuristics can even be so "loose" as to be vague. But in a world where tasks and problems are rarely mathematically precise,

[3]The *Conditions of Learning* (New York: Holt, Rinehart and Winston, 1970), p. 193.

[4]E. James Archer, "The Psychological Nature of Concepts," in H. J. Klausmeier and C. W. Harris, eds., *Analysis of Concept Learning* (New York: Academic Press, 1966), pp. 37–44; David P. Ausubel, *The Psychology of Meaningful Verbal Behavior* (New York: Grune and Stratton, 1963); Robert M. Gagné, "Problem Solving," in Arthur W. Melton, ed., *Categories of Human Learning* (New York: Academic Press, 1964), pp. 293–317; George A. Miller, *Language and Communication* (New York: McGraw-Hill, 1951).

[5]George Katona, *Organizing and Memorizing* (New York: Columbia Univ. Press, 1940); Roger N. Shepard, Carl I. Hovland, and Herbert M. Jenkins, "Learning and Memorization of Classifications," *Psychological Monographs,* 75, No. 13 (1961) (entire No. 517); Robert S. Woodworth, *Dynamics of Behavior* (New York: Henry Holt, 1958), chs. 10–12.

[6]The *Conditions of Learning,* pp. 190–91.

[7]Karl Dunker, "On Problem Solving," *Psychological Monographs,* 58, No. 5 (1945) (entire No. 270); George A. Polya, *How to Solve It* (Princeton: Princeton University Press, 1945); George A. Miller, Eugene Galanter, and Karl H. Pribram, *Plans and the Structure of Behavior* (New York: Henry Holt, 1960).

heuristic rules become the most appropriate, the most functional rules available to us: "a heuristic does not guarantee the optimal solution or, indeed, any solution at all; rather, heuristics offer solutions that are good enough most of the time."[8]

Plans

People don't proceed through problem situations, in or out of a laboratory, without some set of internalized instructions to the self, some program, some course of action that, even roughly, takes goals and possible paths to that goal into consideration. Miller, Galanter, and Pribram have referred to this course of action as a plan: "A plan is any hierarchical process in the organism that can control the order in which a sequence of operations is to be performed" (p. 16). They name the fundamental plan in human problem-solving behavior the TOTE, with the initial T representing a *test* that matches a possible solution against the perceived end-goal of problem completion. O represents the clearance to *operate* if the comparison between solution and goal indicates that the solution is a sensible one. The second T represents a further, post-operation, *test* or comparison of solution with goal, and if the two mesh and problem solution is at hand the person *exits* (E) from problem-solving behavior. If the second test presents further discordance between solution and goal, a further solution is attempted in TOTE-fashion. Such plans can be both long-term and global and, as problem solving is underway, short-term and immediate.[9] Though the mechanicality of this information-processing model renders it simplistic and, possibly, unreal, the central notion of a plan and an operating procedure is an important one in problem-solving theory; it at least attempts to metaphorically explain what earlier cognitive psychologists could not—the mental procedures (see pp. 115–116) underlying problem-solving behavior.

Before concluding this section, a distinction between heuristic rules and plans should be attempted; it is a distinction often blurred in the literature, blurred because, after all, we are very much in the area of gestating theory and preliminary models. Heuristic rules seem to function with the flexibility of plans. Is, for example, "If the car won't start, try x, y, or z" a heuristic or a plan? It could be either, though two qualifications will mark it as heuristic rather than plan. (A) Plans subsume and sequence heuristic and algorithmic rules. Rules are usually "smaller," more discrete cognitive capabilities; plans can become quite large and complex, composed of a series of ordered algorithms, heuristics, and further planning "sub-routines." (B) Plans, as was mentioned earlier, include criteria to determine successful goal-attainment and, as well, include "feedback" processes—ways to incorporate and use information gained from "tests" of potential solutions against desired goals.

One other distinction should be made: that is, between "set" and plan. Set, also called "determining tendency" or "readiness,"[10] refers to the fact that people often approach problems with habitual ways of reacting, a predisposition, a tendency to perceive or function in one way rather than another. Set, which can be established through instructions or, consciously or

---

[8]Lyle E. Bourne, Jr., Bruce R. Ekstrand, and Roger L. Dominowski, *The Psychology of Thinking* (Englewood Cliffs, N.J.: Prentice-Hall, 1971).

[9]John R. Hayes, "Problem Topology and the Solution Process," in Carl P. Duncan, ed., *Thinking: Current Experimental Studies* (Philadelphia: Lippincott, 1967), pp. 167–81.

[10]Hulda J. Rees and Harold E. Israel, "An Investigation of the Establishment and Operation of Mental Sets," *Psychological Monographs,* 46 (1925) (entire No.210).

unconsciously, through experience, can assist performance if it is appropriate to a specific problem,[11] but much of the literature on set has shown its rigidifying, dysfunctional effects.[12] Set differs from plan in that set represents a limiting and narrowing of response alternatives with no inherent process to shift alternatives. It is a kind of cognitive habit that can limit perception, not a course of action with multiple paths that directs and sequences response possibilities.

The constructs of rules and plans advance the understanding of problem solving beyond that possible with earlier, less developed formulations. Still, critical problems remain. Though mathematical and computer models move one toward more complex (and thus more real) problems than the earlier research, they are still too neat, too rigidly sequenced to approximate the stunning complexity of day-to-day (not to mention highly creative) problem-solving behavior. Also, information-processing models of problem-solving are built in logic theorems, chess strategies, and simple planning tasks. Even Gagné seems to feel more comfortable with illustrations from mathematics and science rather than with social science and humanities problems. So although these complex models and constructs tell us a good deal about problem-solving behavior, they are still laboratory simulations, still invoked from the outside rather than self-generated, and still founded on the mathematico-logical.

Two Carnegie-Mellon researchers, however, have recently extended the above into a truly real, amorphous, unmathematical problem-solving process—writing. Relying on protocol analysis (thinking aloud while solving problems), Linda Flower and John Hayes have attempted to tease out the role of heuristic rules and plans in writing behavior.[13] Their research pushes problem-solving investigations to the real and complex and pushes, from the other end, the often mysterious process of writing toward the explainable. The latter is important, for at least since Plotinus many have viewed the composing process as unexplainable, inspired, infused with the transcendent. But Flower and Hayes are beginning, anyway, to show how writing generates from a problem-solving process with rich heuristic rules and plans of its own. They show, as well, how many writing problems arise from a paucity of heuristics and suggest an intervention that provides such rules.

This paper, too, treats writing as a problem-solving process, focusing, however, on what happens when the process dead-ends in writer's block. It will further suggest that, as opposed to Flower and Hayes' students who need more rules and plans, blockers may well be stymied by possessing rigid or inappropriate rules, or inflexible or confused plans. Ironically enough, these are occasionally instilled by the composition teacher or gleaned from the writing textbook.

[11]Ibid.; Melvin H. Marx, Wilton W. Murphy, and Aaron J. Brownstein, "Recognition of Complex Visual Stimuli as a Function of Training with Abstracted Patterns," *Journal of Experimental Psychology,* 62 (1961), 456–60.

[12]James L. Adams, *Conceptual Blockbusting* (San Francisco: W. H. Freeman, 1974); Edward DeBono, *New Think* (New York: Basic Books, 1958); Ronald H. Forgus, *Perception* (New York: McGraw-Hill, 1966), ch. 13; Abraham Luchins and Edith Hirsch Luchins, *Rigidity of Behavior* (Eugene: Univ. of Oregon Books, 1959); N. R. F. Maier, "Reasoning in Humans. 1. On Direction," *Journal of Comparative Psycholog,.* 10 (1920), 115–43.

[13]"Plans and the Cognitive Process of Writing," paper presented at the National Institute of Education Writing Conference, June 1977; "Problem Solving Strategies and the Writing Process," *College English,* 39 (1977), 449–61. See also footnote 2.

"ALWAYS GRAB YOUR AUDIENCE"—THE BLOCKERS

In high school, *Ruth* was told and told again that a good essay always grabs a reader's attention immediately. Until you can make your essay do that, her teachers and textbooks putatively declaimed, there is no need to go on. For Ruth, this means that beginning bland and seeing what emerges as one generates prose is unacceptable. The beginning is everything. And what exactly is the audience seeking that reads this beginning? The rule, or Ruth's use of it, doesn't provide for such investigation. She has an edict with no determiners. Ruth operates with another rule that restricts her productions as well: if sentences aren't grammatically "correct," they aren't useful. This keeps Ruth from toying with ideas on paper, from the kind of linguistic play that often frees up the flow of prose. These two rules converge in a way that pretty effectively restricts Ruth's composing process.

The first two papers I received from *Laurel* were weeks overdue. Sections of them were well written; there were even moments of stylistic flair. But the papers were late and, overall, the prose seemed rushed. Furthermore, one paper included a paragraph on an issue that was never mentioned in the topic paragraph. This was the kind of mistake that someone with Laurel's apparent ability doesn't make. I asked her about this irrelevant passage. She knew very well that it didn't fit, but believed she had to include it to round out the paper. "You must always make three or more points in an essay. If the essay has less, then it's not strong." Laurel had been taught this rule both in high school and in her first college English class; no wonder, then, that she accepted its validity.

As opposed to Laurel, *Martha* possesses a whole arsenal of plans and rules with which to approach a humanities writing assignment, and, considering her background in biology, I wonder how many of them were formed out of the assumptions and procedures endemic to the physical sciences.[14] Martha will not put pen to first draft until she has spent up to two days generating an outline of remarkable complexity. I saw one of these outlines and it looked more like a diagram of protein synthesis or DNA structure than the time-worn pattern offered in composition textbooks. I must admit I was intrigued by the aura of process (vs. the static appearance of essay outlines) such diagrams offer, but for Martha these "outlines" only led to self-defeat: the outline would become so complex that all of its elements could never be included in a short essay. In other words, her plan locked her into the first stage of the composing process. Martha would struggle with the conversion of her outline into prose only to scrap the whole venture when deadlines passed and a paper had to be rushed together.

Martha's "rage for order" extends beyond the outlining process. She also believes that elements of a story or poem must evince a fairly linear structure and thematic clarity, or—perhaps bringing us closer to the issue—that analysis of a story or poem must provide the linearity or clarity that seems to be absent in the text. Martha, therefore, will bend the logic of her analysis to reason ambiguity out of existence. When I asked her about a strained paragraph in her paper on Camus' "The Guest," she said, "I didn't want to admit that it [the story's conclusion] was just hanging. I tried to force it into meaning."

---

[14]Jane, a student not discussed in this paper, was surprised to find out that a topic paragraph can be rewritten after a paper's conclusion to make that paragraph reflect what the essay truly contains. She had gotten so indoctrinated with psychology's (her major) insistence that a hypothesis be formulated and then left untouched before an experiment begins that she thought revision of one's "major premise" was somehow illegal. She had formed a rule out of her exposure to social science methodology, and the rule was totally inappropriate for most writing situations.

Martha uses another rule, one that is not only problematical in itself, but one that often clashes directly with the elaborate plan and obsessive rule above. She believes that humanities papers must scintillate with insight, must present an array of images, ideas, ironies gleaned from the literature under examination. A problem arises, of course, when Martha tries to incorporate her myriad "neat little things," often inherently unrelated, into a tightly structured, carefully sequenced essay. Plans and rules that govern the construction of impressionistic, associational prose would be appropriate to Martha's desire, but her composing process is heavily constrained by the non-impressionistic and non-associational. Put another way, the plans and rules that govern her exploration of text are not at all synchronous with the plans and rules she uses to discuss her exploration. It is interesting to note here, however, that as recently as three years ago Martha was absorbed in creative writing and was publishing poetry in high school magazines. Given what we know about the complex associational, often non-neatly-sequential nature of the poet's creative process, we can infer that Martha was either free of the plans and rules discussed earlier or they were not as intense. One wonders, as well, if the exposure to three years of university physical science either established or intensified Martha's concern with structure. Whatever the case, she now is hamstrung by conflicting rules when composing papers for the humanities.

Mike's difficulties, too, are rooted in a distortion of the problem-solving process. When the time of the week for the assignment of writing topics draws near, Mike begins to prepare material, strategies, and plans that he believes will be appropriate. If the assignment matches his expectations, he has done a good job of analyzing the professor's intentions. If the assignment *doesn't* match his expectations, however, he cannot easily shift approaches. He feels trapped inside his original plans, cannot generate alternatives, and blocks. As the deadline draws near, he will write something, forcing the assignment to fit his conceptual procrustian bed. Since Mike is a smart man, he will offer a good deal of information, but only some of it ends up being appropriate to the assignment. This entire situation is made all the worse when the time between assignment of topic and generation of product is attenuated further, as in an essay examination. Mike believes (correctly) that one must have a plan, a strategy of some sort in order to solve a problem. He further believes, however, that such a plan, once formulated, becomes an exact structural and substantive blueprint that cannot be violated. The plan offers no alternatives, no "sub-routines." So, whereas Ruth's, Laurel's, and some of Martha's difficulties seem to be rule-specific ("always catch your audience," "write grammatically"), Mike's troubles are more global. He may have strategies that are appropriate for various writing situations (e.g., "for this kind of political science assignment write a compare/contrast essay"), but his entire approach to formulating plans and carrying them through to problem solution is too mechanical. It is probable that Mike's behavior is governed by an explicitly learned or inferred rule: "Always try to 'psych out' a professor." But in this case this rule initiates a problem-solving procedure that is clearly dysfunctional.

While Ruth and Laurel use rules that impede their writing process and Mike utilizes a problem-solving procedure that hamstrings him, *Sylvia* has trouble deciding which of the many rules she possesses to use. Her problem can be characterized as cognitive perplexity; some of her rules are inappropriate, others are functional; some mesh nicely with her own definitions of good writing, others don't. She has multiple rules to invoke, multiple paths to follow, and that very complexity of choice virtually paralyzes her. More so than with the previous four students, there is probably a strong emotional dimension to Sylvia's blocking, but the cognitive difficulties are clear and perhaps modifiable.

Sylvia, somewhat like Ruth and Laurel, puts tremendous weight on the crafting of her first paragraph. If it is good, she believes the rest of the essay will be good. Therefore, she will spend up to five hours on the initial paragraph: "I won't go on until I get that first paragraph down." Clearly, this rule—or the strength of it—blocks Sylvia's production. This is one problem. Another is that Sylvia has other equally potent rules that she sees as separate, uncomplementary injunctions: one achieves "flow" in one's writing through the use of adequate transitions; one achieves substance to one's writing through the use of evidence. Sylvia perceives both rules to be "true," but several times followed one to the exclusion of the other. Furthermore, as I talked to Sylvia, many other rules, guidelines, definitions were offered, but none with conviction. While she *is* committed to one rule about initial paragraphs, and that rule is dysfunctional, she seems very uncertain about the weight and hierarchy of the remaining rules in her cognitive repertoire.

"IF IT WON'T FIT MY WORK, I'LL CHANGE IT"—THE NON-BLOCKERS

Dale, Ellen, Debbie, Susan, and Miles all write with the aid of rules. But their rules differ from blockers' rules in significant ways. If similar in content, they are expressed less absolutely— e.g., "*Try* to keep audience in mind." If dissimilar, they are still expressed less absolutely, more heuristically—e.g., "I can use as many ideas in my thesis paragraph as I need and then develop paragraphs for each idea." Our non-blockers do express some rules with firm assurance, but these tend to be simple injunctions that free up rather than restrict the composing process, e.g., "When stuck, write!" or "I'll write what I can." And finally, at least three of the students openly shun the very textbook rules that some blockers adhere to: e.g., "Rules like 'write only what you know about' just aren't true. I ignore those." These three, in effect, have formulated a further rule that expresses something like: "If a rule conflicts with what is sensible or with experience, reject it."

On the broader level of plans and strategies, these five students also differ from at least three of the five blockers in that they all possess problem-solving plans that are quite functional. Interestingly, on first exploration these plans seem to be too broad or fluid to be useful and, in some cases, can barely be expressed with any precision. Ellen, for example, admits that she has a general "outline in [her] head about how a topic paragraph should look" but could not describe much about its structure. Susan also has a general plan to follow, but, if stymied, will quickly attempt to conceptualize the assignment in different ways: "If my original idea won't work, then I need to proceed differently." Whether or not these plans operate in TOTE-fashion, I can't say. But they do operate with the operate-test fluidity of TOTEs.

True, our non-blockers have their religiously adhered-to rules: e.g., "When stuck, write," and plans, "I couldn't imagine writing without this pattern," but as noted above, these are few and functional. Otherwise, these non-blockers operate with fluid, easily modified, even easily discarded rules and plans (Ellen: "I can throw things out") that are sometimes expressed with a vagueness that could almost be interpreted as ignorance. There lies the irony. Students that offer the least precise rules and plans have the least trouble composing. Perhaps this very lack of precision characterizes the functional composing plan. But perhaps this lack of precision simply masks habitually enacted alternatives and sub-routines. This is clearly an area that needs the illumination of further research.

And then there is feedback. At least three of the five non-blockers are an Information-Processor's dream. They get to know their audience, ask professors and T.A.s specific questions about assignments, bring half-finished products in for evaluation, etc. Like Ruth, they realize the importance of audience, but unlike her, they have specific strategies for obtaining and utilizing feedback. And this penchant for testing writing plans against the needs of the audience can lead to modification of rules and plans. Listen to Debbie:

> In high school I was given a formula that stated that you must write a thesis paragraph with *only* three points in it, and then develop each of those points. When I hit college, I was given longer assignments. That stuck me for a bit, but then I realized that I could use as many ideas in my thesis paragraph as I needed and then develop paragraphs for each one. I asked someone about this and then tried it. I didn't get any negative feedback, so I figured it was o.k.

Debbie's statement brings one last difference between our blockers and non-blockers into focus. It has been implied above, but needs specific formulation: the goals these people have, and the plans they generate to attain these goals, are quite mutable. Part of the mutability comes from the fluid way the goals and plans are conceived, and part of it arises from the effective impact of feedback on these goals and plans.

ANALYZING WRITER'S BLOCK

Algorithms Rather Than Heuristics

In most cases, the rules our blockers use are not "wrong" or "incorrect"—it is good practice, for example, to "grab your audience with a catchy opening" or "craft a solid first paragraph before going on." The problem is that these rules seem to be followed as though they were algorithms, absolute dicta, rather than the loose heuristics that they were intended to be. Either through instruction, or the power of the textbook, or the predilections of some of our blockers for absolutes, or all three, these useful rules of thumb have been transformed into near-algorithmic urgencies. The result, to paraphrase Karl Dunker, is that these rules do not allow a flexible penetration into the nature of the problem. It is this transformation of heuristic into algorithm that contributes to the writer's block of Ruth and Laurel.

Questionable Heuristics Made Algorithmic

Whereas "grab your audience" could be a useful heuristic, "always make three or more points in an essay" is a pretty questionable one. Any such rule, though probably taught to aid the writer who needs structure, ultimately transforms a highly fluid process like writing into a mechanical lockstep. As heuristics, such rules can be troublesome. As algorithms, they are simply incorrect.

Set

As with any problem-solving task, students approach writing assignments with a variety of orientations or sets. Some are functional, others are not. Martha and Jane (see footnote 14), coming out of the life sciences and social sciences respectively, bring certain methodological orientations with them—certain sets or "directions" that make composing for the humanities a difficult, sometimes confusing, task. In fact, this orientation may cause them to misperceive the task. Martha has formulated a planning strategy from her predisposition to see processes in terms of linear, interrelated steps in a system. Jane doesn't realize that she can revise the statement that "committed" her to the direction her essay has taken. Both of these students are stymied because of formative experiences associated with their majors—experiences, perhaps, that nicely reinforce our very strong tendency to organize experiences temporally.

The Plan that Is Not a Plan

If fluidity and multi-directionality are central to the nature of plans, then the plans that Mike formulates are not true plans at all but, rather, inflexible and static cognitive blueprints.[15] Put another way, Mike's "plans" represent a restricted "closed system" (vs. "open system") kind of thinking, where closed system thinking is defined as focusing on "a limited number of units or items, or members, and those properties of the members which are to be used are known to begin with and do not change as the thinking proceeds," and open system thinking is characterized by an "adventurous exploration of multiple alternatives with strategies that allow redirection once 'dead ends' are encountered."[16] Composing calls for open, even adventurous thinking, not for constrained, no-exit cognition.

Feedback

The above difficulties are made all the more problematic by the fact that they seem resistant to or isolated from corrective feedback. One of the most striking things about Dale, Debbie, and Miles is the ease with which they seek out, interpret, and apply feedback on their rules, plans, and productions. They "operate" and then they "test," and the testing is not only against some internalized goal, but against the requirements of external audience as well.

Too Many Rules—"Conceptual Conflict"

According to D. E. Berlyne, one of the primary forces that motivate problem-solving behavior is a curiosity that arises from conceptual conflict—the convergence of incompatible beliefs or ideas. In *Structure and Direction in Thinking*,[17] Berlyne presents six major types of conceptual conflict, the second of which he terms "perplexity":

---

[15]Cf. "A plan is flexible if the order of execution of its parts can be easily interchanged without affecting the feasibility of the plan . . . the flexible planner might tend to think of lists of things he had to do, the inflexible planner would have his time planned like a sequence of cause-effect relations. The former could rearrange his lists to suit his opportunities, but the latter would be unable to strike while the iron was hot and would generally require considerable 'lead-time' before he could incorporate any alternative sub-plans" (Miller, Galanter, and Pribram, p. 120).

[16]Frederic Bartlett, *Thinking* (New York: Basic Books, 1958), pp. 74–76.

[17]*Structure and Direction in Thinking* (New York: John Wiley, 1965), p 255.

This kind of conflict occurs when there are factors inclining the subject toward each of a set of mutually exclusive beliefs. (p. 257)

If one substitutes "rules" for "beliefs" in the above definition, perplexity becomes a useful notion here. Because perplexity is unpleasant, people are motivated to reduce it by problem-solving behavior that can result in "disequalization":

Degree of conflict will be reduced if either the number of competing . . . [rules] or their nearness to equality of strength is reduced. (p. 259)

But "disequalization" is not automatic. As I have suggested, Martha and Sylvia hold to rules that conflict, but their perplexity does *not* lead to curiosity and resultant problem-solving behavior. Their perplexity, contra Berlyne, leads to immobilization. Thus "disequalization" will have to be effected from without. The importance of each of, particularly, Sylvia's rules needs an evaluation that will aid her in rejecting some rules and balancing and sequencing others.

A NOTE ON TREATMENT

Rather than get embroiled in a blocker's misery, the teacher or tutor might interview the student in order to build a writing history and profile: How much and what kind of writing was done in high school? What is the student's major? What kind of writing does it require? How does the student compose? Are there rough drafts or outlines available? By what rules does the student operate? How would he or she define "good" writing? etc. This sort of interview reveals an incredible amount of information about individual composing processes. Furthermore, it often reveals the rigid rule or the inflexible plan that may lie at the base of the student's writing problem. That was precisely what happened with the five blockers. And with Ruth, Laurel, and Martha (and Jane) what was revealed made virtually immediate remedy possible. Dysfunctional rules are easily replaced with or counter-balanced by functional ones if there is no emotional reason to hold onto that which simply doesn't work. Furthermore, students can be trained to select, to "know which rules are appropriate for which problems."[18] Mike's difficulties, perhaps because plans are more complex and pervasive than rules, took longer to correct. But inflexible plans, too, can be remedied by pointing out their dysfunctional qualities and by assisting the student in developing appropriate and flexible alternatives. Operating this way, I was successful with Mike. Sylvia's story, however, did not end as smoothly. Though I had three forty-five minute contacts with her, I was not able to appreciably alter her behavior. Berlyne's theory bore results with Martha but not with Sylvia. Her rules were in conflict, and perhaps that conflict was not exclusively cognitive. Her case keeps analyses like these honest; it reminds us that the cognitive often melds with, and can be overpowered by, the affective. So while Ruth, Laurel, Martha, and Mike could profit from tutorials that explore the rules and plans in their writing behavior, students like Sylvia may need more extended, more affectively oriented counseling sessions that blend the instructional with the psychodynamic.

---

[18]Flower and Hayes, "Plans and the Cognitive Process of Writing," p. 26.

Follow-Up Questions and Activities

1. Discuss the worst thing you were taught about writing. What was the underlying idea that supported this notion? In what ways do you think the notion was harmful?

2. Analyze and discuss what you have found most difficult if you have written in a foreign language.

3. Using some of the techniques for invention discussed in Spack's article, conduct your own study and report to the class. If you are currently teaching writing, have your students experiment with and discuss these techniques.

4. Spack suggests that invention is "an art that can be taught as part of a creative process of discovery and communication." Write an essay in which you discuss whether you believe that invention can or cannot be taught. Support your ideas with either the empirical data of others or your own study.

5. Do a study, using tape recordings, interviews, or some other method, in which you investigate students' writing blocks. You could make this a comparison between L1 and L2 writing.

6. Discuss several potential writing blocks and the teaching method that could be employed to solve them. Are there any that are particular to students writing in a second language?

7. Rose states, "Students who offer the least precise rules and plans have the least trouble composing. Perhaps this very lack of precision characterizes the functional composing plan. But perhaps this lack of precision simply masks habitually enacted alternatives and sub-routines." Conduct a study in which you explore whether writers who seem to "offer the least precise rules" do indeed follow rules and routines that they are not aware of. Discuss the implications for teaching in the report of your study.

8. Do a study in which you compare student essays that were done with and without the benefit of a prewriting discussion. What are the results and implications for teaching?

5

REVISION

EDITOR'S INTRODUCTION

One of the things that distinguishes experienced from inexperienced writers, according to Nancy Sommers, is the way in which they view revision. Inexperienced writers rarely go beyond lexical changes in their drafts, while experienced writers use early drafts for the discovery and exploration of ideas, reserving later drafts for stylistic changes. Students need to see revision as the process of returning to a draft and beginning again, creating new ideas and relationships. Ann M. Johns feels that discussing reader expectations with ESL students during the course of their writing can greatly assist them in learning how to revise their papers. Teachers can point out, for example, where students have made promises to the reader that have not been kept.

Prereading Questions

1. How has your process of revision changed over the years? What brought about this change?

2. How do you think the ESL/EFL teacher can best help students learn to revise effectively?

Revision Strategies of Student Writers and Experienced Adult Writers

NANCY SOMMERS

Although various aspects of the writing process have been studied extensively of late, research on revision has been notably absent. The reason for this, I suspect, is that current models of the writing process have directed attention away from revision. With few exceptions, these models are linear; they separate the writing process into discrete stages. Two representative models are Gordon Rohman's suggestion that the composing process moves from prewriting to writing to rewriting and James Britton's model of the writing process as a series of stages described in metaphors of linear growth, conception—incubation—production.[1] What is striking about these theories of writing is that they model themselves on speech: Rohman defines the writer in a way that cannot distinguish him from a speaker ("A writer is a man who . . . puts [his] experience into words in his own mind"—p. 15); and Britton bases his theory of writing on what he calls (following Jakobson) the "expressiveness" of speech.[2] Moreover, Britton's study itself follows the "linear model" of the relation of thought and language in speech proposed by Vygotsky, a relationship embodied in the linear movement "from the motive which engenders a thought to the shaping of the thought, *first* in inner speech, *then* in meanings of words, and *finally* in words" (quoted in Britton et al., p. 40). What this movement fails to take into account in its linear structure—"first . . . then . . . finally"— is the recursive shaping of thought by language; what it fails to take into account is *revision*. In these linear conceptions of the writing process revision is understood as a separate stage at the end of the process—a stage that comes after the completion of a first or second draft and one that is temporally distinct from the prewriting and writing stages of the process.[3]

From "Revision Strategies of Student Writers and Experienced Adult Writers" by N. Sommers, 1980, College Composition and Communication, 31, pp. 378–388. Copyright 1980 by the National Council of Teachers of English. Reprinted with permission.

[1]D. Gordon Rohman and Albert O. Wlecke, "Pre-writing: The Construction and Application of Models for Concept Formation in Writing," Cooperative Research Project No. 2174, U.S. Office of Education, Department of Health, Education and Welfare; James Britton, Anthony Burgess, Nancy Martin, Alex McLeod, Harold Rosen, *The Development of Writing Abilities (11–18)* (London: Macmillan Education, 1975).

[2]Britton is following Roman Jakobson, "Linguistics and Poetics," in T. A. Sebeok, *Style in Language* (Cambridge, Mass: MIT Press, 1960).

[3]For an extended discussion of this issue see Nancy Sommers, "The Need for Theory in Composition Research," *College Composition and Communication, 30* (February 1979), 46–49.

The linear model bases itself on speech in two specific ways. First of all, it is based on traditional rhetorical models, models that were created to serve the spoken art of oratory. In whatever ways the parts of classical rhetoric are described, they offer "stages" of composition that are repeated in contemporary models of the writing process. Edward Corbett, for instance, describes the "five parts of a discourse"—*inventio, dispositio, elocutio, memoria, pronuntiatio*—and, disregarding the last two parts since "after rhetoric came to be concerned mainly with written discourse, there was no further need to deal with them,"[4] he produces a model very close to Britton's conception [*inventio*], incubation [*dispositio*], production [*elocutio*]. Other rhetorics also follow this procedure, and they do so not simply because of historical accident. Rather, the process represented in the linear model is based on the irreversibility of speech. Speech, Roland Barthes says, "is irreversible":

> A word cannot be retracted, except precisely by saying that one retracts it. To cross out here is to add: if I want to erase what I have just said, I cannot do it without showing the eraser itself (I must say: *"or rather . . . " "I expressed myself badly . . . "*); paradoxically, it is ephemeral speech which is indelible, not monumental writing. All that one can do in the case of a spoken utterance is to tack on another utterance.[5]

What is impossible in speech is *revision:* like the example Barthes gives, revision in speech is an afterthought. In the same way, each stage of the linear model must be exclusive (distinct from the other stages) or else it becomes trivial and counterproductive to refer to these junctures as "stages."

By staging revision after enunciation, the linear models reduce revision in writing, as in speech, to no more than an afterthought. In this way such models make the study of revision impossible. Revision, in Rohman's model, is simply the repetition of writing; or to pursue Britton's organic metaphor, revision is simply the further growth of what is already there, the "preconceived" product. The absence of research on revision, then, is a function of a theory of writing which makes revision both superfluous and redundant, a theory which does not distinguish between writing and speech.

What the linear models do produce is a parody of writing. Isolating revision and then disregarding it plays havoc with the experiences composition teachers have of the actual writing and rewriting of experienced writers. Why should the linear model be preferred? Why should revision be forgotten, superfluous? Why do teachers offer the linear model and students accept it? One reason, Barthes suggests, is that "there is a fundamental tie between teaching and speech," while "writing begins at the point where speech becomes *impossible.*"[6] The spoken word cannot be revised. The possibility of revision distinguishes the written text from speech. In fact, according to Barthes, this is the essential difference between writing and speaking. When we must revise, when the very idea is subject to recursive shaping by language, then speech becomes inadequate. This is a matter to which I will return, but first we should examine, theoretically, a detailed exploration of what student writers as distinguished from experienced adult writers *do* when they write and rewrite their work. Dissatisfied with

---

[4]*Classical Rhetoric for the Modern Student* (New York: Oxford University Press, 1965), p. 27.

[5]Roland Barthes, "Writers, Intellectuals, Teachers," in *Image-Music-Text*, trans. Stephen Heath (New York: Hill and Wang, 1977), pp. 190–191.

[6]"Writers, Intellectuals, Teachers," p. 190.

both the linear model of writing and the lack of attention to the process of revision, I conducted a series of studies over the past three years which examined the revision processes of student writers and experienced writers to see what role revision played in their writing processes. In the course of my work the revision process was redefined as *a sequence of changes in a composition—changes which are initiated by cues and occur continually throughout the writing of a work.*

METHODOLOGY

I used a case study approach. The student writers were twenty freshmen at Boston University and the University of Oklahoma with SAT verbal scores ranging from 450-600 in their first semester of composition. The twenty experienced adult writers from Boston and Oklahoma City included journalists, editors, and academics. To refer to the two groups, I use the terms *student writers* and *experienced writers* because the principal difference between these two groups is the amount of experience they have had in writing.

Each writer wrote three essays, expressive, explanatory, and persuasive, and rewrote each essay twice, producing nine written products in draft and final form. Each writer was interviewed three times after the final revision of each essay. And each writer suggested revisions for a composition written by an anonymous author. Thus extensive written and spoken documents were obtained from each writer.

The essays were analyzed by counting and categorizing the changes made. Four revision operations were identified: deletion, substitution, addition, and reordering. And four levels of changes were identified: word, phrase, sentence, theme (the extended statement of one idea). A coding system was developed for identifying the frequency of revision by level and operation. In addition, transcripts of the interviews in which the writers interpreted their revisions were used to develop what was called a *scale of concerns* for each writer. This scale enabled me to codify what were the writer's primary concerns, secondary concerns, tertiary concerns, and whether the writers used the same scale of concerns when revising the second or third drafts as they used in revising the first draft.

REVISION STRATEGIES OF STUDENT WRITERS

Most of the students I studied did not use the terms *revision* or *rewriting*. In fact, they did not seem comfortable using the word *revision* and explained that revision was not a word they used, but the word their teachers used. Instead, most of the students had developed various functional terms to describe the type of changes they made. The following are samples of these definitions:

> *Scratch Out and Do Over Again:* "I say scratch out and do over, and that means what it says. Scratching out and cutting out. I read what I have written and I cross out a word and put another word in; a more decent word or a better word. Then if there is somewhere to use a sentence that I have crossed out, I will put it there."

> *Reviewing:* "Reviewing means just using better words and eliminating words that are not needed. I go over and change words around."

Reviewing: "I just review every word and make sure that everything is worded right. I see if I am rambling; I see if I can put a better word in or leave one out. Usually when I read what I have written, I say to myself, 'that word is so bland or so trite,' and then I go and get my thesaurus."

Redoing: "Redoing means cleaning up the paper and crossing out. It is looking at something and saying, no that has to go, or no, that is not right."

Marking Out: "I don't use the word rewriting because I only write one draft and the changes that I make are made on top of the draft. The changes that I make are usually just marking out words and putting different ones in."

Slashing and Throwing Out: "I throw things out and say they are not good. I like to write like Fitzgerald did by inspiration, and if I feel inspired then I don't need to slash and throw much out."

The predominant concern in these definitions is vocabulary. The students understand the revision process as a rewording activity. They do so because they perceive words as the unit of written discourse. That is, they concentrate on particular words apart form their role in the text. Thus one student quoted above thinks in terms of dictionaries, and, following the eighteenth-century theory of words parodied in *Gulliver's Travels,* he imagines a load of things carried about to be exchanged. Lexical changes are the major revision activities of the students because economy is their goal. They are governed, like the linear model itself, by the Law of Occam's razor that prohibits logically needless repetition: redundancy and superfluity. Nothing governs speech more than such superfluities; speech constantly repeats itself precisely because spoken words, as Barthes writes, are expendable in the cause of communication. The aim of revision according to the students' own description is therefore to clean up speech; the redundancy of speech is unnecessary in writing, their logic suggests, because writing, unlike speech, can be reread. Thus one student said, "Redoing means cleaning up the paper and crossing out." The remarkable contradiction of cleaning by marking might, indeed, stand for student revision as I have encountered it.

The students place a symbolic importance on their selection and rejection of words as the determiners of success or failure for their compositions. When revising, they primarily ask themselves: can I find a better word or phrase? A more impressive, not so cliched, or less hum-drum word? Am I repeating the same word or phrase too often? They approach the revision process with what could be labeled as a "thesaurus philosophy of writing"; the students consider the thesaurus a harvest of lexical substitutions and believe that most problems in their essays can be solved by rewording. What is revealed in the students' use of the thesaurus is a governing attitude toward their writing: that the meaning to be communicated is already there, already finished, already produced, ready to be communicated, and all that is necessary is a better word "rightly worded." One student defined revision as "redoing"; "redoing" meant "just using better words and eliminating words that are not needed." For the students, writing is translating: the thought to the page, the language of speech to the more formal language of prose, the word to its synonym. Whatever is translated, an original text already exists for students, one which need not be discovered or acted upon, but simply communicated.[7]

The students list repetition as one of the elements they most worry about. This cue signals to them that they need to eliminate the repetition either by substituting or deleting words or phrases. Repetition occurs, in large part, because student writing imitates—transcribes—

---

[7]Nancy Sommers and Ronald Schleifer, "Means and Ends: Some Assumptions of Student Writers," *Composition and Teaching.* (in press).

speech: attention to repetitious words is a manner of cleaning speech. Without a sense of the developmental possibilities of revision (and writing in general) students seek, on the authority of many textbooks, simply to clean up their language and prepare to type. What is curious, however, is that students are aware of lexical repetition, but not conceptual repetition. They only notice the repetition if they can "hear" it; they do not diagnose lexical repetition as symptomatic of problems on a deeper level. By rewording their sentences to avoid the lexical repetition, the students solve the immediate problem, but blind themselves to problems on a textual level; although they are using different words, they are sometimes merely restating the same idea with different words. Such blindness, as I discovered with student writers, is the inability to "see" revision as a process: the inability to "re-view" their work again, as it were, with different eyes, and to start over.

The revision strategies described above are consistent with the students' understanding of the revision process as requiring lexical changes but not semantic changes. For the students, the extent to which they revise is a function of their level of inspiration. In fact, they use the word *inspiration* to describe the ease or difficulty with which their essay is written, and the extent to which the essay needs to be revised. If students feel inspired, if the writing comes easily, and if they don't get stuck on individual words or phrases, then they say that they cannot see any reason to revise. Because students do not see revision as an activity in which they modify and develop perspectives and ideas, they feel that if they know what they want to say, then there is little reason for making revisions.

The only modification of ideas in the students' essays occurred when they tried out two or three introductory paragraphs. This results, in part, because the students have been taught in another version of the linear model of composing to use a thesis statement as a controlling device in their introductory paragraphs. Since they write their introductions and their thesis statements even before they have really discovered what they want to say, their early close attention to the thesis statement, and more generally the linear model, function to restrict and circumscribe not only the development of their ideas, but also their ability to change the direction of these ideas.

Too often as composition teachers we conclude that students do not willingly revise. The evidence from my research suggests that it is not that students are unwilling to revise, but rather that they do what they have been taught to do in a consistently narrow and predictable way. On every occasion when I asked students why they hadn't made any more changes, they essentially replied, "I knew something larger was wrong, but I didn't think it would help to move words around." The students have strategies for handling words and phrases and their strategies helped them on a word or sentence level. What they lack, however, is a set of strategies to help them identify the "something larger" that they sensed was wrong and work from there. The students do not have strategies for handling the whole essay. They lack procedures or heuristics to help them reorder lines of reasoning or ask questions about their purposes and readers. The students view their compositions in a linear way as a series of parts. Even such potentially useful concepts as "unity" or "form" are reduced to the rule that a composition, if it is to have form, must have an introduction, a body, and a conclusion, or the sum total of the necessary parts.

The students decide to stop revising when they decide that they have not violated any of the rules for revising. These rules, such as "Never begin a sentence with a conjunction" or "Never end a sentence with a preposition," are lexically cued and rigidly applied. In general, students will subordinate the demands of the specific problems of their text to the demands of the rules. Changes are made in compliance with abstract rules about the product, rules that quite often do not apply to the specific problems in the text. These revision strategies are teacher-based, directed towards a teacher-reader who expects compliance with rules—with pre-existing "conceptions"—and who will only examine parts of the composition (writing comments about those parts in the margins of their essays) and will cite any violations of rules in those parts. At best the students see their writing altogether passively through the eyes of former teachers or their surrogates, the textbooks, and are bound to the rules which they have been taught.

REVISION STRATEGIES OF EXPERIENCED WRITERS

One aim of my research has been to contrast how student writers define revision with how a group of experienced writers define their revision processes. Here is a sampling of the definitions from the experienced writers:

Rewriting: "It is a matter of looking at the kernel of what I have written, the content, and then thinking about it, responding to it, making decisions, and actually restructuring it."

Rewriting: "I rewrite as I write. It is hard to tell what is a first draft because it is not determined by time. In one draft, I might cross out three pages, write two, cross out a fourth, rewrite it, and call it a draft. I am constantly writing and rewriting. I can only conceptualize so much in my first draft—only so much information can be held in my head at one time; my rewriting efforts are a reflection of how much information I can encompass at one time. There are levels and agenda which I have to attend to in each draft."

Rewriting: "Rewriting means on one level, finding the argument, and on another level, language changes to make the argument more effective. Most of the time I feel as if I can go on rewriting forever. There is always one part of a piece that I could keep working on. It is always difficult to know at what point to abandon a piece of writing. I like this idea that a piece of writing is never finished, just abandoned."

Rewriting: "My first draft is usually very scattered. In rewriting, I find the line of argument. After the argument is resolved, I am much more interested in word choice and phrasing."

Revising: "My cardinal rule in revising is never to fall in love with what I have written in a first or second draft. An idea, sentence, or even a phrase that looks catchy, I don't trust. Part of this idea is to wait a while. I am much more in love with something after I have written it than I am a day or two later. It is much easier to change anything with time."

Revising: "It means taking apart what I have written and putting it back together again. I ask major theoretical questions of my ideas, respond to those questions, and think of proportion and structure, and try to find a controlling metaphor. I find out which ideas can be developed and which should be dropped. I am constantly chiseling and changing as I revise."

The experienced writers describe their primary objective when revising as finding the form or shape of their argument. Although the metaphors vary, the experienced writers often use structural expressions such as "finding a framework," "a pattern," or "a design" for their argument. When questioned about this emphasis, the experienced writers responded that since their first drafts are usually scattered attempts to define their territory, their objective in the second draft is to begin observing general patterns of development and deciding what should be included and what excluded. One writer explained, "I have learned from experience that I need to keep writing a first draft until I figure out what I want to say. Then in a second draft, I begin to see the structure of an argument and how all the various sub-arguments which are buried beneath the surface of all those sentences are related." What is described here is a process in which the writer is both agent and vehicle. "Writing," says Barthes, unlike speech, "develops like a seed, not a line,"[8] and like a seed it confuses beginning and end, conception and production. Thus, the experienced writers say their drafts are "not determined by time," that rewriting is a "constant process," that they feel as if (they) "can go on forever." Revising confuses the beginning and end, the agent and vehicle; it confuses, *in order to find,* the line of argument.

After a concern for form, the experienced writers have a second objective: a concern for their readership. In this way, "production" precedes "conception." The experienced writers imagine a reader (reading their product) whose existence and whose expectations influence their revision process. They have abstracted the standards of a reader and this reader seems to be partially a reflection of themselves and functions as a critical and productive collaborator—a collaborator who has yet to love their work. The anticipation of a reader's judgment causes a feeling of dissonance when the writer recognizes incongruities between intention and execution, and requires these writers to make revisions on all levels. Such a reader gives them just what the students lacked: new eyes to "re-view" their work. The experienced writers believe that they have learned the causes and conditions, the product, which will influence their reader, and their revision strategies are geared towards creating these causes and conditions. They demonstrate a complex understanding of which examples, sentences, or phrases should be included or excluded. For example, one experienced writer decided to delete public examples and add private examples when writing about the energy crisis because "private examples would be less controversial and thus more persuasive." Another writer revised his transitional sentences because "some kinds of transitions are more easily recognized as transitions than others." These examples represent the type of strategic attempts these experienced writers use to manipulate the conventions of discourse in order to communicate to their reader.

But these revision strategies are a process of more than communication; they are part of the process of *discovering meaning* altogether. Here we can see the importance of dissonance; at the heart of revision is the process by which writers recognize and resolve the dissonance they sense in their writing. Ferdinand de Saussure has argued that meaning is differential or "diacritical," based on differences between terms rather than "essential" or inherent qualities of terms. "Phonemes," he said, "are characterized not, as one might think, by their own positive quality but simply by the fact that they are distinct."[9] In fact, Saussure bases his entire *Course in General Linguistics* on these differences, and such differences are dissonant; like musical dissonances which gain their significance from their relationship to the "key" of the composition which itself is determined by the whole language, specific language (parole) gains its meaning from the system of language (langue) of which it is a manifestation and part. The musical composition—a "composition" of parts—creates its "key" as in an over-all structure

---

[8]*Writing Degree Zero in Writing Degree Zero and Elements of Semiology,* trans. Annette Lavers and Colin Smith (New York: Hill and Wang, 1968) p. 20.

[9]*Course in General Linguistics,* trans. Wade Baskin (New York, 1966), p. 119.

which determines the value (meaning) of its parts. The analogy with music is readily seen in the compositions of experienced writers: both sorts of composition are based precisely on those structures experienced writers seek in their writing. It is this complicated relationship between the parts and the whole in the work of experienced writers which destroys the linear model; writing cannot develop "like a line" because each addition or deletion is a reordering of the whole. Explicating Saussure, Jonathan Culler asserts that "meaning depends on difference of meaning."[10] But student writers constantly struggle to bring their essays into congruence with a predefined meaning. The experienced writers do the opposite: they seek to discover (to create) meaning in the engagement with their writing, in revision. They seek to emphasize and exploit the lack of clarity, the differences of meaning, the dissonance, that writing as opposed to speech allows in the possibility of revision. Writing has spatial and temporal features not apparent in speech—words are recorded in space and fixed in time—which is why writing is susceptible to reordering and later addition. Such features make possible the dissonance that both provokes revision and promises, from itself, new meaning.

For the experienced writers the heaviest concentration of changes is on the sentence level, and the changes are predominantly by addition and deletion. But, unlike the students, experienced writers make changes on all levels and use all revision operations. Moreover, the operations the students fail to use—reordering and addition—seem to require a theory of the revision process as a totality—a theory which, in fact, encompasses the *whole* of the composition. Unlike the students, the experienced writers possess a non-linear theory in which a sense of the whole writing both precedes and grows out of an examination of the parts. As we saw, one writer said he needed "a first draft to figure out what to say," and "a second draft to see the structure of an argument buried beneath the surface." Such a "theory" is both theoretical and strategical; once again, strategy and theory are conflated in ways that are literally impossible for the linear model. Writing appears to be more like a seed than a line.

Two elements of the experienced writers' theory of the revision process are the adoption of a holistic perspective and the perception that revision is a recursive process. The writers ask: what does my essay as a *whole* need for form, balance, rhythm, or communication? Details are added, dropped, substituted, or reordered according to their sense of what the essay needs for emphasis and proportion. This sense, however, is constantly in flux as ideas are developed and modified; it is constantly "re-viewed" in relation to the parts. As their ideas change, revision becomes an attempt to make their writing consonant with that changing vision.

The experienced writers see their revision process as a recursive process—a process with significant recurring activities—with different levels of attention and different agenda for each cycle. During the first revision cycle their attention is primarily directed towards narrowing the topic and delimiting their ideas. At this point, they are not as concerned as they are later about vocabulary and style. The experienced writers explained that they get closer to their meaning by not limiting themselves too early to lexical concerns. As one writer commented to explain her revision process, a comment inspired by the summer 1977 New York power failure: "I feel like Con Edison cutting off certain states to keep the generators going. In first and second drafts, I try to cut off as much as I can of my editing generator, and in a third draft, I try to cut off some of my idea generators, so I can make sure that I will actually finish the essay." Although the experienced writers describe their revision process as a series of different levels or cycles, it is inaccurate to assume that they have only one objective for each cycle and that

---

[10]Jonathan Culler, *Saussure* (Penguin Modern Masters Series; London: Penguin Books, 1976), p. 70.

each cycle can be defined by a different objective. The same objectives and sub-processes are present in each cycle, but in different proportions. Even though these experienced writers place the predominant weight upon finding the form of their argument during the first cycle, other concerns exist as well. Conversely, during the later cycles, when the experienced writers' primary attention is focused upon stylistic concerns, they are still attuned, although in a reduced way, to the form of the argument. Since writers are limited in what they can attend to during each cycle (understandings are temporal), revision strategies help balance competing demands on attention. Thus, writers can concentrate on more than one objective at a time by developing strategies to sort out and organize their different concerns in successive cycles of revision.

It is a sense of writing as discovery—a repeated process of beginning over again, starting out new—that the students failed to have. I have used the notion of dissonance because such dissonance, the incongruities between intention and execution, governs both writing and meaning. Students do not see the incongruities. They need not rely on their own internalized sense of good writing and to see their writing with their "own" eyes. Seeing in revision—seeing beyond hearing—is at the root of the word *revision* and the process itself; current dicta on revising blind our students to what is actually involved in revision. In fact, they blind them to what constitutes good writing altogether. Good writing disturbs: it creates dissonance. Students need to seek the dissonance of discovery, utilizing in their writing, as the experienced writers do, the very difference between writing and speech—the possibility of revision.

ACKNOWLEDGMENT

The author wishes to express her gratitude to Professor William Smith, University of Pittsburgh, for his vital assistance with the research reported in this article and to Patrick Hays, her husband, for extensive discussion and critical editorial help.

Nancy Sommers is currently Director of Expository Writing at Harvard University.

The ESL Student and the Revision Process: Some Insights from Schema Theory

ANN M. JOHNS *San Diego State University*

An increasing number of immigrant, bilingual, and international students are enrolled in college and university basic writing classrooms across the United States. Though at some universities, nonnative students are assigned exclusively to ESL classes; at others, most are enrolled in classes designed for native-speakers of English, either because they are too advanced for ESL classes or because there is an insufficient number of ESL classes to accommodate them. At San Diego State University, for instance, nearly 50 percent of the students in the second semester basic writing course do not speak English in their homes (Johns, "Academic Skills").

When these students appear in native-speaker basic writing classes, their instructors are faced with new challenges; for these students, barriers to proficient writing often differ considerably from those faced by their English-speaking classmates. Since much of these students' ESL instruction may have been focused on sentence-level errors, they have not produced much English discourse. Because of this, teachers find that at the discourse level these students often have difficulties producing writing which is considered coherent by English-speaking readers, i.e., text which meets English-speaker expectations for topic organization and development (Carrell, "Cohesion" and Ulijn). These coherence problems may be difficult for the teachers to address, for they involve reader expectations which are seldom discussed in textbooks; and, for the students, meeting readers' expectations often involves abandoning the structures for organizing content which are basic to their first languages and therefore central to the manner in which they develop ideas (see, e.g., Kaplan "Contrastive Grammar" and Walters).

To enable ESL students to produce English text which is "reader-considerate," which meets the expectations of speakers of English (Armbruster & Anderson "Producing"), it is necessary to work with their writing at the discourse level, and to discuss with them the expectations of English readers. The focus, then, is upon the interaction between reader and text, and upon the students' understanding that audiences speaking different languages may require different approaches to topic development and organization.

Useful in developing instruction which focuses upon reader-text interaction are the insights and pedagogical strategies of schema-theoretical approaches, based upon the notion that "what we [as readers] understand of something is a function of our past experience or background knowledge" (Carrell, "Role of Schemata" and Miller & Kintsch).

SCHEMA THEORY

The term "schema" was first used by the cognitive psychologist Bartlett, in 1932, to describe "an active principle in our memory which organizes elements of recall into structural wholes" (15). Rumelhart, drawing on the substantial consensus that has arisen in the field of cognitive science in the past fifty years, has recently spoken of a schema theory in this way:

> A schema theory is basically a theory about knowledge—a theory about how knowledge is represented and about how that representation facilitates the use of knowledge in particular ways. According to schema theories, all knowledge is packaged into units. These units are the schemata. Embedded in these packets of knowledge, in addition to knowledge itself, is information about how this knowledge is to be used. A schema, then, is a data structure for representing our knowledge about all concepts. . . . Perhaps the central function of schemata is in the construction of an interpretation of an event, object or situation. . . . The total set of schemata we have available for interpreting our world in a sense constitutes our private theory of the nature of reality. The total set of schemata instantiated at a particular moment in time constitutes our internal model of the situation we face at that moment in time or, in the case of reading a text, a model of the situation depicted by the text (23).

The "knowledge units" of which Rumelhart speaks are also referred to as "topic types" or "conceptual frames." These units consist of content slots, "for each constituent element in the knowledge structure" (Anderson and Bower 369). The slots "consistently co-occur over a wide range of different topics" (Johns & Davies 9). Schema theorists believe, then, that there are canonical knowledge units with predictable content slots that reflect the expectations of the native-speaker reader. For example, in a text in which the knowledge unit is Physical Structure, readers expect content slots for *part, location, property,* and *function* to be filled with information from this discourse, not once, but several times (Johns & Davies). A newspaper article of the Accident Type (the knowledge unit) has seven slots (not all of which are obligatory), including *the nature of the accident, the setting, the cause, victims, comparison with other accidents, comments on the accident, public figures involved* (Zuck & Zuck).

Schema theorists posit that when a person begins to read a text, one or several sets of schemata, consisting of knowledge units, their content slots, and the networks of which they are a part (Anderson & Bower), are instantiated. The reader mentally revises—or discards—this set to accommodate the content and the structure of the text (Minsky) and uses the set to organize and store information from the text in memory (Meyer, Schank & Abelson).

The degree to which readers grasp intended meaning from and remember text depends, to a large extent, upon whether the reader-selected schemata are consistent with those of the text writer. If the reader lacks the necessary schema set, or if s/he selects an alternative set, s/he will have difficulty appropriately processing and recalling the discourse. If, for example, a Chinese writer of English develops a topic using the "eight-legged essay form," common in traditional Chinese rhetoric (Kaplan), then the English reader may not have appropriate schema set to process the text. Therefore, the text may be incoherent to the reader.

Most of the work in schema theory research and model building has been done on the knowledge units of stories (Mandler & Johnson). From "story grammar" work have come some valuable contributions to classroom teaching (Mavrogenes, Rand). Recently, however, there has been research completed to discover knowledge units and their slots as reflected in written scientific texts (Johns & Davies) and history texts (Armbruster & Anderson).

READER EXPECTATIONS AND REVISION

In this paper, discussion of the application of schema-theoretical approaches to ESL writing will focus on the first revision of an essay by a Chinese-speaking student, a sophomore enrolled in a second-semester basic writing class at San Diego State University. This student, whom I will call "You-min," completed this draft on the topic "Discuss a Problem in Your Community" during a two-hour class period.

In assigning this essay, I followed a consistent approach in my classes—that of asking students to produce writing without prior instruction in form. This approach is followed because it is important to focus upon the generation of ideas and the establishment of meaning before the imposition of structure (Murray). Like Zamel, I believe that:

> As students continue to develop their ideas in writing, considerations of organization and logical development come into play. The question, then, is not of choosing to attend to organization or not, but of when and how to do so (154).

This particular essay, by You-min, was selected for several reasons. First, though it contains sentence-level errors, it is at the discourse level where English-speaker reader expectations are not fulfilled, i.e., where coherence breaks down. Second, it was chosen because an increasing number of refugee and international students enrolled in colleges in this country are from the Orient. Many of these students are of Chinese origin (including some Vietnamese and Laotians) or influenced by Chinese culture (including Koreans and Japanese). Third, it was chosen because it seems to be characterized by the "Oriental circular development" described by Kaplan, which, though it may be consistent with the schema sets of Chinese speakers, is not consistent with those of the English readers for whom the student is writing. Kaplan notes that this type of development does not meet English reader expectation because:

> There is a lot of seemingly unnecessary wandering around the topic. The papers are characterized by an inability to get to the point and stick with it: in the traditional sense (i.e., American rhetorical traditional), they lack unity and coherence (12).

In approaching the revision of this essay, I acted as English reader and text processor for You-min as we worked through the text. Using schema-theoretical concepts and aided by articles on prediction (Pearson & Johnson) and on modeling of the reading process (Davey), I demonstrated how the English-speaker might impose a schema set and then seek out organization and meaning from text.

I began by explaining reader expectations, and how these are established by the writer. To illustrate my point, I drew a tree diagram (Figure 1, p. 143), simplified from those in artificial intelligence literature, to show how reader expectations are elicited by the writer text. These expectations are first elicited by the title and the introductory paragraph (Dooling &

Lachman). We read You-min's title, which is "How to Solve the Problem of Teenagers." From my instantiated schemata, I predicted that the text would be of a Problem/Solution type. The title was recorded next to the Problem/Solution heading on the Expectation Chart. Also noted were the content slots to be filled: *situation, problem, causes* (often embedded in problem or situation), *responses or solutions,* and *evaluation* (Hoey).

With You-min, I then looked at the introduction:

> In the past five years, juvenile delinquency increased to almost thirty percent of the overall crime in Hong-Kong. This remarkable increase put the police department to pay more attention to the teenagers. The delinquents were around twelve to eighteen years old and mostly involved in burglary, robbery and group fighting.

In this paragraph, three of the five content slots of Problem/Solution texts are alluded to: *situation, problem,* and *responses or solutions.* As reader, I asked myself (and You-min, the writer) the following questions: "What is the situation?" "What is the problem?" "What are the responses to the problem?" The answers, as prerevealed in this paragraph, are ones upon which You-min, the writer, and I agree. The *situation* is "Hong Kong in the past five years." The problem is "increase in juvenile delinquency." The *response* to the problem is "to pay more attention to the teenagers." As we answered each question, I continued to add to the Expectation Network of the Problem/Solution text, showing that from the reader's content-slot predictions, established by the title and first paragraph, must stem all content included in the coherent text.

You-min and I then moved to the first internal paragraph and the lower nodes on the network chart:

> Juvenile delinquency is an increasing problem in nowaday society around the world. Why is it increasing, is a controversial question to whether is the society, the parents, the education system or the teenagers themselves. Almost 90% of the arrested delinquents complained that they were either abused by their parents or did not feel any love in their family. There is always a generation gap between parents and adolescents, the one's who think that already grown up and mature, but their parents usually deny. Problems start to create from this point and things getting worse without the parents attention. Especially in Hong Kong is overpopulated, and modernized small city. They have not much time to pay attention to their children. Also, the education system derives a lot of pressure to the youngsters because of the limited number of universities and technical colleges in this small place. All this stress on those teenagers makes them either to face it or to escape from it—get into crime or dope. Nowadays the delinquents are sent to a special training center to teach them skills and make them to participate in recreation activities to bring back hope to them and become good citizen. Beside this, there are voluntary professional psychologists, socialist to from a non-profit organization to help solving their personal problems. More recreation centers and library were increasing by been built to give teenagers a place to spend their time meaningfully. In another way, law has been set up to let nobody under 21 is allowed to go into bar, dance rooms or any other place where alcohol or sex is involved. Group gathering in public place is limited under police department permission to avoid any group fighting occur.

I asked You-min under which category or content slot the new information (in "nowaday society around the world") in the first sentence of this paragraph should go. We decided that it should go under *situation.* Yet a different situation, "in Hong Kong in the past five years," had already been established. She was able to see the first possibility for incoherence between text and reader, in her failure to keep her promise made in the introduction. I recorded this first breakdown in the network chart—as under "Situation" in Figure 2.

We then moved to the second sentence in this paragraph, in which You-min first begins to fill the *causes* slot. Here, she mentions four causes, "the society, the parents, the education system, and the teenagers themselves." I recorded these causes under the appropriate content slot, stating that as reader I expected each of them to be discussed. In fact, only two causes were mentioned in any detail, "the parents" and "the education system." Again, You-min saw a possible breakdown in coherence as the expectations of the reader for all four causes were not fulfilled. We recorded this breakdown on expectation network.

I then turned as reader to the next content slot discussed in her essay, "Responses," noting to You-min that the reader may expect a change in content slot to be signaled by indentation. We looked at the introduction and saw that the prerevealed response is "put the police department to pay more attention to the teenagers"; yet in the text You-min has mentioned special training centers, psychologists, socialists, recreation centers, and libraries, in addition to the contributions of the police department. We marked this on the network chart, again showing a possible breakdown in coherence due to confusion with the slot information which had been prerevealed in the introduction.

Because the Evaluation slot of the essay had not yet been filled, I, as reader, expected the final paragraph to be devoted to content in this slot:

> The adolescents who are the most need care and love an away that they want the public looks at them as adults, create an increasing problem in society. This problem, people think, should gather the parents, the teachers, the socialists and the police effort to find out the solution.

As You-min and I read this part of the text, I speculated that she might be evaluating the responses by suggesting new ones, e.g., "gather the parents, the teacher, the socialists and the police." This isn't clear, however, since some of the solutions mentioned have been suggested previously in the text. Again, there is a possible breakdown in coherence between reader and text.

When I finished the reader-expectations processing of the essay and we examined the completed Expectation Network Chart (Figure 2, p. 144), You-min could see exactly where the possible breakdowns between the reader's expectations and writer take place. We reviewed the questions about the content (e.g., "What is the situation?"), the answers for which should be placed in the higher nodes of the Expectation Network Chart, and made revisions on the chart. Next, we made revisions on the chart so that what was prerevealed was actually mentioned in the essay. She was then ready to begin the "holistic revision" process, which, incidentally, was quite successful.

This approach, based upon the schema-theoretical concern for the interaction between writer and text, has become very important to revision instruction in my classrooms. My ESL students have benefited from the guidance which it provides and the freedom within the question constraints which it allows. I find this type of teacher intercession in the revision process superior to isolated comments in the margins, for the questions and the Expectation Network Charts give the writers assistance in revising in an organized manner from the top down.

However, this technique could become formulaic if employed incorrectly. Therefore it is necessary to mention its appropriate place in the revision process, noting what must proceed and follow it and emphasizing that allowances for writer meaning and reader interpretation must always be made. It must first be pointed out that You-min and I began to discuss the problem-solution categories and reader expectations only after she had completed her first draft and established a problem-solution structure for her discourse. It is she who imposed form upon her text. My responsibility was to assist her in making that form more coherent for the English reader, by suggesting the questions that must be answered and the types of answers to the questions that are expected, i.e., how the content slots should be filled to be consistent with what she had prerevealed in the title and the first paragraphs.

There are a number of activities which follow this exercise as well, all of which are devoted to increasing the writer's understanding of audience and of the variation in text which is possible, even within the problem-solution constraints. One such activity involves the distribution of copies of this essay to the class, who, individually or in groups, come up with a series of questions, prompted by what was prerevealed in the introduction and the initial sentences in the paragraphs (Johns, "Learning First"). This multiple-audience technique is particularly valuable in a class such as You-min's, in which the majority of her classmates are English speakers. After hearing these questions, You-min may attempt to answer some of them by revising the paper; or, as is often the case, she may find that her classmates' questions parallel mine since, as English speakers, we approach the text with similar schema sets. In further revisions, You-min is encouraged to experiment, exploring how various alternatives to topic development and other coherence features might satisfy her as writer as well as meet English readers' expectations. Sometimes she is asked to write about the same subject to a variety of audiences (e.g., her sociology professor, her mother), predicting the questions they might ask and answering them within the text.

The aim of this technique, then, is to give students a systematic method for predicting audience expectations, for filling content slots of a particular type of data structure such as problem-solution. As basic writers increase their proficiency and their knowledge of audience becomes more complete, they no longer need this guidance. Their intended meaning, and a number of other features such as use of metadiscourse (Kopple), become more important to the development of an essay which satisfies the writer and meets reader expectations.

Figure 1

Model Expectation Network Chart
Knowledge Unit: Problem/Solution

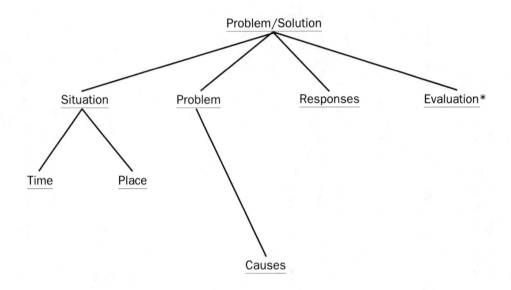

*Nonobligatory

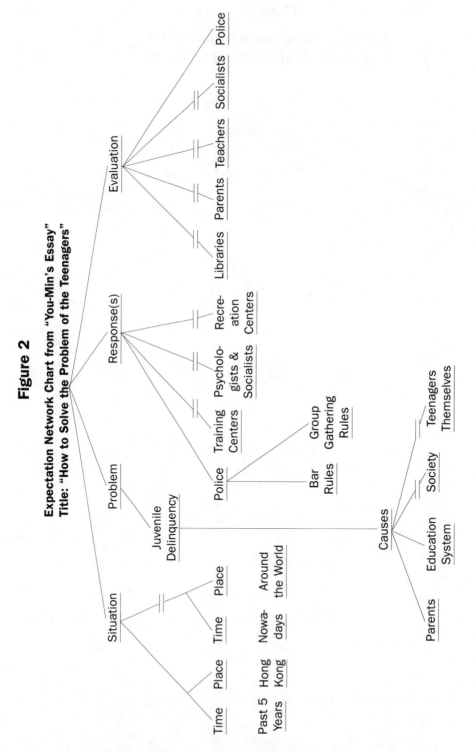

Figure 2

Expectation Network Chart from "You-Min's Essay"
Title: "How to Solve the Problem of the Teenagers"

= Indicates a breakdown between expectations of content and the manner in which slots have been filled.

REFERENCES

Anderson, John Robert, and Gordon H. Bower. *Human Associative Memory.* Washington, DC: Winston, 1973.

Armbruster, Bonnie B., and Thomas H. Anderson. *Structure for Explanations in History Textbooks or So What If Governor Stanford Missed the Spike and Hit the Rail?* Technical Rept. 252. Urbana-Champaign: University of Ilinois, Center for the Study of Reading, 1982.

———. *Producing "Considerate" Expository Text: Or Easy Reading Is Damned Hard Writing.* Reading Education Rept. 45. Urbana-Champaign: University of Illinois, Center for the Study of Reading, 1984.

Bartlett, Frederic Charles. *Remembering.* London: Cambridge UP, 1932.

Carrell, Patricia. "Cohesion Is Not Coherence." *TESOL Quarterly* 16.4 (1982): 479–488.

———. "Some Issues in Studying the Role of Schemata, or Background Knowledge in Second Language Comprehension." *Reading in a Foreign Language* 1.2 (1983): 81–92.

Davey, Beth. "Think-Aloud: Modeling the Cognitive Processes of Reading Comprehension." *Journal of Reading* 27.1 (1983): 219–224.

Dooling, D. James, and Roy Lachman. "Effects of Comprehension on Retention of Prose." *Journal of Experimental Psychology* 88.2 (1971): 216–222.

Hoey, Michael. *Signaling in Discourse.* Discourse Analysis Monograph 6. Birmingham, AL: English Language Research Unit, University of Birmingham, 1979.

———. *On the Surface of Discourse.* New York: Allen and Unwin, 1983.

Johns, Ann M. "Academic Skills 150: A Needs Assessment." Unpublished Rept., 1985a.

———. "Putting Learning First: Promoting Coherence in Academic Writing." Paper presented at the 19th Annual TESOL Convention, New York, 1985b.

Johns, Tim, and Florence Davies. "Text as a Vehicle for Information: The Classroom Use of Written Texts in Teaching Reading in a Foreign Language." *Reading in a Foreign Language* 1.1 (1983): 1–19.

Kaplan, Robert B. "Contrastive Grammar: Teaching Composition to the Chinese Students." Journal of English as a Second Language 3.1 (1968): 1–13.

———. "Cultural Thought Patterns in Intercultural Education." *Composing in a Second Language.* Ed. Sandra McKay. Rowley, MA: Newbury, 1984. 43–62.

Kopple, William V. "Some Exploratory Discourse on Metadiscourse." *College Composition and Communication* 36.1 (1985): 82–93.

Mandler, Jean M., and Nancy S. Johnson. "Remembrance of Things Parsed: Story Structure and Recall." *Cognitive Psychology* 9.1 (1977): 111–151.

Mavrogenes, Nancy A. "Teaching Implications of the Schemata Theory of Comprehension." *Reading World* 11.4 (1983): 195–305.

Meyer, Bonnie J. *The Organization of Prose and Its Effects on Memory.* Amsterdam: North Holland Publishing, 1975.

Miller, James R., and Walter Kintsch. "Readability and Recall of Short Prose Passages: A Theoretical Analysis." *Journal of Experimental Psychology: Human Learning and Memory* 6.4 (1980): 335-353.

Minsky, Martin. "A Framework for Representing Knowledge." *Psychology of Computer Vision.* Ed. P. Winston. New York: McGraw, 1975.

Murray, Donald M. *A Writer Teaches Writing.* Boston: Houghton, 1968.

Pearson, P. David, and Dale D. Johnson. *Teaching Reading Comprehension.* New York: Holt, 1978.

Rand, Muriel K. "Story Schema: Theory, Research and Practice." *The Reading Teacher.* 37.4 (1984): 377–382.

Rumelhart, David E. "Understanding Understanding." *Understanding Reading Comprehension.* Ed. J. Flood. Newark, DE: International Reading Association, 1984.

Schank, Roger C., and Robert P. Abelson. *Scripts, Plans, Goals and Understanding.* New York: Wiley, 1977.

Ulijn, Jan M. "Reading for Professional Purposes: Psycholinguistic Evidence in a Cross-linguistics Perspective." *Reading for Professional Purposes.* Ed. A. K. Pugh and Jan M. Ulijn. London: Heinemann, 1984.

Walters, Keith. "Topical Structures in the English Essays of Arabic Speakers." Paper presented at the 19th Annual TESOL Convention, New York, 1985.

Zamel, Vivian. "The Author Responds." *TESOL Quarterly* 18.1 (1984): 154–157.

Zuck, Joyce G., and L.V. Zuck. "Scripts: An Example from Newspaper Texts." *Reading in a Foreign Language* 2.1 (1984): 147–155.

Follow-Up Questions and Activities

1. Discuss and compare the revision processes of people in your class. Can any generalizations be made about these processes?

2. Discuss the ways in which a teacher can promote the revision of student papers. This could be a series of sample lesson plans, an annotated list of teaching strategies, or some other type of presentation.

3. Compare the writing blocks discussed by Rose in Chapter 4 to the problems students encounter during the rewrite process, suggesting ways to help students solve rewrite problems.

4. Interview experienced first- and second-language writers and find out how they revise. You could make this a comparative study.

5. Sommers quotes Barthes's statement that "writing," unlike speech, "develops like a seed, not a line." Conduct a study of both experienced and inexperienced writers and attempt to determine if the "seed" and "line" metaphor applies to their respective writing activities. In a follow-up paper, discuss the implications for teaching.

6. Johns states that her student was "encouraged to experiment, exploring how various alternatives to topic development and other coherence features might satisfy her as writer as well as meet the English readers' expectations." Have ESL students write both an academic paper and a personal essay on the same topic, and then have the students report on the advantages and/or disadvantages they perceive between the two types of writing. Present your findings in an essay of your own.

7. Compare Johns's approach to teaching revision to the approaches of Sommers in this chapter, Spack in Chapter 4, Flower in Chapter 3, or those of other authors. Sommers's article in Chapter 6 could also be used for this purpose. What patterns emerge that would be helpful for the writing instructor?

6

TEACHER FEEDBACK

EDITOR'S INTRODUCTION

All writers can benefit from the detached view of their work an editor can provide. According to Nancy Sommers, however, teachers should avoid making comments on students' early drafts as though they were final drafts, because this encourages students to focus on the surface level of their texts. Students should concentrate instead on revising structure and meaning, and teachers should make comments that advance these deeper purposes. This is perhaps especially important for ESL teachers and students, whose attention tends to be directed to surface-level problems. Vivian Zamel demonstrates how a teacher, despite the best of intentions, can miss the writer's intent by paying too much attention to surface details. Written comments, of course, are not the only way to respond to student writing. Lynn M. Goldstein and Susan M. Conrad find that having one-on-one oral conferences with students is an excellent way to explore the deeper purposes of a paper. They suggest that students who actively negotiate the meaning of their texts during a conference tend to make more substantial changes in revision.

Prereading Questions

1. How would you respond to your students' writing? What areas would you pay attention to first and last?

2. Discuss the kinds of feedback to your writing that you have had from teachers. What kinds of feedback did you find most helpful?

Responding to Student Writing

NANCY SOMMERS

More than any other enterprise in the teaching of writing, responding to and commenting on student writing consumes the largest proportion of our time. Most teachers estimate that it takes them at least 20 to 40 minutes to comment on an individual student paper, and those 20 to 40 minutes times 20 students per class, times eight papers, more or less, during the course of a semester add up to an enormous amount of time. With so much time and energy directed to a single activity, it is important for us to understand the nature of the enterprise. For it seems, paradoxically enough, that although commenting on student writing is the most widely used method for responding to student writing, it is the least understood. We do not know in any definitive way what constitutes thoughtful commentary or what effect, if any, our comments have on helping our students become more effective writers.

Theoretically, at least, we know that we comment on our students' writing for the same reasons professional editors comment on the work of professional writers or for the same reasons we ask our colleagues to read and respond to our own writing. As writers we need and want thoughtful commentary to show us when we have communicated our ideas and when not, raising questions from a reader's point of view that may not have occurred to us as writers. We want to know if our writing has communicated our intended meaning and, if not, what questions or discrepancies our reader sees that we, as writers, are blind to.

In commenting on our students' writing, however, we have an additional pedagogical purpose. As teachers, we know that most students find it difficult to imagine a reader's response in advance, and to use such responses as a guide in composing. Thus, we comment on student writing to dramatize the presence of a reader, to help our students to become that questioning reader themselves, because, ultimately, we believe that becoming such a reader will help them to evaluate what they have written and develop control over their writing.[1]

Even more specifically, however, we comment on student writing because we believe that it is necessary for us to offer assistance to student writers when they are in the process of composing a text, rather than after the text has been completed. Comments create the motive for doing something different in the next draft; thoughtful comments create the motive for revising. Without comments from their teachers or from their peers, student writers will revise in a consistently narrow and predictable way. Without comments from readers, students assume that their writing has communicated their meaning and perceive no need for revising the substance of their text.[2]

From "Responding to Student Writing" by N. Sommers, 1982, College Composition and Communication, *33, pp. 148–156. Copyright 1982 by the National Council of Teachers of English. Reprinted with permission.*

[1]C. H. Knoblach and Lil Brannon, "Teacher Commentary on Student Writing: The State of the Art," *Freshmen English News,* 10 (Fall, 1981), 1–3.

[2]For an extended discussion of revision strategies of student writers see Nancy Sommers, "Revision Strategies of Student Writers and Experienced Adult Writers," *College Composition and Communication,* 31 (December, 1980), 378–388.

Yet as much as we as informed professionals believe in the soundness of this approach to responding to student writing, we also realize that we don't know how our theory squares with teachers' actual practice—do teachers comment and students revise as the theory predicts they should? For the past year my colleagues, Lil Brannon, Cyril Knoblauch, and I have been researching this problem attempting to discover not only what messages teachers give their students through their comments, but also what determines which of these comments the students choose to use or to ignore when revising. Our research has been entirely focused on comments teachers write to motivate revisions. We have studied the commenting styles of thirty-five teachers at New York University and the University of Oklahoma, studying the comments these teachers wrote on first and second drafts, and interviewing a representative number of these teachers and their students. All teachers also commented on the same set of three student essays. As an additional reference point, one of the student essays was typed into a computer that had been programmed with the "Writer's Workbench," a package of twenty-three programs developed by Bell Laboratories to help computers and writers work together to improve a text rapidly. Within a few minutes, the computer delivered editorial comments on the student's text, identifying all spelling and punctuation errors, isolating problems with wordy or misused phrases, and suggesting alternatives, offering a stylistic analysis of sentence types, sentence beginnings, and sentence lengths, and finally, giving our freshman essay a Kincaid readability score of eighth grade, which, as the computer program informed us, "is a low score for this type of document." The sharp contrast between the teachers' comments and those of the computer highlighted how arbitrary and idiosyncratic most of our teachers' comments are. Besides, the calm, reasonable language of the computer provided quite a contrast to the hostility and mean-spiritedness of most of the teachers' comments.

The first finding from our research on styles of commenting is that *teachers' comments can take students' attention away from their own purposes in writing a particular text and focus that attention on the teachers' purpose in commenting.* The teacher appropriates the text from the student by confusing the student's purpose in writing the text with her own purpose in commenting. Students make the changes the teacher wants rather than those that the student perceives are necessary, since the teachers' concerns imposed on the text create the reasons for the subsequent changes. We have all heard our perplexed students say to us when confused by our comments: "I don't understand how you want me to change this" or "Tell me what you want me to do." In the beginning of the process there was the writer, her words, and her desire to communicate her ideas. But after the comments of the teacher are imposed on the first or second draft, the student's attention dramatically shifts from "This is what I want to say," to "This is what you, the teacher, are asking me to do."

This appropriation of the text by the teacher happens particularly when teachers identify errors in usage, diction, and style in a first draft and ask students to correct these errors when they revise; such comments give the student an impression of the importance of these errors that is all out of proportion to how they should view these errors at this point in the process. The comments create the concern that these "accidents of discourse" need to be attended to before the meaning of the text is attended to.

It would not be so bad if students were only commanded to correct errors, but, more often than not, students are given contradictory messages; they are commanded to edit a sentence to avoid an error or to condense a sentence to achieve greater brevity of style, and then told in the margins that the particular paragraph needs to be more specific or to be developed more. An example of this problem can be seen in the following student paragraph:

wordy – be precise   *which Sunday?*   *comma / needed*   *word choice*

Every year [on one Sunday in the middle of January] tens of millions of people <u>cancel</u> all

wordy

events, plans or work to watch the Super Bowl. This audience includes [little boys and girls, old

Be specific – what reasons?

people, and housewives and men.] <u>Many reasons</u> have been given to explain why the Super Bowl

and why   *what spots?)*   *awkward*

has become so popular ~~that~~ commercial (spots cost up to $100,000.00. <u>One explanation is that</u>

another what?   *↓ spelling*

<u>people</u> like to take sides and root for a team. <u>Another</u> is that some people like the pagentry and

too colloquial

excitement of the event. These reasons alone, however, do not explain <u>a happening</u> as big as the

Super Bowl.

{ You need to do more research

{ The paragraph needs to be expanded in order to be more interesting to a reader

In commenting on this draft, the teacher has shown the student how to edit the sentences, but then commands the student to expand the paragraph in order to make it more interesting to a reader. The interlinear comments and the marginal comments represent two separate tasks for this student; the interlinear comments encourage the student to see the text as a fixed piece, frozen in time, that just needs some editing. The marginal comments, however, suggest that the meaning of the text is not fixed, but rather that the student still needs to develop the meaning by doing some more research. Students are commanded to edit and develop at the same time; the remarkable contradiction of developing a paragraph after editing the sentences in it represents the confusion we encountered in our teachers' commenting styles. These different signals given to students, to edit and develop, to condense and elaborate, represent also the failure of teachers' comments to direct genuine revision of the text as a whole.

Moreover, the comments are worded in such a way that it is difficult for students to know what is the most important problem in the text and what problems are of lesser importance. No scale of concerns is offered to a student, with the result that a comment about spelling or a comment about an awkward sentence is given weight equal to a comment about organization or logic. The comment that seemed to represent this problem best was one teacher's command to his student: "Check your commas and semi-colons and think more about what you are thinking about." The language of the comments makes it difficult for a student to sort out and decide what is most important and what is least important.

When the teacher appropriates the text for the student in this way, students are encouraged to see their writing as a series of parts—words, sentences, paragraphs—and not as a whole discourse. The comments encourage students to believe that their first drafts are finished drafts, not invention drafts, and that all they need to do is patch and polish their writing. That is, teachers' comments do not provide their students with an inherent reason for revising the structure and meaning of their texts, since the comments suggest to students that the meaning of their text is already there, finished, produced, and all that is necessary is a better word or phrase. The processes of revising, editing, and proofreading are collapsed and reduced to a single trivial activity, and the students' misunderstanding of the revision process as a rewording activity is reinforced by their teachers' comments.

It is possible, and it quite often happens, that students follow every comment and fix their texts appropriately as requested, but their texts are not improved substantially, or, even worse, their revised drafts are inferior to their previous drafts. Since the teachers' comments take the students' attention away from their own original purposes, students concentrate more, as I have noted, on what the teachers commanded them to do than on what they are trying to say. Sometimes students do not understand the purpose behind their teachers' comments and take these comments very literally. At other times students understand the comments, but the teacher has misread the text and the comments, unfortunately, are not applicable. For instance, we repeatedly saw comments in which teachers commanded students to reduce and condense what was written, when in fact what the text really needed at this stage was to be expanded in conception and scope.

The process of revising always involves a risk. But, too often revision becomes a balancing act for students in which they make the changes that are requested but do not take the risk of changing anything that was not commented on, even if the students sense that other changes are needed. A more effective text does not often evolve from such changes alone, yet the student does not want to take the chance of reducing a finished, albeit inadequate, paragraph to chaos—to fragments—in order to rebuild it, if such changes have not been requested by the teacher.

The second finding from our study is that *most teachers' comments are not text-specific and could be interchanged, rubber-stamped, from text to text.* The comments are not anchored in the particulars of the students' texts, but rather are a series of vague directives that are not text-specific. Students are commanded to "Think more about [their] audience, avoid colloquial language, avoid the passive, avoid prepositions at the end of sentences or conjunctions at the beginning of sentences, be clear, be specific, be precise, but above all, think more about what [they] are thinking about." The comments on the following student paragraph illustrate this problem:

Begin by telling your reader
what you are going to write about   *avoid –"one of the"*
In the sixties it was drugs, in the seventies it was rock and roll. Now in the eighties, <u>one of</u>

                                                            elaborate
the most controversial subjects is nuclear power. The United States is <u>in great need of its own</u>

source of power. Because of environmentalists, coal is not an acceptable source of energy. [Solar
            be specific   *avoid –"it seems"*
and wind power have not yet received the technology necessary to use them,] <u>It seems</u> that

nuclear power is the only feasible means right now for obtaining self-sufficient power. However,

Think more about your reader

Thesis sentence needed

too large a percentage of the population are against nuclear power claiming it is unsafe. With as

be precise

many problems as the United States is having concerning energy, it seems a shame that the public

is so quick to "can" a very feasible means of power. Nuclear energy should not be given up on,

but rather, more nuclear plants should be built.

One could easily remove all the comments from this paragraph and rubber-stamp them on another student text, and they would make as much or as little sense on the second text as they do here.

We have observed an overwhelming similarity in the generalities and abstract commands given to students. There seems to be among teachers an accepted, albeit unwritten canon for commenting on student texts. This uniform code of commands, requests, and pleadings demonstrates that the teacher holds a license for vagueness while the student is commanded to be specific. The students we interviewed admitted to having great difficulty with these vague directives. The students stated that when a teacher writes in the margins or as an end comment, "choose precise language," or "think more about your audience," revising becomes a guessing game. In effect, the teacher is saying to the student, "Somewhere in this paper is imprecise language or lack of awareness of an audience and you must find it." The problem presented by these vague commands is compounded for the students when they are not offered any strategies for carrying out these commands. Students are told that they have done something wrong and that there is something in their text that needs to be fixed before the text is acceptable. But to tell students that they have done something wrong is not to tell them what to do about it. In order to offer a useful revision strategy to a student, the teacher must anchor that strategy in the specifics of the student's text. For instance, to tell our student, the author of the above paragraph, "to be specific," or "to elaborate," does not show our student what questions the reader has about the meaning of the text, or what breaks in logic exist, that could be resolved if the writer supplied specific information; nor is the student shown how to achieve the desired specificity.

Instead of offering strategies, the teachers offer what is interpreted by students as rules for composing; the comments suggest to students that writing is just a matter of following the rules. Indeed, the teachers seem to impose a series of abstract rules about written products even when some of them are not appropriate for the specific text the student is creating.[3] For instance, the student author of our sample paragraph presented above is commanded to follow the conventional rules for writing a five paragraph essay—to begin the introductory paragraph by telling his reader what he is going to say and to end the paragraph with a thesis sentence. Somehow these abstract rules about what five-paragraph products should look like do not seem applicable to the problems this student must confront when revising, nor are the rules specific strategies he could use when revising. There are many inchoate ideas ready to be

---

[3]Nancy Sommers and Ronald Schleifer, "Means and Ends: Some Assumptions of Student Writers," *Composition and Teaching*, 2 (December, 1980), 69–76.

exploited in this paragraph, but the rules do not help the student to take stock of his (or her) ideas and use the opportunity he has, during revision, to develop those ideas.

The problem here is a confusion of process and product; what one has to say about the process is different from what one has to say about the product. Teachers who use this method of commenting are formulating their comments as if these drafts were finished drafts and were not going to be revised. Their commenting vocabularies have not been adapted to revision and they comment on first drafts as if they were justifying a grade or as if the first draft were the final draft.

Our summary finding, therefore, from this research on styles of commenting is that the news from the classroom is not good. For the most part, teachers do not respond to student writing with the kind of thoughtful commentary which will help students to engage with the issues they are writing about or which will help them think about their purposes and goals in writing a specific text. In defense of our teachers, however, they told us that responding to student writing was rarely stressed in their teacher-training or in writing workshops; they had been trained in various prewriting techniques, in constructing assignments, and in evaluating papers for grades, but rarely in the process of reading a student text for meaning or in offering commentary to motivate revision. The problem is that most of us as teachers of writing have been trained to read and interpret literary texts for meaning, but, unfortunately, we have not been trained to act upon the same set of assumptions in reading student texts as we follow in reading literary texts.[4] Thus, we read student texts with biases about what the writer should have said or about what he or she should have written, and our biases determine how we will comprehend the text. We read with our preconceptions and preoccupations, expecting to find errors, and the result is that we find errors and misread our students' texts.[5] We find what we look for; instead of reading and responding to the meaning of a text, we correct our students' writing. We need to reverse this approach. Instead of finding errors or showing students how to patch up parts of their texts, we need to sabotage our students' conviction that the drafts they have written are complete and coherent. Our comments need to offer students revision tasks of a different order of complexity and sophistication from the ones that they themselves identify, by forcing students back into the chaos, back to the point where they are shaping and restructuring their meaning.[6]

For if the content of a student text is lacking in substance and meaning, if the order of the parts must be rearranged significantly in the next draft, if paragraphs must be restructured for logic and clarity, then many sentences are likely to be changed or deleted anyway. There seems to be no point in having students correct usage errors or condense sentences that are likely to disappear before the next draft is completed. In fact, to identify such problems in a text at this early first draft stage, when such problems are likely to abound, can give a student a disproportionate sense of their importance at this stage in the writing process.[7] In responding

---

[4]Janet Emig and Robert P. Parker, Jr., "Responding to Student Writing: Building a Theory of the Evaluating Process," unpublished papers, Rutgers University.

[5]For an extended discussion of this problem see Joseph Williams, "The Phenomenology of Error," *College Composition and Communication*, 32 (May 1981), 152–168.

[6]Ann Berthoff, *The Making of Meaning* (Montclair, NJ: Boynton/Cook Publishers, 1981).

[7]W. U. McDonald, "The Revising Process and the Marking of Student Papers," *College Composition and Communication*, 24 (May 1978), 167–170.

to our students' writing, we should be guided by the recognition that it is not spelling or usage problems that we as writers first worry about when drafting and revising of our texts.

We need to develop an appropriate level of response for commenting on a first draft, and to differentiate that from the level suitable to a second or third draft. Our comments need to be suited to the draft we are reading. In a first or second draft, we need to respond as any reader would, registering questions, reflecting befuddlement, and noting places where we are puzzled about the meaning of the text. Comments should point to breaks in logic, disruptions in meaning, or missing information. Our goal in commenting on early drafts should be to engage students with the issues they are considering and help them clarify their purposes and reasons in writing their specific text.

For instance, the major rhetorical problem of the essay written by the student who wrote the first paragraph (the paragraph on nuclear power) quoted above was that the student had two principal arguments running through his text, each of which brought the other into question. On the one hand, he argued that we must use nuclear power, unpleasant as it is, because we have nothing else to use; though nuclear energy is a problematic source of energy, it is the best of a bad lot. On the other hand, he also argued that nuclear energy is really quite safe and therefore should be our primary resource. Comments on this student's first draft need to point out this break in logic and show the student that if we accept his first argument, then his second argument sounds fishy. But if we accept his second argument, his first argument sounds contradictory. The teacher's comments need to engage this student writer with this basic rhetorical and conceptual problem in his first draft rather than impose a series of abstract commands and rules upon his text.

Written comments need to be viewed not as an end in themselves—a way for teachers to satisfy themselves that they have done their jobs—but rather as a means for helping students to become more effective writers. As a means for helping students, they have limitations; they are, in fact, disembodied remarks—one absent writer responding to another absent writer. The key to successful commenting is to have what is said in the comments and what is done in the classroom mutually reinforce and enrich each other. Commenting on papers assists the writing course in achieving its purpose; classroom activities and the comments we write to our students need to be connected. Written comments need to be an extension of the teacher's voice—an extension of the teacher as reader. Exercises in such activities as revising a whole text or individual paragraphs together in class, noting how the sense of the whole dictates the smaller changes, looking at options, evaluating actual choices, and then discussing the effect of these changes on revised drafts—such exercises need to be designed to take students through the cycles of revising and to help them overcome their anxiety about revising: that anxiety we all feel at reducing what looks like a finished draft into fragments and chaos.

The challenge we face as teachers is to develop comments which will provide an inherent reason for students to revise; it is a sense of revision as discovery, as a repeated process of beginning again, as starting out new, that our students have not learned. We need to show our students how to seek, in the possibility of revision, the dissonances of discovery—to show them through our comments why new choices would positively change their texts, and thus to show them the potential for development implicit in their own writing.

Nancy Sommers is currently Director of Expository Writing at Harvard University.

Responding to Student Writing

VIVIAN ZAMEL *University of Massachusetts at Boston*

The following description, entitled, "Portrait of the English Teacher as a Tired Dog," appears in a recent reference work for teachers of writing:

> It is a November midnight, Johnny Carson has just ended, and throughout the block the last lights flick off—all but one that is. A single orange light blooms in the darkness. It is the English teacher, weary-eyed, cramped of leg, hand, and brain, sifting listlessly, but doggedly through piles of themes, circling, marking, grading, commenting, guilt-ridden because the students were promised that the papers would be returned last week. The fifth cup of coffee grows cold and bitter. Just one more paper. And then one more. And then . . . (Judy 1981:208).

That writing teachers spend a great deal of time responding to their students' papers is a truism. According to one estimate (Sommers 1982), teachers take at least 20 to 40 minutes to comment on an individual paper. While little data of this sort exist for ESL teachers of writing,[1] anecdotal evidence suggests that we too invest a great proportion of our instructional time responding to our students' compositions.

TEACHERS' RESPONSES TO STUDENT WRITING: L1 SETTINGS

Given the fact that writing teachers believe, by virtue of the time and effort invested, that their responses provide critical information to students about their writing performance, it is interesting to note that until very recently, little attention was paid to the nature of these responses. Recently, however, attempts have been made to describe and investigate teachers' responses to student writing, since these responses are believed to reflect underlying assumptions about the nature and function of writing. As two researchers recently put it:

> The attitudes that teachers have toward writing strongly influence their own teaching practices, particularly their evaluation of student writing. Their beliefs . . . serve as filters that train their attention to qualities (or lack thereof) in student writing (Beach and Bridwell 1984:312).

These investigations reveal that despite the findings of process-oriented studies and their implications for the teaching of writing, practice lags far behind research and theory (see, for example, Young 1978, M. Rose 1981, Hairston 1982, Burhans 1983, Friedmann 1983) and that this is especially the case for teachers' responses.

From "Responding to Student Writing" by V. Zamel, 1985, TESOL Quarterly, *19, pp. 79–101. Copyright 1985 by Teachers of English to Speakers of Other Languages. Reprinted by permission.*

[1]See, however, Cumming (1983), whose analysis of the think-aloud protocols of three ESL teachers revealed that two of these teachers spent approximately 40 minutes responding to an ESL text.

Sommers' (1982) study, for example, of teachers' comments—comments that were "intended to motivate revision"—indicates that they "take students' attention away from their own purposes in writing a particular text and focus that attention on the teachers' purpose in commenting" (149). According to Murray, "we want our students to perform to the standards of other students, to study what we plan for them to study and to learn from it what we or our teachers learned" (1984:7). As a result, students revise according to the changes that teachers impose on the text.

Other researchers have studied the ways in which teachers appropriate their students' writing by establishing themselves as authorities. Teachers have been found to apply uniform, inflexible standards to their students' texts and to respond according to the extent to which these texts conform to or deviate from these standards (Moran 1981). They have been found to pre-empt control of important decision-making processes, allowing their own "ideal texts to dictate choices that properly belong to writers" (Brannon and Knoblauch 1982:159). Students are thus given to understand that what they wanted to say is not as important as what their teachers wanted them to say. Furthermore, these "ideal texts" may interfere with the teachers' ability to read and interpret texts, with the result that texts may be misread and comments and reactions may be inaccurate, misleading, or inappropriate (Greenbaum and Taylor 1981, Sommers 1982). In the face of their teachers' critical judgments, students are unlikely to make any effort to establish that their meaning has been misconstrued; "the writer avoids or alters meaning rather than risk [the teacher's] disapproval" (Schwartz 1983:556).

When teachers appropriate writing in this way, they are obviously viewing texts as products to be judged and evaluated. Their responses, therefore, do not take into account "the writer's intention and the actual playing out of that intention in the process of composing" or the "writer's relation to audience in any full way" (M. Rose 1983:116). Thus, the changes and revisions that students incorporate not only may fail to clarify what they intended to communicate but may have little to do with what was originally intended (see, for example, Brannon and Knoblauch 1982, Freedman 1984).

That texts are viewed as fixed and final products is further corroborated by the overwhelming evidence that teachers attend to surface-level features in what should otherwise be considered first drafts (see, for example, Collins 1981, Moran 1981, Murray 1982, Sommers 1982). Teachers seemingly "find it difficult to respond to student writing unless they can respond to it as a final draft" (Butturff and Sommers 1980:99–100) and therefore focus on problems of mechanics, usage, and style. Responding in this way to local concerns creates in students a rather limited notion of composing and reinforces the understanding that these concerns must be dealt with at the outset. I use the word *reinforces* here because studies of revising strategies indicate that it is surface-level features of writing that inexperienced writers attend to (see, for example, Beach 1976, Sommers 1980, Faigley and Witte 1981, Rubin 1983, Witte 1983). As Flower and Hayes put it, these writers are "locked in by the myopia" of their "low level goals" (1981:379).

This is not to say that teachers in fact do not believe that certain features of writing are more important than others (see, for example, Griffin 1982), but that the impression their responses create is that local errors are either as important as, if not more important than, meaning-related concerns. And this is the impression that stays with students. For example, in a recent study by Schwartz (1984), students were asked to indicate which passage a professor would prefer: one that was clear but lifeless or one that was colorful and creative but flawed mechanically. Students chose the first, assuming that "grammatical errors are more powerful in effect than voice" (60).

Because teachers often address both minor infelicities and larger issues of rhetoric and content in the same version of a text, their responses are frequently contradictory; while interlinear comments address the text as a finished product to be edited, marginal comments view the text as still developing and evolving (Sommers 1982:151). For example, mechanical errors might be pinpointed at the same time that students are being asked to elaborate upon an idea or make it more interesting. Students who receive mixed messages of this kind may be confused because they have no way of knowing whether to focus on the meaning-level changes suggested or the local problems pinpointed. Furthermore, they may recognize—although the teacher seemingly does not—that additional clarification may obviate the necessity of making these local changes. But students typically do not have to resolve this conflict, for although instructors suggest revision, they paradoxically do not provide for further revision or require it (Johnson 1979). As one researcher has indicated, students may read the comments on their papers, but they rarely write "subsequent drafts in which they can act upon the comments, and thus the improvements desired by their teachers rarely occur" (Ziv 1984:362).

Students are further likely to be confused by the contradictory ways in which different teachers respond. Teachers apply very different and even conflicting standards, based on different experiences, orientations, expectations, preconceptions, and biases (see for example, Griffin 1982, Siegel 1982, Purves 1984). This variation in teachers' responses is confirmed by a number of investigations (Hake 1978, Harris 1979). Schwartz (1984) found that when two pieces of discourse are read by two different readers, the very text that pleases one reader may irritate the other. Another recent study (Freedman 1984) found that teachers' expectations of and assumptions about student writing determine their responses to student writing. Even teachers' anxiety about their own ability to write may be a contributing factor to the way teachers respond to students' texts (Gere, Schuessler, and Abbott 1984). Williams' (1981) study of standards of evaluation indicates that conflicting and contradictory standards are as evident in handbooks and grammar texts as they are in teachers' responses. Given the variation in teachers' responses and the tendency of textbooks to reinforce or even promote this variation, it is no wonder that teachers' responses have been found to be "idiosyncratic" and "arbitrary" (Sommers 1982:149).

Another major finding is that most teachers' comments are not "text-specific and could be interchanged from text to text" (Sommers 1982:152). Instead of specific strategies, questions, and suggestions that might help students reshape their texts, students are given vague prescriptive advice (see, for example, Butturff and Sommers 1980, E. Miller 1982, G. Smith 1982, Winterowd 1983)—perhaps because, as one trainer of writing teachers has suggested, teachers are not capable of doing "accurate or creative diagnoses of student writing" (Moran 1981:70). These vague prescriptions take the form of marks and comments that represent "complex meanings . . . which remain locked in [the teacher's] head" (Butler 1980:270). While teachers may assume that these prescriptions have "universally-accepted definitions" that transmit the same "values" to their students, this is not the case (Schwartz 1984). As one study

(Ziv 1984) has indicated, when cues remain implicit, whether at the conceptual, structural, or sentential level, these responses are often misunderstood, misinterpreted, and unhelpful to students in their efforts to rethink the problems being addressed.

TEACHERS' RESPONSES TO STUDENT WRITING: L2 SETTINGS

For the same reasons that researchers are exploring the ways in which teachers respond to student writing in L1 settings—to discover both the kinds of responses they make and the underlying assumptions about writing that these responses reflect—we should be investigating the responses of ESL writing teachers. Studies of teachers' responses in L2 settings (of the sort carried out by Brannon and Knoblauch 1982, Siegel 1982, Sommers 1982, and Schwartz 1984) are practically nonexistent.

This is not to say, however, that ESL teachers have no guidelines to follow when responding to student writing. On the contrary, a descriptive survey (Cumming 1983) of responding procedures outlines the techniques and practices that have been recommended to ESL professionals and that are "seemingly implemented on a regular basis" (2) by these teachers. The following illustrates one such recommendation:

> Error correction is crucial for learning the writing skill, and correction techniques are essentially the same for controlled and free composition. Using a set list of correction symbols, teachers indicate student errors focusing on the teaching point and previously learned patterns (Bruder and Furey 1979:71).

It is obvious from the survey that despite the recent influence of process-oriented research (see, for example, Taylor 1981, Zamel 1982, 1983, Raimes 1983, Spack and Sadow 1983), teachers are still by and large concerned with the accuracy and correctness of surface-level features of writing and that error identification—the practice of searching for and calling attention to error—is still the most widely employed procedure for responding to ESL writing. Cumming offers the following rationale for this almost obsessive preoccupation with error:

> Error-identification appears to be ingrained in the habitual practices of second language teachers who perhaps by reason of perceiving their role solely as instructors of the formal aspects of "language" therefore restrict their activities to operations exclusively within the domain of formal training rather than that of cognitive development (1983:6).

Current research tells us very little about ESL teacher's responses to student writing. We know that teachers respond imprecisely and inconsistently to errors (Hendrickson 1980). Experimental studies have been undertaken to determine whether certain correction strategies seem to be more effective than others (see, for example, Cardelle and Corno 1981, Chaudron 1983, Cohen 1983, Robb, Ross, and Shortreed 1984). While studies of this sort help us explore the effects of certain feedback treatments, they clearly do not increase our understanding of what teachers actually do in response to their students' written texts.

One investigation (Vann, Meyer, and Lorenz 1984) that attempted to determine how teachers respond to ESL writing examined the responses of university faculty from various academic disciplines. Unfortunately, the texts evaluated consisted of isolated sentences containing typical ESL errors rather than total units of discourse. Thus, while the findings of this study—particularly those that indicate that variables such as age and academic area seem to influence how faculty react to certain errors—are intriguing, responding to errors in sentences out of context is so unlike what professors typically do that the findings probably bear little relationship to real responding behavior.[2]

One recent study (Cumming 1983) does provide insight into how ESL teachers respond to student writing. An examination of these teachers' responses to the same student paper suggests that error identification is in fact the most widely employed technique, that teachers' responses to the same text differ, and that the application of error-identification techniques varies considerably. Analysis of the think-aloud protocols of three of the teachers provides other interesting data. For example, particular responding techniques seem to affect how teachers view and react to the text. It is not surprising, given these differences, that these teachers "differ[ed] markedly in their assessments" (21) of the written text. This study certainly begins to ask the right question about ESL teachers' responses and provides revealing data. However, as in other experimental studies, the teachers were responding within a context created by the researcher. They may have been influenced not only by what they thought the researcher was looking for, particularly as they thought aloud about their responding processes, but by the very act of responding aloud. Thus, the extent to which their responses represent their actual reactions to and comments about authentic texts in real instructional settings cannot be determined.

THE PRESENT STUDY

Given the limitations of previous studies of ESL teachers' responses to student writing, I set out to investigate actual teacher responses. I examined the comments, reactions, and markings that appeared on compositions assigned and evaluated by teachers in their own university-level ESL writing classes. It should be noted that these compositions were originally collected to establish files of student writing, not to study teachers' responses. Thus, it is unlikely that the teachers' responses were influenced by the artificial conditions prevailing in an experimental situation.

The responding behaviors of 15 teachers were analyzed. In all but three cases, I was able to examine the way each of these teachers responded to three or more students, and in most cases there were at least two different papers for each student. Altogether, I studied 105 student texts, not including revisions of the same text. Since each teacher responded to different students and the different papers they each wrote, I was satisfied that the responses were in fact representative of these teachers' responding behavior.

---

[2]My own explanatory examination of how university faculty respond to ESL writing raises additional questions about the Vann, Meyer, and Lorenz (1984) study and its findings. My analysis indicates that faculty do not react according to some hierarchy of error types. Rather, they apply certain modes of responding: reacting to all errors, reacting to very few errors, or not reacting to any. Furthermore, whatever the level of response to error, these professors seemed to be mainly concerned with how well students presented their ideas about the content studied. It is important to note the problematical nature of the Vann, Meyer, and Lorenz investigation and to undertake further research on faculty responses within genuine writing contexts, since these responses may have implications for composition curricula.

The findings are consistent with much of what has been found about the responses of L1 writing teachers. ESL writing teachers misread student texts, are inconsistent in their reactions, make arbitrary corrections, write contradictory comments, provide vague prescriptions, impose abstract rules and standards, respond to texts as fixed and final products, and rarely make content-specific comments or offer specific strategies for revising the text.

What is particularly striking about these ESL teachers' responses, however, is that the teachers overwhelmingly view themselves as language teachers rather than writing teachers; they attend primarily to surface-level features of writing and seem to read and react to a text as a series of separate sentences or even clauses, rather than as a whole unit of discourse. They are in fact so distracted by language-related local problems that they often correct these without realizing that a much larger meaning-related problem has totally escaped their notice. Williams describes the phenomenon this way:

> It is the difference between reading for typographical errors and reading for content. When we read for typos, letters constitute the field of attention; content becomes virtually inaccessible. When we read for content, semantic structures constitute the field of attention; letters—for the most part—recede from our consciousness (1981:154).

Let us now look at specific responses:

1. I work at a office. At work everyone ~~try~~ *tries* to do their job but we also socialize with each other. There are moments when you think everything is going wrong and nobody care~~s~~ about you. ~~On~~ *One* [does] moment [that] you are really [are] down, ~~they come up with~~ *but then the people you work with do* some action that really surprises you. They really show a great deal of human love, charity and helping hands.

[ ]= omit; word not needed

Note in particular the changes made in the fourth sentence of this text. The teacher has misread the text, for he has failed to recognize that *does* for this particular student is the graphic representation of *those*, a fact which I discovered when the student read the paper aloud. In addition to appropriating the text in this way, the incorporated changes make the text less coherent than the student's own version. The student's intention was to say "on those moments," which refers directly to the preceding sentence.

In Example 2, we see a similar misinterpretation of a text:

2. I asked him why didn't you return the extra change back to her. He said No "Why should I?" I said because you should be honest, *He* answered honest for what? for money *confusing*

I said yes. He answered I'll be honest for something else but not for money, I was so

ᔕhocked and surprised by his answer that I didn't tell him anything else. He kept his

money and became my ~~enemie~~ *enemy.* that was a lesson to me ~~It (tough)~~ thought *I* me *to myself* how

money could change someone *'s* personality and honesty In a second a~~ll~~ *.all* I did was wish

that my *other* friends ~~couldn't act~~ *will never act* the same way in a similar situation.

Notice that the teacher in this case had some clue about the student's intention. By looking at the student's own crossed-out spelling in the parentheses in the third to the last line, one can see that he was trying to say, "It taught me." But the teacher read the word *thought* and changed the surrounding context so that it would accommodate this misread word. As a result, the text becomes less coherent than it originally was.

When teachers misread the text, their recommendations or corrections are often imprecise or inaccurate:

3. Sharing the same concern, Phillipa Strum in "Women at Work: Is Discrimination Real?"

word order
said that ~~even there has been~~ the Equal Rights Amendment, Discrimination Against

women at work regardless of age still exists in the U.S.A.

4. But much of the American parents' teachings was towards making their children become

good Americans and believe in the value of work and build up their self-confidence in

order for them in later years, to challenge different situations and to be successful.

if
Especially they wanted their children to understand that th̶e̶ upward mobility was

believed to be accomplished through an individual's hard work.

In Example 3, rewording the underlined phrase does not deal appropriately with the grammatical problem. In Example 4, the addition of *if* establishes a different relationship between the last two sentences and creates a structural error.

In responding to student texts, teachers often attend to local concerns and are seemingly unaffected by the larger, meaning-related problems:

5. The result was that there was no significant differences among the groups on measures of

emotional adjustment, delinquency, I.Q., visual-motor coordination, and academic

performance. Not only no significant differences, but also the children who took stimula *[verb?]* *[s.]*

for many years, their *[had]* heart rate increased and blood pressure, too.

6. I'm affraid *[SP]* of being immersed in water. For instance when I go to the beach I don't go far

away in the water. This is the way to describe my particular fear of water. However ,

essential and dangerous are two best words to describe how water is good for life and at

the same time it is also dangerous. How could *[VT]* I explain to people that I am affraid *[VT]* *[SP]* of

water since I was when since I was 5 years old.

Note how the teacher's focus at the end of Example 5 results in his missing the illogical relationship between the two sentences. In Example 6, the teacher fails to address the problematical nature of this paragraph and focuses instead on issues of lesser concern.

Because teachers commonly respond to certain problems but not others, their reactions seem arbitrary and idiosyncratic. This indicates that some things catch the teacher's attention while others do not or that errors most easily dealt with are the ones identified[3]:

7. Television is very popular among children, and these days children cannot live without

it. However, it is a big controversy that whether TV can give *[have a]* good influence on children

or not

Television can help to socialize *[word choice]* children without any efforts. They can learn from

---

[3]I am well aware of the argument that responses cannot be characterized as arbitrary without taking into account the context of the instruction and that these responses may have been deliberate and purposeful. However, an examination of students' entire texts reveals such inconsistent reactions to the same types of problems in the same text that these responses appear far more arbitrary than intentional.

television what is good and what is bad from them to do. Also they can learn from

television easily the things which they cannot see or touch directly. Those things are ~~lifes~~ *lives*

of animals and ~~lifes~~ *lives* of ~~different country's children~~ *from different countries.* However, there are some arguements

that television ~~gives~~ *has a* negative influence on children. Parents sometimes ~~give~~ *overuse* television to *word order*

children instead of playing with them as it is easier way to make children calm.

In this example, one is struck by both the language items corrected and those left uncorrected. Why, for example, is the verb changed from *give* to *have*, while the larger grammatical problem is not addressed? Does the sentence read better as a result of the changed verb? Do any of these corrections illustrate an underlying assumption that certain errors need attending to before others?

In addition to reacting idiosyncratically to textual problems, teachers often provide vague and abstract responses that do not enable students to revise their texts. Comments like "What do you mean?" "Word form," "Wrong word," "Can you say this more concisely?" or "Be careful with run-ons" appear repeatedly; revisions of the same text, however, indicate that such comments are of little help to the student, as is readily apparent from Examples 8 to 11:

Original	Revision
8. There is a final step that the bride	There is a final step that the bride
has to make. She has to go back to	has to make. She has to go back to
visit her family three days after she	visit her family three days after she
get marry *ets* ~~also must eat the rice~~ *ied*	get marry additional, she must eats
~~cooked the day before.~~ *REW write a new sentence*	the overnight rice.

9. All the apartments built with new

styles were perfectly gorgeous and

magnificent. (But is was

INC SEN unbelievable that when I visited

New York City.) It was in a terrible

condition.

All the apartments built with new

styles were perfectly gorgeous and

magnificent. It was unbelievable

that when I visited New York City.

It was in a terrible condition.

10. The foreman walked with a limp.

He walked through the plant

limping like a broken man over his

?—

prime. His face looked like it never

seen laughter. He was big from

head to toe. He looked like a bear.

The foreman walked with a limp.

He wlaked through the plant

limping. He looked like a sore

loser.

11. At that time, I was baffled by the

?
beautiful scenery helpness with

happiness yet in the firm grasp of

some sustaining power because it *awkward in this sentence*

seemed very short as a trip for

only two days. I feel that I have a *will always*
                              ∧

unique feeling of this significant

holiday.

At the time, I was baffled by the

beautiful scenery which symbolize

with happiness yet in my life.

Although its a short holiday for

only two days. I feel that I will

always have a unique feeling of

this significant holiday.

These examples are revealing, since the intent of these teachers' responses is ostensibly to draw students' attention to and help them understand their problems and how to revise their texts effectively.

While it is obvious that all of these examples illustrate teachers' responses to shorter pieces of text, the responses in fact reflect how teachers respond to whole texts. ESL teachers, viewing their students as language learners rather than developing writers, treat students' texts as final products to be edited.

This is not to say, however, that ESL teachers do not address issues of content and organization as well. Most of the texts that I examined indicate that they do. Since most first drafts were seemingly read as final drafts, however, students did not have to take responsibility for addressing these important features of writing. Furthermore, since teachers' comments about these larger concerns were couched in the same sort of vague and abstract terms used for localized errors, it is unlikely that students could have made substantial revisions, even if they had been required to do so.

The following comments are typical of how teachers dealt with content-related and organizational problems:

> Organization O.K. However, you did not understand the topic you were assigned. I cannot understand a lot of what you are saying.

> What are your subtopics? Make them explicit in your introduction and make sure your paragraphs elaborate on them.

> Although you have an introduction, developing sentences and conclusion, there's no clear T.S., nor do individual sentences clearly relate.

> This is a really excellent narrative but I do not really see any description here. You also have some other compositional changes to make in sentence, paragraph formation.

> Well-organized and well-developed in most cases, but the last point isn't well discussed.

> Interesting examples and observations about people. A few unclear ideas and references, however.

> Getting away from Topic

> A few confusing parts

> You need to support your opinion by giving details and you need to organize your thoughts a little better.

> The argument remains a little superficial.

> I'd like to see a general introduction, something to interest your reader.

> This is well-organized, but some of your paragraphs need developing.

> Some of your statements are so general that I don't know what you mean.

This last comment ironically underscores the fact that we are not very good models for our students, for while we fault them for being too general and imprecise, we are just as vague when we attempt to communicate with them.

Obviously, responses like these do not provide students with clear and explicit strategies for revising the text. They are not content-specific and could easily be appended to any student text. Rarely was a question asked or a suggestion made that gave students real direction. Rarely did a comment indicate a reaction to the actual ideas and content presented. When such comments did appear, they were perceptibly different and clearly demonstrated what happens when one reads and interacts with the text instead of evaluating it. For example, in response to a student's unsuccessful attempt to explain the effects of the energy crisis, a teacher remarked:

> The question is not "Are these energy sources decreasing?" but "How will the energy crisis change our modern life style?" You will need to be a lot more specific in your composition. See if you can answer the following question: How will the energy crisis affect agricultural production, industry and personal comfort?

Or, in response to a student's rather limited composition on the changing American family, this same teacher offered the following:

> So far you have only told me your opinion; you haven't told me why you believe what you do. You need to tell me what social, political and economic factors are putting pressure on the family to change. You stop just when it's getting interesting!

It is obvious from these responses that the teacher expected these texts to be revised in a dramatic and substantial way. One should also note that the numerous surface-level errors in these texts were not dealt with at all; this challenges the belief, illustrated in the following response of another teacher, that meaning cannot or should not be addressed when texts show signs of faulty grammar:

> If people can't understand you, it doesn't help to have some very intelligent or interesting ideas. I am not saying that you do not work hard enough—I know that you do—but rather to let you know you have a problem. When you rewrite this, I want you to concentrate on the language only. Don't even try to change or improve the content. Try to learn from rewriting how you should express your ideas in clearer and more correct language.

Compared with the two previous responses, this teacher's response communicates to the student a very different notion of what revising entails and what is important in writing.

The vague commentary of teachers often reflects the assumption that learning to write depends upon the application and mastery of rules and prescriptions. One response in particular demonstrates the extent to which the application of these formulaic guidelines interferes with a genuine reading of student writing. Reacting to a student's text, the teacher writes:

> What is this? Is this free writing? If not, where is your free writing? If this is a paragraph, there should be five sentences here.

Furthermore, teachers' responses reveal remarkable contradictions:

> You show a deep theoretical understanding of the problem but you need more detail.

> You explain this quite nicely. It's clear why you liked it although you could have analyzed its appeal more deeply.

> Very well thought out and well-written although the first body paragraph is better than the other two.

While these comments illustrate messages that are internally contradictory, there are larger contradictions as well, similar to those that Sommers (1982) identified in her study. At the same time that teachers addressed major issues of content and development in the responses that sometimes appeared in the margin, but primarily at the end of a text, they worked at polishing the text by identifying, reacting to, or correcting errors. It has apparently not occurred to these teachers that the major revisions suggested and the interlinear responses are at odds with one another. In the face of these incongruous types of comments, students are not likely to know which type of response deserves a higher priority.

From the revisions that I examined, it is quite obvious that the marginal and end comments notwithstanding, students revise on the basis of local corrections and that teachers approve of and accept these superficially better texts. For example, in response to one student's composition, a teacher suggested that one of the paragraphs be developed further and even provided some specific questions to consider. The revision, however, incorporated the teacher's grammatical corrections and did not address the questions at all. The response to the second draft: "Good! Almost error-free! Very good in organization and development!" Despite our best intentions, our responses communicate conflicting and constricting notions about the nature of writing.

This dilemma was captured well by one teacher, a student in one of my graduate courses, whom I encouraged to study her own responding behaviors:

> Whenever ESL writing students have turned in their compositions to me, I have felt a rush of mixed emotions: excitement at the prospect of reading their ideas, but at the same time utter dread of the monumental task of dealing with all those errors! I usually start out with good intentions of focusing primarily on the students' message and attending to only the "most important" errors; but all too often, I end up plowing through each paper, systematically circling, crossing out, putting brackets around, and/or revising every usage error I find. A few days later, the students get back a paper "of a different color [ink] from what they originally wrote," (according to my Vietnamese students). They read through the corrected paper once, (if I'm lucky), making mental note of the errors, (with or without understanding; to be filed in short-term memory), and then put away (or throw away?) that completed venture, ready to try their luck again at the next assignment.

She then poses the question, "Is anything really gained by the experience?" Her own answer to this question, after she examined both her responses and their effect on student writing, was an unqualified no. This corroborates the findings of other research, which makes clear the insignificant effects of teacher's responses (see, for example, Butturff and Sommers 1980, Haswell 1983, Carroll 1984, Ziv 1984).

IMPLICATIONS

We all have the opportunity to study our own responding behaviors. Each of us can become a researcher, or more accurately, an ethnographer, and analyze the rich data available to us. For example, we can try to keep logs of the types of responses we make and the degree to which these responses are incorporated into student revisions. If we are not asking for revisions, this of course tells us something as well. Just as we ask students to reread their writing, we can reread our responses and see whether they make as much sense to us as they did when we wrote them. We can ask students to tell us whether or not they understand our responses and to indicate those that they do not. In this way we can better understand what we are asking students to do, what students are learning (both about the specific point addressed and about the writing process in general), and the extent to which this enterprise helps students develop as writers.[4]

We are likely to discover, as a result of such self-exploration, that we need to change our responding behavior so that students can better understand how to revise their writing. We must recognize that students may not be able to use our comments and markings, for our responses may represent very complex reactions which they are incapable of applying to their texts. Therefore, we need to replace vague commentary and references to abstract rules and principles with text-specific strategies, directions, guidelines, and recommendations. Responses of this sort reveal to the writer the confusion that the reader may have experienced and make obvious how to deal with these problems.

Offering text-specific comments and reactions means that instead of a single standard for evaluating a text, we must adopt a flexible standard that takes into account the constraints of the tasks. Rather than a concern with whether or not a particular form was applied to the construction of the text, the concern is with the communicative effectiveness of the text (Brannon and Knoblauch 1982, Siegel 1982). Thus, the questions that we raise in responding to a text can better address the crucial dimensions of composing: for example, the author's intention and the audience.

Furthermore, applying a flexible rather than an absolute standard reminds us that the cognitive demands of a task determine what students produce on paper. Attempting to deal with intellectually complex and demanding writing assignments may result in breakdowns or setbacks that may not be evident in other kinds of writing (Clark 1980, Freedman and Pringle 1980, S. Miller 1980). To respond to these breakdowns and setbacks without taking into account the writing contexts undermines students' efforts to deal with challenging composing tasks. Responding in such a way reflects the notion that composing is a matter of writing texts that conform to the models and paradigms imposed by the teacher or textbook. As a result of such responses, students are less likely to take the kinds of risks necessary for their development as writers.

It is not enough, however, to respond more specifically and substantively or to employ more flexible criteria. Students must be provided the time and opportunity to apply these criteria and incorporate these responses into their texts. They must be made to understand that texts evolve, that revision is to be taken literally as a process of re-seeing one's text, and that this re-seeing is an integral and recursive aspect of writing. Thus, rather than responding to texts as fixed and final products, we should be leading students through the "cycles of revision" (Butturff and Summers 1980:103), for evaluating work while it may conceivably be changed "interferes with, or ends, any sense of work in progress" (S. Miller 1982:181). By providing assistance before an essay is considered finished, we are facilitating more writing and reinforcing the idea that continual clarification and exploration may be necessary before one's meaning becomes articulated. As Sommers puts it:

> We need to sabotage our students' conviction that the drafts they have written are completed and coherent. Our comments need to offer students revision tasks . . . by forcing students back into chaos, back to the point where they are shaping and restructuring their meaning (1982:154).

---

[4]In addition to investigating teacher's responses and how these responses affect student writing within real instructional settings, we need to examine the context for these responses. In this way we can begin to understand how instruction and responses reinforce one another.

Furthermore, we need to establish priorities in our responses to drafts and subsequent revisions and encourage students to address certain concerns before others. As Purves (1984) suggests, we need to play a whole range of roles as readers of student writing and adopt those that are appropriate for the various stages of a developing text. By probing, challenging, raising questions, and pinpointing ambiguities, we can help students understand that meaning-level issues are to be addressed first. This understanding is especially crucial in the ESL writing classroom, where students may be convinced that accuracy and correctness are of primary importance and where, because of their concern with language and their inexperience with writing, they may be trying to attend to all of the various demands of composing simultaneously.

We need to realize that what is true for language acquisition, as we understand it from Krashen (1982), also applies to learning to write: monitoring student output while that output is in the process of developing may not only be unproductive, but may inhibit further development (Winterowd 1980, Pringle 1983). Thus, we need to refrain from reading texts the way most of us currently do. We should hold in abeyance our reflex-like reactions to surface-level concerns and give priority to meaning, for "by worrying about mistakes in writing before we have helped students with the more important problem of adequately representing meaning . . . we may be teaching students to do the same" (Collins 1981:202). By reading primarily for error, instead of responding to the substance of students' writing, we create a situation in which genuine change even at the more superficial level is unlikely:

> To insist only on technical propriety is to underestimate [the] power [of composing] as a heuristic . . . Conversely, to accentuate the role of composing in discovering new knowledge is to show students why their writing matters, therefore to increase their motivation to write, and therefore, ultimately, to increase the likelihood of improvement because they have become more aware of the purpose and value of making meaning (Knoblauch and Brannon 1983:468).

To respond by participating in the making of meaning means that we no longer present ourselves as authorities but act instead as consultants, assistants, and facilitators. Thus, rather than making assumptions about the text, taking control of it, and offering judgmental commentary that "unbalances the teacher-student equilibrium in an authentic learning situation" (Haswell 1983:600), we need to establish a collaborative relationship with our students, drawing attention to problems, offering alternatives, and suggesting possibilities. In this sort of relationship, student and teacher can exchange information about what the writer is trying to communicate and the effect that this communication has had upon the reader and can "negotiate ways to bring actual effect as closely in line with desired intention as possible" (Brannon and Knoblauch 1982:162).

This dynamic interchange and negotiation is most likely to take place when writers and readers work together face-to-face (see, for example, Berthoff 1980, Beach 1982, Murray 1982, A. Rose 1982, Spear 1982). Instead of limiting our responses to written comments and reactions, which by their very nature are "disembodied remarks" (Sommers 1982:155) that proceed in only one direction, we should set up collaborative sessions and conferences during which important discoveries can be made by both reader and writer. The reader can discover the underlying meaning and logic of what may appear to be an incoherent text and instruct the writer how to reshape, modify, and transform the text; the writer can simultaneously discover what lies behind and motivates the complex reactions of the reader and help the reader understand a text that up to this point may have been ambiguous, elusive, or unintelligible.

In light of what we can learn from and teach each other during this reciprocal, dialectical process, we should all begin to re-examine our typical approaches to responding to writing and attempt to teach, as Murray puts it, "where the student is, not where the teacher wishes the student was" (1982:144). We should consider how we can respond as genuine and interested readers rather than as judges and evaluators. We should try to respond not to secretaries, but to authors, a distinction that F. Smith (1983) draws between the act of proofreading transcriptions of our own texts and that of reading original texts created by others. What all of this means, then, is that we should respond not so much to student writing but to student writers.

ACKNOWLEDGMENTS

This article is a revised version of a paper presented at the 18th Annual TESOL Convention in Houston, March 1984.

REFERENCES

Beach, Richard. 1976. Self-evaluation strategies of extensive revisers and nonrevisers. *College Composition and Communication* 27(2):160–164.

Beach, Richard. 1982. The pragmatics of self-assessing. In *Revising*, Ronald A. Sudol (Ed.), 71–83. Urbana, Illinois: National Council of Teachers of English.

Beach, Richard, and Lillian S. Bridwell. 1984. The instructional context. In *New directions in composition research*, Richard Beach and Lillian S. Bridwell (Eds.), 309–314. New York: Guilford Press.

Berthoff, Ann E. 1980. Learning the uses of chaos. In *Reinventing the rhetorical tradition*, Aviva Freedman and Ian Pringle (Eds.), 75–78. Conway, Arkansas: Canadian Council of Teachers of English.

Brannon, Lil, and C. H. Knoblauch. 1982. On students' rights to their own texts: a model of teacher response. *College Composition and Communication* 33(2):157–166.

Bruder, Mary Newton, and Patricia R. Furey. 1979. The writing segment of an intensive program for students of English as a second language. *Journal of Basic Writing* 2(2):67–84.

Burhans, Clinton S. 1983. The teaching of writing and the knowledge gap. *College English* 45(7):639–656.

Butler, John F. 1980. Remedial writers: the teacher's job as corrector of papers. *College Composition and Communication* 31(3):270–277.

Butturff, Douglas R., and Nancy I. Sommers. 1980. Placing revision in a reinvented rhetorical tradition. In *Reinventing the rhetorical tradition*, Aviva Freedman and Ian Pringle (Eds.), 99–104. Conway, Arkansas: Canadian Council of Teachers of English.

Cardelle, Maria, and Lyn Corno. 1981. Effects on second language learning of variations in written feedback on homework assignments. *TESOL Quarterly* 15(3):251–261.

Carroll, Joyce Armstrong. 1984. Process into product: teacher awareness of the writing process affects students' written products. In *New directions in composition research*, Richard Beach and Lillian S. Bridwell (Eds.), 315–333. New York: Guilford Press.

Chaudron, Craig. 1983. Evaluating writing: effects of feedback on revision. Paper presented at the 17th Annual TESOL Convention, Toronto, March 1983.

Clark, Michael. 1980. There is no such thing as good writing (so what are we looking for?). In *Reinventing the rhetorical tradition*, Aviva Freedman and Ian Pringle (Eds.), 129–135. Conway, Arkansas: Canadian Council of Teachers of English.

Cohen, Andrew. 1983. Reformulating second language compositions: a potential source of learner input. Paper presented at the 17th Annual TESOL Convention, Toronto, March 1983.

Collins, James L. 1981. Speaking, writing and teaching for meaning. In *Exploring speaking-writing relationships: connections and contrasts*, Barry M. Kroll and Roberta J. Vann (Eds.), 198–214. Urbana, Illinois: National Council of Teachers of English.

Cumming, Alister. 1983. Teachers' procedures for responding to the writing of students of English as a second language. Paper presented at the 16th Annual Canadian Council of Teachers of English Convention, Montreal, May 1983.

Faigley, Lester, and Stephen Witte. 1981. Analyzing revision. *College Composition and Communication* 32(4):400–414.

Flower, Linda, and John R. Hayes. 1981. A cognitive process theory of writing. *College Composition and Communication* 32(4):365-387.

Freedman, Aviva, and Ian Pringle. 1980. Writing in the college years: some indices of growth. *College Composition and Communication* 31(3):311–324.

Freedman, Sarah Warshauer. 1984. The registers of student and professional expository writing: influences on teachers' responses. In *New Directions in composition research*, Richard Beach and Lillian S. Bridwell (Eds.), 334–347. New York: Guilford Press.

Friedmann, Thomas. 1983. Teaching error, nurturing confusion: grammar texts, tests, and teachers in the developmental English class. *College English* 45(4):390–399.

Gere, Ann Ruggles, Brian F. Schuessler, and Robert D. Abbott. 1984. Measuring teachers' attitudes toward writing instruction. In *New directions in composition research*, Richard Beach and Lillian S. Bridwell (Eds.), 348–361. New York: Guilford Press.

Greenbaum, Sidney, and John Taylor. 1981. The recognition of usage errors by instructors of freshman composition. *College Composition and Communication* 32(2):169–174.

Griffin, C. W. 1982. Theory of responding to student writing: the state of the art. *College Composition and Communication* 33(3):296–301.

Hairston, Maxine. 1982. The winds of change: Thomas Kuhn and the revolution in the teaching of writing. *College Composition and Communication* 33(1):76–88.

Hake, Rosemary. 1978. With no apology: teaching to the test. *Journal of Basic Writing* 1(4):39–62.

Harris, Muriel. 1979. Contradictory perceptions of rules for writing. *College Composition and Communication* 30(2):218–220.

Haswell, Richard H. 1983. Minimal marking. *College English* 45(6):600–604.

Hendrickson, James M. 1980. Error correction in foreign language teaching: recent theory, research and practice. In *Readings on English as a second language*, Kenneth Croft (Ed.), 153–173. Cambridge, Massachusetts: Winthrop.

Johnson, Paula. 1979. Writing face to face. *Journal of Basic Writing* 2(2):7–18.

Judy, Stephen N. 1981. *Explorations in the teaching of English*. New York: Harper and Row.

Knoblauch, C. H., and Lil Brannon. 1983. Writing as learning through the curriculum. *College English* 45(5):465–474.

Krashen, Stephen D. 1982. *Principles and practice in second language acquisition*. New York: Pergamon Press.

Miller, Edmund. 1982. 'But it's just my opinion': understanding conflict with students about the expression of opinion. In *Revising,* Ronald A. Sudol (Ed.), 149–155. Urbana, Illinois: National Council of Teachers of English.

Miller, Susan. 1980. Rhetorical maturity: definition and development. In *Reinventing the rhetorical tradition*, Aviva Freedman and Ian Pringle (Eds.), 119–127. Conway, Arkansas: Canadian Council of Teachers of English.

Miller, Susan. 1982. How writers evaluate their own writing. *College Composition and Communication* 33(2):176–183.

Moran, Charles. 1981. A model for teacher training programs in the field of writing. *Journal of Basic Writing* 3(2):64–78.

Murray, Donald M. 1982. Teaching the other self: the writer's first reader. *College Composition and Communication* 33(2):140–147.

Murray, Donald M. 1984. Writing and teaching for surprise. *College English* 46(1):1–7.

Pringle, Ian. 1983. Why teach style? a review essay. *College Composition and Communication* 34(1):91–98.

Purves, Alan C. 1984. The teacher as reader: an anatomy. *College English* 46(3):259–265.

Raimes, Ann. 1983. Anguish as a second language? remedies for composition teachers. In *Learning to write: first language/second language*, Aviva Freedman, Ian Pringle, and Janice Yalden (Eds.), 258–272. New York: Longman.

Robb, Thomas N., Steven Ross, and Ian Shortreed. 1984. A large-scale study of feedback methods in EFL composition. Paper presented at the 18th Annual TESOL Convention, Houston, March 1984.

Rose, Alan. 1982. Spoken versus written criticisms of student writing: some advantages of the conference method. *College Composition and Communication* 33(3):326–330.

Rose, Mike. 1981. Sophisticated, ineffective books—the dismantling of process in composition texts. *College Composition and Communication* 32(1):65–74.

Rose, Mike. 1983. Remedial writing courses: a critique and a proposal. *College English* 45(2):109–128.

Rubin, Donnalee. 1983. Evaluating freshman writers: what do students really learn? *College English* 45(4):373–379.

Schwartz, Mimi. 1983. Revision profiles: patterns and implications. *College English* 45(6):549–558.

Schwartz, Mimi. 1984. Response to writing: a college-wide perspective. *College English* 46(1):55–62.

Siegel, Muffy E. A. 1982. Responses to student writing from new composition faculty. *College Composition and Communication* 33(3):302–309.

Smith, Frank. 1983. Writing: authors vs. secretaries. Paper presented at the 17th Annual TESOL Convention, Toronto, March 1983.

Smith, Gayle L. 1982. Revision and improvement: making the connection. In *Revising*, Ronald A. Sudol (Ed.), 132–139. Urbana, Illinois: National Council of Teachers of English.

Sommers, Nancy. 1980. Revision strategies of student writers and experienced writers. *College Composition and Communication* 31(4):378–388.

Sommers, Nancy. 1982. Responding to student writing. *College Composition and Communication* 33(2):148–156.

Spack, Ruth, and Catherine Sadow. 1983. Student-teacher working journals in EFL freshman composition. *TESOL Quarterly* 17(4):575–593.

Spear, Karen I. 1982. Empathy and revision. In *Revising*, Ronald A. Sudol (Ed.), 156–162. Urbana, Illinois: National Council of Teachers of English.

Taylor, Barry P. 1981. Content and written form: a two-way street. *TESOL Quarterly* 15(1):5–13.

Vann, Roberta J., Daisy E. Meyer, and Frederick O. Lorenz. 1984. Error gravity: a study of faculty opinion of ESL errors. *TESOL Quarterly* 18(3):427–440.

Williams, Joseph M. 1981. The phenomenology of error. *College Composition and Communication* 32(2):152–168.

Winterowd, Ross W. 1980. Developing a composition program. In *Reinventing the rhetorical tradition*, Aviva Freedman and Ian Pringle (Eds.), 157–171. Conway, Arkansas: Canadian Council of Teachers of English.

Winterowd, Ross W. 1983. From classroom practice into psycholinguistic theory. In *Learning to write: first language/second language*, Aviva Freedman, Ian Pringle, and Janice Yalden (Eds.), 237–246. New York: Longman.

Witte, Stephen. 1983. Topical structure and invention: an exploratory study. *College Composition and Communication* 34(3):313–341.

Young, Richard E. 1978. Paradigms and problems: needed research in rhetorical invention. In *Research on composing*, Charles Cooper and Lee Odell (Eds.), 29–47. Urbana, Illinois: National Council of Teachers of English.

Zamel, Vivian. (1982). Writing: The process of discovering meaning. *TESOL Quarterly*, 16(2), 195–210.

Zamel, Vivian. (1983). The composing processes of advanced ESL students: Six case studies. *TESOL Quarterly*, 17(2), 165–187.

Student Input and Negotiation of Meaning in ESL Writing Conferences

LYNN M. GOLDSTEIN *Monterey Institute of International Studies*

SUSAN M. CONRAD *Central Washington University*

Student-teacher writing conferences are widely recommended in composition pedagogy and many claims have been made about their role in helping students become more effective writers. These claims, however, remain unverified for second language writers because none of the research has examined the discourse that takes place in conferences or the relationship between this discourse and subsequent revision for these writers. In fact, most claims for both native-speaker and ESL writers are based on the participants' impressions of, or attitudes towards, conferences.

In a study of native speakers, Carnicelli (1980) reviewed students' evaluative comments towards their conferences. On the basis of these, he concluded that conferences are a more effective means of feedback than are written comments because conferences allow students to express their opinions and needs, and to clarify teachers' comments when they are not understood: "If a teacher's response is unclear the student can simply ask for an explanation" (p. 108).

Zamel (1985) and Sokmen (1988) reach similar conclusions for conferences with nonnative speakers. Zamel discovered that ESL students often found written comments difficult to understand. Thus, she suggests that teachers need to hold conferences with students because "dynamic interchange and negotiation is most likely to take place when writers and readers work together face-to-face" (p. 97). Sokmen concurs, stating that "responding in conferences is more effective than in writing because you, the teacher, can interact dynamically with the students to understand the intent" (p. 5).

The above claims, however, are based not on an examination of discourse that actually occurs in conferences, but on students' and teachers' evaluations of conferences. The few studies that have examined actual discourse have focused on native-speaker conferences. Freedman and Katz (1987) analyzed transcripts of several conferences and found that the discourse within these conferences had predictable parts: openings, student-initiated comments and questions, teacher-initiated comments and questions, reading of the paper, and closings. Examining one conference in detail, they discovered that the teacher and student followed interactional rules that "placed the conference somewhere between" (p. 77) conversational turn-taking rules described by Sacks, Schegloff, and Jefferson (1974) and the rules of classroom turn-taking as described by Mehan (1979). While the teacher initiated many questions to guide the student, the student supplied the direction and content of the conference. Freedman and Katz hypothesized that a student's input and control of the discourse accounts for the effectiveness of conferences in improving student writing. However, they did not actually look at the relationship between these factors and subsequent revisions or papers to test this.

Walker and Elias (1987) compared the discourse in conferences rated highly by tutors and students to those rated poorly. Highly rated conferences were characterized by a focus on the student, with a discussion of criteria for successful writing and with an evaluation of the student's work. Low-rated conferences were dominated by the tutor and contained repeated requests for explanations, either by the tutor or student or both. Since success in this study is defined by tutor and student evaluation, there is no discussion of whether writing or revisions that occurred after the more "successful" conferences were more effective than those that occurred after less successful conferences.

Researchers have also studied the variation among students in the discourse they produce within conferences. Freedman and Sperling (1985) examined the conferences of four native-speaker students: two high-achieving students and two low-achieving students. The high-achieving students elicited more praise from the teachers while low-achieving students tended to nominate topics that "alienated" (p. 128) the teachers. Freedman and Sperling conclude that the interactions in conferences vary and that "these differences in conversational interaction signal the possibility of differential instruction" (p. 128). These researchers do not, however, examine the relationship between such "differential instruction" and student success.

The relationship between the discourse created in conferences and subsequent revision or overall writing improvement has been studied by Jacobs and Karliner (1977). They compared the conferences of two native-speaker students to determine if the differences in the roles played by teacher and student corresponded to differences in the revisions made in subsequent drafts. They found that the student who engaged in exploratory talk and who initiated more discussion in the conference made revisions that contained deeper analysis of the subject. In contrast, the student who deferred to the teacher, with the teacher acting as an expert who gives suggestions even before hearing the student's ideas, made more surface-level changes and never solved the deeper problems in content. Jacobs and Karliner conclude that the type of verbal interaction within the conference does influence the type of subsequent revision made.

We must be cautious in extending the conclusions of these studies to ESL student-teacher conferences. First, there is very little research that examines actual conference discourse and/or conference discourse in relation to subsequent revision. Second, we cannot extrapolate from studies where the subjects were native speakers of English because we cannot assume that nonnative speakers will behave in conferences in the same ways that native speakers behave.

THE STUDY

In our study we sought to answer the following questions:

1. To what extent do ESL writing conferences ensure student input?
2. To what extent is meaning negotiated in ESL writing conferences? (See Figure 1 for a definition of *negotiation of meaning*.)
3. What is the relationship between the discourse in the conference and successful revision in the subsequent draft?

The Educational Context

Subjects were selected from 21 students in an advanced ESL composition class at a large urban university. The teacher was an experienced ESL composition instructor who had been using conferences as an integral part of her courses for the previous four years. The students wrote multiple drafts of expository papers, had a scheduled 20-minute conference every other week to discuss the draft they were working on, and received written feedback on another draft in the week between conferences. The teacher did not read the drafts that were discussed in conference until the actual conference and students were asked to be ready to identify areas they wanted to discuss when they came to conference.

METHODOLOGY

Subjects

Three students were selected from three different cultural backgrounds. The students had roughly equivalent proficiency, as determined by a holistic evaluation of all the papers each had written during the semester. They were in the last course of an ESL sequence that leads to Freshman Composition. Each demonstrated a working knowledge of academic rhetoric, and evidenced only relatively minor and infrequent sentence-level problems.

Two women and one man, all in their 20s, participated in the study. All three were full-time matriculated students in their junior year majoring in a science. All had been in the United States for six years and were fluent speakers of English who evidenced no difficulty in understanding or participating in spoken discourse. Two of the subjects, Tranh (from Vietnam) and Zohre (from Iran), had attended high school in their native countries; Marigrace (from the Philippines) had attended public high school in the United States.

Data Collection

With the students' permission, the teacher taped all the conferences and collected copies of each draft of every paper. Oral data consisted of tapes of ten 20-minute conferences, three each for Zohre and Marigrace, and four for Tranh. Written data consisted of two drafts each of 10 papers (three papers each for Zohre and Marigrace, and four for Tranh). One draft of each paper was written before the conference and was discussed in the conference, and the other draft of the paper was written after the conference.

Conference Data Analysis

The 10 tapes of the conferences were transcribed orthographically. Our first attempts to apply established discourse analysis systems to the data did not account for elements that appeared important in the conferences. As has been the case for other researchers (Walker & Elias, 1987; Freedman & Sperling, 1985; van Lier, 1988), it became obvious that our data should suggest the categories, rather than be made to fit imposed categories. Consequently, we looked for recurring patterns and variations across students that suggested to us how the discourse was structured and what the roles of each participant were in the discourse. As new patterns and variations emerged, we went back and coded them in conferences that we had already analyzed. Through this iterative process, we identified seven features (see Table 1) for coding. After we had finished analyzing all the conferences once, we went through them two more times (independently and then together) to ensure that our analysis was consistent across all conferences.

After the features were identified and coded on the transcripts, we obtained frequency counts per conference for types of discourse structures, topic nominations, invited nominations, turns per episode, questions, and negotiations. We then calculated mean frequencies per category for each student's conferences.

Analysis of Revision and Negotiation

One of the goals of this research was to look at the relationship between what was discussed in conference and what was revised in the subsequent draft. We recognize that many other revisions may have occurred that were not discussed in conference and that many other rhetorical problems may have remained in the drafts. However, we decided to limit ourselves in this study to an examination of only those revisions that were discussed in the conference. Our overall goal was to determine what elements (if any) in the conference discourse concerning revision appeared to influence whether and how the students revised those areas.

After we had analyzed the conference transcripts, we looked at the student papers. We compared the conference draft to that written subsequently, examining those places in the papers that had been identified in the conferences as needing revision. Through this process, a pattern began to emerge: Revisions seemed to occur when they had been negotiated in the conference. Working with this hypothesis, we went back to the transcripts and identified all the discussions of revision and categorized them on the basis of whether negotiation had taken place. We again compared the draft being conferenced with the one written after the conference, this time to discover which revisions had been made and how successful these had been. In the determination of successful revision, each of the researchers analyzed the written data individually, then compared and discussed categorizations, reaching consensus on what was successful or not, and why. Next, we compared negotiated discussions of revision to nonnegotiated ones to see the degree to which each resulted in successful, unsuccessful, or no revision.

We defined successful revisions as those we judged had solved or improved upon a rhetorical problem discussed in the conference while being consistent with the writer's purpose, main point, and audience. This also allowed us to credit as successful those revisions that solved the rhetorical problem under discussion even if, when a strategy had been discussed in conference, the student chose to use a different one.

FIGURE 1

Discourse Features

Episodes: These are subunits of conferences, with a conference made up of a series of episodes. Each episode has a unique combination of topic and purpose such that a change in either or both signifies a new episode. Episodes could be interrupted by others, continuing at the end of the interruption.

Discourse Structure: Each episode was characterized by a particular discourse structure. Six types of structures emerged from the data.

1. Teacher talks and student backchannels.[1]
2. Teacher questions and student answers.
3. Teacher talks and student talks.
4. Student talks and teacher backchannels.
5. Student questions and teacher answers.
6. A combination of the above.

Topic Nomination: The participant who introduced either a new topic and/or new purpose, effectively changing to a new episode, was said to have nominated the topic of the new episode.

Invited Nomination: An invited nomination occurs when the participant nominates the topic in response to a question such as, "What would you like to discuss?"

Turns: A change of speaker signified a new turn, with the exception of backchannels. There are many theoretical positions on whether or not backchannels are turns (see van Lier, 1988, for example). However, these positions vary with the data being analyzed. Thus, we do not count backchannels as turns because, while they showed the listener was attending, in our data they do not expand, comment on, agree or disagree with, or ask for clarification of what the speaker was saying.

Questions: We counted the number of questions asked both by student and teacher. This category contains only those questions not used for negotiation (see below).

Negotiation: Two types of negotiation were identified. *Negotiation of meaning*, identified in many second langue acquisition studies (see, for example, Long, 1983) refers to confirmation checks, comprehension checks, and clarification requests.

   Negotiation of revision took place not when meaning needed to be clarified, but when revision strategies needed to be clarified. These consisted of (a) the student confirming the teacher's suggestion of a need for revision or the use of a revision strategy (for example, saying, "So you are suggesting that I should change the order of these"); (b) either the teacher checking to see if the student had understood a discussion of revision options or a student checking (for example, the teacher saying, "So what strategies can you use to revise this?"); (c) the student checking, while the need for revision was being discussed, to see if it would be appropriate to revise in a certain way (for example, the student saying, "What do you think if I added this example here?"); (d) the student stating that he or she did not understand either why a revision would be necessary or how to revise.

---

[1]*Backchannels* are verbal devices such as *um-hum, yeah*, and *um* that indicate that a listener is attending to a speaker.

   To illustrate, Tranh wrote a first draft about discrimination in which he had confused types of discrimination with causes of discrimination and in which he had arrived at a superficial discussion. In the conference, the teacher elicited the fact that Tranh's purpose was to examine the causes of discrimination so that people could arrive at solutions to it. The teacher and

Tranh then went on to examine whether or not his purpose had been achieved, discovering that it had not been and that Tranh was confused about the difference between cause and type of discrimination. As the conference unfolded, they jointly generated possible causes of discrimination and discussed how to focus on and develop only those parts of his paper related to his purpose.

After the conference, Tranh rewrote his introduction making it fit his purpose; he kept in causes he had discussed in the previous draft while he eliminated any discussion from the previous draft on types of discrimination; he expanded his discussion of causes by adding ones he had not mentioned in his previous draft; he provided concrete illustrations for some of the causes he was writing about; he completely rewrote his conclusion to be consistent with his purpose. These revisions were judged successful since they solved rhetorical problems of the previous draft. Importantly, he was able to decide on his own which parts of the text fit his purpose and should remain and which didn't and should be removed. Also, he was able to generate causes that were not in his previous draft and that had not been discussed in conference.

It is important to note that our definition of success is "local": We were examining only the relationship between revisions discussed in the conference and the revisions that appeared in the subsequent draft. We recognize that future research needs to address rhetorical issues not discussed in the conference, as well as the long-term effects of conferencing on writing quality and revision.

RESULTS

Conference Data

The mean scores for each discourse feature and discourse structure are displayed in Tables 1 and 2. These scores demonstrate that there was much variation across the students in the amount of interactional work they did in their conferences. Frequencies for individual conferences are not reported because there was little or no variation across each student's conferences.

The three students differed greatly in the amount of input they contributed. First, the degree to which each set the agenda can be seen in the percent of nominations (see Table 1). While Zohre and Tranh contributed roughly half of the topic nominations, Marigrace contributed only one fifth. Second, these three students differed in how much interactional work they did building the discourse (see Table 2). Tranh consistently did more work than Zohre, who in turn consistently did more than Marigrace. Although Zohre and Tranh made about the same percent of topic nominations (Table 1), twice as many of Zohre's nominations were invited nominations (41% for Zohre vs. 20% for Tranh). Marigrace's nominations, in addition to being relatively infrequent (19.50%), were often invited (42.88% of her nominations were invited). Marigrace was also more often invited to contribute input to the conference in other ways. For example, the teacher frequently used questions (14 times per conference) with Marigrace; in contrast, she asked far fewer questions of Zohre and Tranh (6 and 6.75 per conference respectively), who more often voluntarily contributed to the conferences.

TABLE 1
Comparison of Student Input: Discourse Features

Discourse features per conference	Student[a]		
	M	Z	T
Nominations made by student (%)	19.50	47.30	50.00
Of student nominations, % invited	42.88	41.00	20.00
Turns per episode (M)[b]	2.33	3.68	5.94
Questions asked by student (M)[b]	1.43	2.33	4.50
Questions asked by teacher (M)[b]	14.00	6.00	6.75
Negotiations made by student (%)	33.20	55.75	60.78
Negotiations made by student (M)[b]	1.66	6.30	7.75

[a] M = Marigrace, Z = Zohre, T = Tranh.
[b] M = mean number

The students also differed in the degree to which they clarified meaning (Table 1). Marigrace was responsible for only 33.20% of the meaning negotiations (mean per conference = 1.66); Zohre was responsible for 55.75% (mean per conference = 6.30) and Tranh for 60.78% (mean per conference = 7.75). This is another measure demonstrating that Tranh did the most conversational work in the conferences, Zohre the next, and Marigrace considerably less than either of the other two.

TABLE 2
Comparison of Student Input: Discourse Structure (%)

Episodes per conference	Student[a]		
	M	Z	T
Conversational work done primarily by teacher			
T questions/S answers	27.27	13.89	3.57
T talks/S backchannels	33.33	36.11	10.71
Total[a]	60.60	50.00	14.28
Student/teacher sharing work			
T talks/S talks	21.21	36.11	53.57
Total[a]	21.21	36.11	53.57
Conversational work done primarily by student			
S questions/T answers	0	8.33	10.71
S talks/T backchannels	0	0	3.57
Total[a]	0	8.33	14.28

Note. Percentages do not total to 100 because the remainder consisted of mixed episodes.
[a] M = Marigrace, Z = Zohre, T = Tranh.

The amount of work that the students did is also reflected in the degree to which they used each type of discourse structure (see Table 2). Those episodes where the student did less work than the teacher (teacher questions/student answers, and teacher talks/student backchannels) occurred most frequently with Marigrace (60.60%), the next most frequently for Zohre (50.00%), and considerably less frequently for Tranh (14.28). In contrast, episodes where the student did more of the work (student questions/teacher answers, and student talks/teacher backchannels) never occurred in Marigrace's conferences, occurred 8.33% of the time in Zohre's conferences, and 14.28% of the time in Tranh's. Episodes in which student and teacher shared the work occurred least frequently for Marigrace (21.21%), more frequently for Zohre (36.11%), and most frequently for Tranh (53.57%).

The Relationship Between Revision and Negotiation

Table 3 presents the results of the analysis of the relationship between the revision of the written drafts and negotiation of revisions. These results support our hypothesis that there is a positive relationship between negotiation and successful revision.

TABLE 3
Negotiations of Revisions (%)

	Student[a]		
	M	**Z**	**T**
Negotiated revisions	(n = 3)	(n = 6)	(n = 12)
Successful	100.00	100.00	91.66
Unsuccessful	0	0	0
No revision			
Nonnegotiated revisions	(n = 6)	(n = 5)	(n = 10)
Successful	33.33	0	20.00
Unsuccessful	66.67	40.00	60.00
No revision	0	60.00	20.00

[a] **M = Marigrace, Z = Zohre, T = Tranh.**

When teacher and student negotiated revisions, the ensuing revisions were almost always successful (see Table 3). In the following excerpt from one of Zohre's conferences, for example, the teacher and Zohre discuss the need to include more concrete details in a paper written as a letter to convince a friend to come for a visit. In lines 9–10 Zohre negotiates by asking if a certain revision strategy would be appropriate, and in lines 27–29 she checks her understanding of the number of examples needed:

T: Um::(teacher reading from Zohre's text) "In addition there are many cheap ethnic restaurants in which can satisfy the taste of an adventurist person." Here's another place where I think that someone could get a real sense of the place um by describing a little bit the kind of food you might get in one particular restaurant a Thai restaurant or something like that

Z: Um

T: the sensations the taste what the food looks like (.)

Z: like ok in different restaurants like I say what kind of food they have

T: Umhum, um: you know if I were if I were gonna write to someone and I was gonna say um you can find many cheap ethnic restaurants you can sa-satisfy the taste of an adventurist person that means a taste I've never tasted before um if I'm an adventurous person I'm gonna try something new. So I'd try to think of something exotic you know for example you could try Thai food and you can taste the hot and sweet flavors in combination with each other with coconut milk um

Z: um

T: make their mouths water

Z: ya

T: you know in a sense. You don't have to the purpose of the paper isn't to describe the restaurant so you don't have to go into any great detail but if you could just have one line the dominant flavors of a particular cuisine I think would make it very vivid

Z: o.k. just one example

T: ya

Z: would be enough

T: ya

In the subsequent draft of the paper Zohre adds details that give the reader a more vivid picture of one of the restaurants:

there are many cheap restaurants in which can satisfy the taste of an adventurist person. For example, there is a Moroccan restaurant which serves you with a spicy lentil based soup, platters of Arabic bread and different entrees, most of which are chicken or lamb stewed with various combinations of fruits and vegetables. In this restaurant you eat with your fingers like North African tradition.

These details were of Zohre's own making, not a copy of those given as an illustration by the teacher. She extracted the principle and applied it to her own writing.

Table 3 shows that all three students, not only Zohre, had a higher percentage of successful revisions when negotiation had taken place. Every time Marigrace and Zohre negotiated, their subsequent revisions were successful. When Tranh negotiated, 91.66% (11/12) of his revisions were successful. None of Tranh's were unsuccessful, but there is one instance where he did not revise despite negotiation. This lack of revision, however, may be due to a discussion between the teacher and Tranh in which this revision was determined to be of relatively minor importance.

In contrast, when the students did not negotiate (i.e., when the teacher made revision suggestions and the student backchanneled), the subsequent revisions were often either unsuccessful or not attempted at all (Table 3). For example, in the same conference referred to above, Zohre did not negotiate when the teacher suggested using more specific details in another part of the paper. Zohre only backchanneled while the teacher spoke:

> T: . . . where I fel– I felt you needed the detail and (teacher reading Zohre's text) "it has really nice and big campus" this
>
> Z: uhuh
>
> T: word "nice" means nothing
>
> Z: oh
>
> T: O.K. what does nice mean
>
> Z: O.K. like I know
>
> T: um you might want to describe the campus briefly
>
> Z: o.k
>
> T: here it's set on a hill lots of green and the architecture you know
>
> Z: ya

The only change Zohre made in her next draft is from "it has really nice and big campus" to "It has a nice and big campus." She did not address the need for specific details.

We can also contrast this excerpt to the previous one: While Zohre did not do a lot of conversational work in either excerpt, in the previous one she did negotiate the revision suggestion, and she acted on that suggestion successfully. She did not act on the nonnegotiated suggestion even though both suggestions addressed the need for more detail.

The relationship between lack of negotiation and unsuccessful/unattempted revision holds for all three students (Table 3). When revisions had not been negotiated, Zohre either revised unsuccessfully (40%) or did not attempt revision at all (60%). While Tranh had some successful revisions (20%) when he didn't negotiate, the majority were unsuccessful (60%) or not attempted (20%). Although Marigrace had the highest number of successful revisions in nonnegotiated instances (33.33%), she still produced a greater number of unsuccessful revisions (66.67%). In three out of the four cases of nonnegotiated successful revision (both of Marigrace's and one of Tranh's), the discussion included specific instructions for very mechanical revisions, such as the switching of the order of two sentences. And, in these cases, the instructions were restated. The simplicity of these revisions and the restatements may explain why, even without negotiation, these revisions were successful.

DISCUSSION

Our results do not support some of the claims that have been made for conferences. Much of the literature suggests that the very act of conferencing (see, for example, Carnicelli, 1980; Zamel, 1985) leads students to contribute input: setting the agenda, making their needs known, expressing their ideas and opinions, and asking questions and clarifying meaning. However, we have not found this to be the case for all the students in this study. Like Jacobs and Karliner (1977) and Freedman and Sperling (1985), we have found variation across students in the way they interact with the teacher in a conference. Marigrace's conferences were characterized by the teacher generating most of the input and doing most of the conversational work: The teacher nominated the topics, the teacher did most of the talking, and the teacher used questions to engage Marigrace in the interaction. Marigrace primarily backchanneled. Tranh's conferences contrasted sharply with those of Marigrace. His were characterized by student and teacher equally contributing topic nominations, questions and talk, and backchannels; they shared in the building of the discourse. Zohre's conferences fell between these extremes. Thus, while a student *may* contribute input to the conference, *may* set the agenda, and *may* negotiate meaning, these are not guaranteed—even in conferences with the same teacher.

Each student who participates in a conference brings to that conference a unique personality that may affect the ways in which that student behaves in the conference. For example, the teacher's impression, before the study began, was that Tranh was the most assertive, Zohre the next, and Marigrace the least. If this is the case this might be one explanation of why Tranh contributed the most input, Zohre somewhat less, and Marigrace the least.

The teacher's role in producing variation in the conference discourse needs to be considered. One possibility is that the teacher may have adjusted to the student's individual discourse style, thus reinforcing it, whether or not this resulted in the student actively participating in the conference. For instance, the greater amount of conversational work done by the teacher in Marigrace's conferences, asking many questions for example, may be an adjustment to Marigrace's lack of voluntary input and may have encouraged her to continue to rely on the teacher to do most of the interactional work in the conference.

However, it is also possible that the teacher gave differential treatment to students for reasons other than the teacher adjusting to the students' own discourse styles, as Freedman and Sperling (1985) suggested in their study. In our study, once students' behaviors in conference and in class had been observed, the teacher may have subconsciously behaved in ways consistent with her expectations of the students. The teacher may have accepted less participation from Marigrace in the conference because she evaluated her as a less capable student on the basis of her initial conferences and revisions. On the other hand, the teacher may have been more encouraging of discussion with students such as Tranh and Zohre who more actively participated in conferences and who revised their papers more successfully.

In addition, as members of diverse cultures, ESL students come with rules of speaking that may conflict with those of U.S. classrooms and with those teachers might like to see operate in conferences. These rules of speaking may also play a role in the students' perceptions of their and their teachers' roles in a conference. As Philips (1972) has demonstrated, for example, students often bring to the classroom rules of speaking from their own cultures that work differently from those of the new culture. In our study, it is possible that the variation we have seen across the three students may result, at least in part, from these students using culturally diverse rules for how much teachers and students control the discourse when interacting with each other.

Students may have also acquired rules of speaking from typical U.S. classrooms that may also conflict with those of the conference. For example, in many U.S. classrooms it is the teacher who typically initiates and questions, the student who responds, and the teacher who evaluates (see, for example, Mehan, 1979). Again, this may result in some students contributing more input than others. In our study, it is possible that Marigrace had been influenced by her high school education in the United States and was consequently following that discourse structure.

In the end, however, regardless of why variation across students existed, the results show that conferences do not necessarily do what the literature claims they do—they do not necessarily result in student input. In sum, instructional events such as conferences are dynamic, lending themselves to the myriad influences and interpretations of their participants.

Conferences also do not necessarily result in revision, and when revision occurs after a conference, it is not always successful. Our data suggest that negotiation of meaning does play a role in subsequent revision and we need to ask why negotiation would lead to more successful revisions. First, just as negotiation clarifies meanings in ordinary conversations, negotiation in the conference may clarify the need for revision and the strategies to undertake the revision. Students, therefore, may understand more clearly what to revise, how to revise, and why they need to do so. In addition, negotiation may lead to better retention of what has been discussed. Negotiation requires the student to be more actively involved in the discussion either by asking questions or answering them, which may lead to better retention (see, for example, Stevick 1976). Finally, it is also possible that students negotiate points where they most clearly see the need for revision; they may already be predisposed to revising in the area being negotiated and may be more interested in discussing how to do so. For example, in Zohre's case, there are several instances where she shows very little interest in the revision the teacher has nominated for discussion, and in fact she does not make these revisions in subsequent drafts.

Although we do not know all the characteristics of discourse that might lead to successful revision, this study suggests that negotiation plays an important role. The student who was conversationally active (Tranh) and the student who was more dependent on teacher input and direction (Marigrace) both demonstrated more successful revisions when negotiation occurred. However, we have seen that despite the claims made, conferences do not ensure that negotiation will take place any more than they necessarily result in a great deal of student input and control.

IMPLICATIONS AND SUGGESTIONS FOR FUTURE RESEARCH

We cannot expect that students will come to writing conferences understanding the purposes of such conferences, the rules of speaking, and the respective roles of the participants. Since the quality of their conferences and revisions can be affected by participant expectations, we must teach students the purposes conferences can serve, and stress that the discourse and the teacher-student relationship can vary greatly between a conference and classroom. In a sense, we need to give students permission to break the rules they may have learned previously and we need to teach them new rules for a new speech event.

This can be accomplished in several ways. Teachers can have students discuss the rules of speaking the students feel govern classroom behavior, making these rules explicit. The teacher can then discuss conferencing with students in terms of the goals of conferences, the roles of participants, and the rules of speaking. Conferences and classrooms can be compared and contrasted so that students understand the differences and gain permission to behave differently in conferences.

Furthermore, our results suggest that students might benefit from explicit instruction concerning the importance of their conversational input and of the negotiation of meaning; in addition, students need to be taught concrete ways to achieve these goals. We have experimented with bringing the transcripts of the students in this study into our ESL writing classes and having our students analyze them. From this, the students have seen the differences among the conferences, and they have learned specific techniques for contributing input and negotiating meaning and revisions.

As teachers, we need to examine our own behaviors as well. One means of doing so is to tape our conferences (with permission from our students) and then examine them with particular questions in mind. For example, we can ask if we control the discourse, thereby discouraging our students from participating in the conference. By coding how and the degree to which the teacher and student nominate topics, and the relative amounts of teacher and student talk, we can begin to answer this question. We can also compare the treatment we give to different students, seeing if all are given equal opportunities to contribute input and negotiate meaning. In addition, we can examine the degree to which we negotiate meaning when we want to clarify for ourselves or for the students. There are many questions to be asked, and taping and analyzing the discourse in our conferences is one means of answering these questions.

In composition research we must move beyond an assessment of the effectiveness of conferences based primarily on student and teacher evaluations. While it is important to know the participants' attitudes towards conferences, and the criteria by which students and teachers judge the effectiveness of conferences, we need to understand how discourse is jointly built by the participants, and what characteristics of the discourse influence "success," defined as either improvements in subsequent revisions or in terms of more positive student attitudes. We also need studies that compare the success of revisions made after conferences with those made after written comments so that we can examine the relative effectiveness of these different forms of feedback.

Finally, ESL composition teachers are indebted to those who teach native speakers and who have conducted research with native-speaker writers. They have taught us much about composing, and over time we have discovered that their findings are often applicable to ESL students. However, while the results of this study are similar to those of Jacobs and Karliner's (1977) study of native speakers, we should keep in mind that ESL students bring with them diverse cultures and languages. This fact argues for more research conducted with an ESL population. There may be, for example, many student characteristics, such as culture, that potentially affect how students conference or how their teachers respond to them. For that matter, teachers may differ greatly from each other in how they interact with their students in conferences (see, for example, Katz, 1988) These factors, among many others, need to be systematically studied since writing conferences are not stable entities but rather, dynamic events affected by context and participants.

ACKNOWLEDGMENTS

This paper is a revised version of presentations made at the 22nd Annual TESOL Convention in Chicago, March 1988; the Second Language Acquisition Forum in Honolulu, March 1988; and the 1989 Conference on College Composition and Communication in Seattle, March 1989. We would like to thank the students who participated in this study and Anne Katz, Joanne Cavallero, Kathi Bailey, Tim Hacker, and two anonymous *TESOL Quarterly* reviewers for their valuable suggestions on the paper.

Susan M. Conrad is currently a doctoral candidate in Applied Linguistics at Northern Arizona University.

REFERENCES

Carnicelli, T. A. (1980). The writing conference: A one-to-one conversation. In T. R. Donovan & B. W. McClelland (Eds.), *Eight approaches to teaching composition* (pp. 101–131). Urbana, IL: NCTE.

Freedman, S., & Katz, A. (1987). Pedagogical interaction during the composing process: The writing conference. In A. Matsuhasi (Ed.), *Writing in real time: Modeling production processes* (pp. 58–80). New York: Academic Press.

Freedman, S., & Sperling, M. (1985). Written language acquisition: The role of response and the writing conference. In S. Freedman (Ed.), *Acquisition of written language: Response and revision* (pp. 106–130). Norwood, NJ: Ablex.

Jacobs, S., & Karliner, A. (1977). Helping writers to think: The effect of speech roles in individual conferences on the quality of thought in student writing. *College English, 38*, 489–505.

Katz, A. (1988). *Responding to student writers: The writing conferences of second language learners*. Unpublished doctoral dissertation, Stanford University, Palo Alto.

Long, M. H. (1983). Native speaker/non-native speaker conversation and the negotiation of comprehensible input. *Applied Linguistics, 4*, 126–141.

Mehan, H. (1979). *Learning lessons: Social organization in the classroom*. Cambridge, MA: Harvard University Press.

Philips, S. U. (1972). Participant structure and communicative competence: Warm Springs children in community and classroom. In C. Cazden, V. Johns, & D. Hymes (Eds.), *Functions of language in the classroom* (pp. 370–394), New York: Teachers College Press.

Sacks, H., Schegloff, E., & Jefferson, G. (1974). A simplest systematics for the organization of turn-taking for conversation. *Language, 50*, 694–735.

Sokmen, A. A. (1988). Taking advantage of conference-centered writing. *TESOL Newsletter, 22*(1), 1, 5.

Stevick, E. W. (1976). *Memory, meaning, and method*. Rowley, MA: Newbury House.

van Lier, L. (1988). *The classroom and the language learner*. London: Longman.

Walker, C. P., & Elias, D. (1987). Writing conference talk: Factors associated with high- and low-rated writing conferences. *Research in the Teaching of English, 21*, 266–285.

Zamel, V. (1985). Responding to student writing. *TESOL Quarterly, 19*(1), 79–97.

Follow-Up Questions and Activities

1. Using sample student essays, demonstrate how you might make comments that focus on a substantial reworking of the text.

2. Many students claim that they want teachers to make extensive comments on their papers. Interview students and find out if this is so. What kind of comments do they prefer, and why? Then, considering the literature on response, discuss whether or not students' wishes should be complied with.

3. Sommers states that "teachers' comments can take students' attention away from their own purposes in writing a particular text and focus that attention on the teachers' purpose in commenting." Conduct a study in which you evaluate teachers' comments on student papers. Write an essay in which you report the patterns you find and whether the teachers' comments seem to substantiate or refute Sommers's thesis. Be certain to comment on the implications for teaching.

4. According to Zamel, "we need to establish priorities in our responses to drafts and subsequent revisions and encourage students to address certain concerns before others." Imagine you are a teacher trainer and have been asked to help beginning ESL/EFL teachers to establish such priorities. How would you go about it?

5. Zamel suggests that the "dynamic interchange and negotiation [between teacher and student] are most likely to take place when writers and readers work together face-to-face." Conduct a study in which you compare the effectiveness of written versus oral comments in relation to helping the student discover the deeper meaning of his or her paper. Then report your findings and their implications for teaching.

6. Observe or tape-record two or more writing conferences with students, transcribe the conversations, and analyze the ways in which you think the conferences were successful.

7. Interview writing teachers or other faculty and investigate whether they have conferences with their students and how they go about them.

8. Discuss the ways in which a teacher can encourage the kind of active participation in the writing conference that Goldstein and Conrad discuss. This could be done as a class presentation.

9. Conduct a study in which you test Goldstein and Conrad's thesis that active participation in the writing conference is followed by substantial revision of student papers.

7

WRITING ASSESSMENT

EDITOR'S INTRODUCTION

Composition teachers often have to evaluate their students' writing in addition to instructing them. Holistic scoring has been commonly used in this regard, particularly for the purpose of making administrative decisions, where judgments have to be made quickly and efficiently. It is often pointed out, however, that holistic scoring does little to help the teacher diagnose particular problems in writing. Christopher C. Burnham finds a possible solution to these problems in the portfolio method of evaluation. According to this method, students typically hand in a portfolio of their work at the end of the course for final evaluation. Burnham points out that the use of portfolios provides teachers with the freedom to make comments on drafts throughout the course, thus encouraging students to recognize the need for revision and to develop a critical attitude toward their work. Because students can revise earlier work at the end of the course, portfolio evaluation also allows them to demonstrate how much they have learned. Peter Elbow also promotes the use of portfolio evaluation as a means of giving both students and the process of writing the attention they deserve. He argues, however, for something that goes beyond both holistic and portfolio evaluation, what he calls "liking." He claims that the best evaluation evolves from a context in which teachers and students share a positive attitude toward their work.

Prereading Questions

1. What form of evaluation have you found the most helpful in your writing career? The least helpful? The most fair? The least fair? What are the implications for teaching?

2. What do you think is the most useful thing you could do to help your students succeed in a standardized institutional writing evaluation?

Portfolio Evaluation: Room to Breathe and Grow

CHRISTOPHER C. BURNHAM *New Mexico State University*

Reviewing more than twenty-five years of research examining the effects of teachers' comments on student writing, C. H. Knoblauch and Lil Brannon draw three conclusions. First, students generally do not comprehend written teacher responses. Second, when students do comprehend the comments, they generally do not know how to use them. And third, when students do use the comments, they do not necessarily produce more effective writing.[1] Similarly, Nancy Sommers examines marginal notations on freshman compositions and concludes that "most teachers' comments are not text-specific and could be interchanged, rubber-stamped, from text to text."[2] The comments may notify a student of a problem in the text, but they help the student neither to understand the problem nor to solve it. These studies and others illustrate the difficulties teachers have responding effectively to student writing.

While researchers are offering these less-than-comforting observations, response and evaluation remain major concerns of inexperienced teachers. Recently, at a workshop for our composition staff, I described the research presented above. Evaluations from that workshop indicated that most of the staff felt the workshop was not helpful but confusing. Presented with research that offers many questions but few answers, teachers felt unready to address the issues on their own. They preferred to continue their present practice even if it accomplished little. If I did not know that their practice was based on process consciousness and multiple drafting, conferences and individualized support for students as learners, I would be dismayed. Given the context, however, I considered the staff's reaction a normal one.

If response and evaluation are major sources of concern, even anxiety, among inexperienced teachers, just as important are the effects our response and evaluation have on writers. The anxiety and insecurity of many freshman writers can be traced directly to hostile or puzzling commentary from previous teachers. In addition, grading is an obsession with some students and can become a major block in the working relationship between student and teacher. What instructor has not been accused of subjectivity and arbitrariness? And how many, even while explaining their practice, have never suspected that the student's claim is at least partly justified? Although the real benefit a writing course offers students is their increased skill as writers and thinkers, their immediate concern, a legitimate one, is the grades

---

From *"Portfolio Evaluation: Room to Breathe and Grow"* in Training the New Teacher of College Composition, *by C. C. Burnham, 1986, C. Bridges, ed. Copyright 1986 by the Naitonal Council of Teachers of English. Reprinted with permission.*

[1]C. H. Knoblauch and Lil Brannon, "Teacher Commentary on Student Writing: The State of the Art," *Freshman English News* 10, no. 2 (Fall 1981): 1.

[2]Nancy Sommers, "Responding to Student Writing," *College Composition and Communication* 33, no. 2 (May 1982): 152. Teacher response to student writing is a theme of two issues of *College Composition and Communication* (vol. 33, nos. 2 and 3, May and October 1982), in which a number of articles elaborate contemporary theory and practice.

they will receive. Anything that can mitigate their sensitivity to grades, anything that helps keep the channels of instruction between students and teachers open, should improve the teaching and learning of writing.

Given the complex problem of response and evaluation, trainers of teachers must give them all the helpful information available, while providing a buffer period during which inexperienced teachers can assimilate that information and practice responding and evaluating. Inexperienced teachers need time to develop their own philosophies of response and evaluation.

Some composition programs use internships or mentor systems to allow new teachers some experience while exempting them from complete responsibility. Others use group evaluation procedures in which instructors are not individually responsible for grading their students.[3] We have developed an alternative procedure that allows instructors the room they need to develop a philosophy and implement it while reserving to them the responsibility for grading. The procedure, portfolio evaluation, incorporates what we know about how students develop as writers by emphasizing process, multiple drafting, and collaborative learning. In addition, portfolio evaluation encourages instructors to become respondents to student writing rather than error-seeking proofreaders. Moreover, portfolio evaluation requires the careful planning and execution not only of the individual course but also of a training program to support teachers using the system, thereby encouraging staff development. Benefits accrue to individual instructors, the students they teach, and the program they teach in.

OVERVIEW

Briefly described, portfolio evaluation works like this. At specific points during the semester, students submit "finished drafts" of papers developed in class workshops. Instructors respond to these drafts not to provide an evaluation with a grade but to provide suggestions for revision as well as some general commentary about the individual's development as a writer. Instructors either accept the finished draft or turn it back for revision. The paper is accepted when the instructor considers the student to have met the specific minimum requirements for that assignment (e.g., the writer is using transitions to show coherence or the writer defends a clear thesis) and the writer is ready to tackle the next assignment in the sequence. When the paper is returned for revision, the instructor offers the feedback that will allow for effective revision. The "revise" notation provides the writer with another opportunity to succeed.

After successfully completing a predetermined number of the semester's assignments, the student can elect to compile a portfolio for final evaluation. Without a portfolio the student receives a C for the course. Students who have not completed the minimum number of finished drafts fail the course.

Qualified students who elect to compile a portfolio and compete for grades higher than C follow this procedure: First, they gather all the work they have done during the semester, review it, and choose examples of their best writing, which can include free-writing, journal writing, or narratives and poems. Then they write short explanations pointing to the features

---

[3]James E. Ford and Gregory Larkin, "The Portfolio System: An End to Backsliding Writing Standards," *College English* 39, no. 8 (Apr. 1978): 950–55.

that make the writing good. These explanations show the criteria that students have developed through the semester to evaluate writing, and require students to make explicit criteria that have been implicit so far.

Second, students choose two previously submitted and approved drafts and revise them substantially in the light of all they have learned about writing during the semester. The students attach the original drafts to the revised papers so the instructor can see the changes the writers have made and the effect these revisions have had.

Third, using the material in the portfolio and their performance in class as "data," students write a short argumentative paper directed to the instructor, asserting that they have earned a particular grade and defending this assertion. Students submit the portfolios to the instructor, who evaluates them and informs students of the success of their portfolios during individual conferences at semester's end.

PREPARATION

The portfolio submitted for final evaluation represents the culmination of the semester's labor, and since so much depends on it the portfolio evaluation procedure must be carefully planned for both instructors and students. For instructors, the work begins before the semester, in a workshop designed to provide information about student writing and practice in responding to and evaluating it, as well as guidance in constructing a comprehensive syllabus for the course. In line with our program's insistence that individual instructors maintain complete responsibility for the sections they teach, we do not have a common syllabus for freshman composition. Rather, we have a comprehensive list of departmentally approved goals and objectives for the course that all instructors use while planning and teaching their individual sections. These goals and objectives include the conventions of standard edited English, the structure and development of paragraphs and papers, various research techniques, a familiarity with the various purposes of writing (including the relation between writing and self-development), and collaborative learning procedures. These are the skills and concepts we have determined students should command when they leave freshman composition. In addition, TAs and new part-time staff use common textbooks that reflect the department's goals and objectives. The training program is keyed to and supports the use of these texts. We believe that making instructors responsible for their own sections makes them more demanding of themselves and in turn more demanding of their students. Ultimately, these increased demands enrich the entire program and the university.

The workshop before the semester begins considers five topics. First we discuss what kinds of response and evaluation frustrate student growth and what kinds encourage growth. We use a Shaughnessy error analysis approach, illustrating that grammar, if it is to be taught effectively, must be taught in the context of the students' own writing. By the end of this part of the workshop inexperienced instructors can note error patterns, focus on those where their efforts have the greatest chance of being effective, and develop instruction that will help students overcome problems.

The second aspect of the workshop is practice in actual responses to papers. Our efforts here focus on developing responses that will result in effective revision. We discuss the benefits of offering positive reinforcement and individualizing summary comments. We respond to a sample paper and critique our responses. We try to look at commentary as an instrument of change rather than evaluation. During the workshop we emphasize that there is no single way to respond effectively, and that principles can guide us but the real test is developing our own ways of responding to individual student needs and strengths.

Third, we spend time discussing and demonstrating workshop and one-on-one conference techniques that can be used to solve problems that might arise once papers are returned. Ideally, each paper should be returned at a short conference during which the instructor checks to make sure the student understands and can act upon the comments that have been made.

Our fourth concern is with ranges of acceptable performance, that is, with standards. Most of our freshman composition instructors have taught in our Basic Writing program, which uses a holistically scored common writing sample at exit. Therefore, our instructors know the procedure for holistic scoring and how to sort and rank papers. They are also aware of the exit criteria for Basic Writing, which in turn become the entrance-level expectations for regular freshman composition. In the workshop, we supply and discuss benchmark papers that illustrate general ranges of acceptable performance. The benchmarks represent ranges of performance rather than specific grades because the grade finally will result from performance in the portfolio rather than on any one assignment. This information gives instructors a sense of the program's standards, permitting them to make informed decisions regarding the acceptability of the finished drafts students submit along the way.

The fifth and final topic is the construction of the course syllabus. Any instructor who will be using the portfolio evaluation procedure must make that clear on his or her syllabus. First, instructors must outline the course requirements in terms of pass/fail. For example, during a fifteen-week semester, students will attempt nine formal assignments. To earn a C and qualify to submit a portfolio, students must complete seven assignments successfully, in addition, of course, to regular attendance and participation in class activities. After listing these minimum requirements, we include the announcement that grades higher than C will be awarded only to those submitting portfolios during the last weeks of class. Although showing such concern for final evaluation so early in the course seems contrary to the objectives of portfolio evaluation, it is the best means of informing students that they will be experiencing an unfamiliar method. Our concern is that the portfolio requirement be clear, and students properly forewarned.

After discussing how to announce the portfolio evaluation on the course syllabus, we spend time generating and responding to the myriad questions students will ask. Instructors must first make the point that the portfolio procedure is designed to benefit the student by taking advantage of the process through which students develop as writers. Since the process is gradual and often unpredictable, with quantum leaps occurring generally late in the semester, revising papers at the end of the course and submitting a portfolio allows students to show the instructor how much they ultimately learned, which is generally much more than the sum of their performances on individual assignments. During the practice question-and-answer session we emphasize that instructors must make clear to students how the "acceptable"/"revise" system will work and the different ways of completing the course. Students must also be warned of the dangers of missing work or falling behind with revisions since the assignments near the end of the course are more demanding than the earlier ones.

Instructors must also announce as a policy that if a paper is not accepted but turned back for revision, it must be revised and resubmitted before the next assignment is due. This policy assures the integrity of the developmental sequence of assignments in the course. Students need to understand that assignment 3 teaches skills needed for successful completion of assignment 4. Just as important, such a revision policy prevents abuses of the system. Inexperienced instructors must be aware of the potential for "irresponsible" revision. Irresponsible revision occurs when students are doing only as much as they must to get by. Instructors can avoid abuses of the system through the revision deadline policy or by using a U (unsatisfactory) grade signifying that the draft which has been submitted or resubmitted cannot be revised and resubmitted. The U grade sends the clear message that the student performance is inadequate.

The point of our attention to the syllabus in the preparatory workshop on portfolio evaluation is to make sure instructors understand the procedure and are able to communicate this understanding to their students. The syllabus serves as an informal contract between instructor and student; it is something both instructors and students must be able to live with.

BEGINNING THE SEMESTER

Once the semester begins, staff support shifts from formal workshops to staff meetings and frequent consultations between experienced portfolio users and novices. The most frequent problem instructors confront is the difficulty many students have adjusting to an ungraded system. At first, most students will express some anxiety, but this is mainly because of the novelty of the system. Soon these students will understand its purpose and benefits. Most respond very favorably to the idea that the drafts they submit can be revised and improved as a result of the feedback of peers and instructors and to the benefits of the learning space provided by portfolios.

There are students, however, who really cannot function without grades, and their special needs must be met. To help these students, we suggest the use of provisional grades. Students are invited to come to instructors during office hours, at which time student and instructor discuss the draft in question. A grade is provided based on the standards that will be invoked at the end of the semester. Instructors use this conference to move from evaluation to instruction. Students needing grades are often anxious and insecure about their writing, and the conference provides the perfect opportunity to offer individualized instruction and build confidence. These students and the opportunities they present are the subject of considerable discussion during informal staff meetings.

Another frequent concern is the need for instructors to send clear messages when responding to submitted drafts. Inexperienced instructors need help writing comments that reinforce what students have done well while pointing out what could and should be done before the paper can be considered strong writing. Practice on sample papers helps instructors develop strategies that allow them to be frank about the need for development and specific about revision while framing comments in supportive language that encourages students to strive to realize the potential of their papers. In addition, instructors must beware of creating unrealistic expectations in students about the quality of their writing, because such expectations will cause problems when portfolios are submitted.

A MIDTERM CONFERENCE

As an additional help to our students, we offer a midterm conference to discuss their progress in the course. These conferences come while there is still sufficient time for the student to withdraw from the class without jeopardy, if necessary, or to make arrangements to salvage the semester. Some instructors offer provisional grades. It must be stressed that these are only provisional grades and that the final grade can come only at the end of the semester with the portfolio.

The most important benefit of the midterm conference is the opportunity to turn some students around. These are the writers whose growth has been very flat and who seem poorly motivated. They depend on grades for motivation. Without grades they are driving toward mediocrity and need an awakening. While they would balk at the very prospect of earning a C, their performance thus far merits a C at best. They need to know, moreover, that doing a portfolio will not automatically result in a higher grade but that it is not too late to begin to work harder and improve their chances for success.

The key is moving from evaluation to instruction. In staff meetings we discuss the midterm conference as a potential motivating tool, a way if need be to shake students out of their complacency and drive them toward realizing their potential. In all instances, the midterm conference ends with the reminder that what has been said has been professional and subject to change through increased effort and the understanding that comes with time and practice.

A CLEARANCE INTERVIEW

The clearance interview is the final preparation for the portfolios. About four weeks before the end of the semester we distribute a comprehensive handout describing the portfolio system. The handout addresses the purpose of portfolio grading, the requirements for qualifying to do a portfolio, instructions on how to put the portfolio together, and end-of-semester deadlines.

The handout announces that anyone wanting to do a portfolio will have to meet with the instructor before a particular date. During this clearance interview, the instructor reviews the student's performance to make sure that the student qualifies in terms of attendance, participation, and the minimum number of accepted drafts. If a student qualifies, the instructor asks if there are any questions about the portfolio procedure. At this time the instructor may provide some needed information. For example, if a student is truly a C student, whose performance has been marginal all semester, the instructor should make clear how much improvement that student must make in the portfolio to break the C barrier. We try to be honest, to make sure some students are aware of the very long road they face. Students must be reminded that substantive improvement, not effort and good will, is the primary criterion by which we finally evaluate portfolios.[4] Given the workload of many college freshmen, and given the time and effort required to compile an effective portfolio, common sense suggests that marginal students are best advised to put their efforts elsewhere. They have

---

[4]An excellent article to begin discussion of this crucial distinction between form and substance, work and quality work, is William Perry's "Examsmanship and the Liberal Arts: A Study in Educational Epistemology," in *Examining Harvard College: A Collection of Essays by Members of the Harvard Faculty* (Cambridge: Harvard Univ. Press, 1963).

already earned C's, and not doing a portfolio frees time to study for calculus or biology or whatever. Students generally appreciate such candor. And any information that can make students more realistic in their expectations makes the final interview easier on student and instructor alike.

The clearance interview allows instructors to remind students of one of the main points of the portfolio system—that students must assume responsibility for their writing and that the instructor's opinion and suggestions for revision must be considered along with peer critiques and, most important, in the light of the criteria for good writing that the students themselves have been developing all semester. When confronted with appeals for specific directions which the student can follow without thinking, the instructor must resist and turn the burden back onto the student: "How do you think the piece can be made better? What new information or argumentative angle do you see developing since you wrote the piece? What new information do the peer review sheets suggest the reader needs?" Instructors must beware of the tendency during the final steps of the portfolio system to undo all the semester's work by changing from respondent to director of revision, thereby allowing students to abandon responsibility for their writing.

EVALUATING PORTFOLIOS

With the submission of portfolios begins a period of intense reading and evaluation. We discuss the process at a staff meeting where veterans of the system share their experience. Instructors must keep several things in mind when they begin to read portfolios. First and most important, they must remember that their role has shifted from respondent to evaluator. Definitions, revisions, and arguments must be considered for what they are, rather than what they could be after revisions. The examples of good writing the students present must be read in the light of the students' own definitions of good writing, and how well those definitions reflect the substance of the course. When reading the good writing examples, instructors should hold their responses until the end, writing only short summary comments stating whether they believe the examples and explanations of good writing are effective or not. Instructors should not explain deficiencies but should note them mentally in case students ask for explanations during the interview.

Reading the revisions is more demanding than reading the examples. Instructors report reading revisions two ways. Some read both the original and all the feedback on it, and then the revision, ultimately comparing the two to gain a specific sense of the changes made and their implicit purpose. Such close reading, however, is time-consuming and often counterproductive. Reading drafts encourages instructors to construct an "ideal" paper, the paper the instructor would write during revision. But only rarely does a student's revision reflect this "ideal" paper. Instructors report getting bogged down trying to understand why a writer followed some bad advice or took a tack that caused rather than solved problems in the paper. Such close reading ultimately reveals what the student did not learn, whereas the purpose of evaluation is to find and reward what the student *did* learn.

The second style of reading is the one preferred by most instructors. Instructors read only the revisions and consider whether they reflect what finished pieces of writing should be. Does each paper state and solve a problem? Does it address an audience effectively? Is it well-structured and logically sound and complete? Is it free from distracting errors or violations of writing conventions?

Instructors using the more holistic style of reading can focus on each revision as a paper in itself and judge whether it meets its own expectations, and how well it meets the specific criteria students, individual instructors, and the whole problem have forged through the semester. Avoiding close comparison with drafts allows instructors to read papers and reward them for what they do rather than penalize them for what they did not do.

Allowing revisions and whole portfolios to exist on their own terms is an issue staff discuss specifically. Reading a portfolio honestly requires considerable forgetting. Beginning to read a portfolio with preconceptions abut a student's ability and potential can lead to reading only to find evidence to confirm those preconceptions. This violates the purpose of the portfolio. Instructors need to read the portfolios to evaluate the writing in front of them, not to defend evaluations built up through the semester.

Since instructors will eventually have to respond to questions raised during the final interview, some shorthand notations in the margins will help serve as reminders of problems or strong points during the interview. Then, after the instructor has read the examples of good writing and found them effective or not, and read the revisions and judged them in the light of individual and program criteria, there is only the argument for a grade left to consider. The argument is generally easy to read and evaluate. Empty arguments betray inflated expectations. No one earns an A just for attending class and turning the work in on time. A's and B's come from the quality of the revisions and from individual growth. Arguments that address these issues specifically are successful and earn the student the grade requested. Arguments that do not address substantive issues receive little consideration. Students must be reminded while compiling portfolios that the final grade will be based on substance and quality as measured by the instructor. Submitting a portfolio does not guarantee a grade higher than a C.

THE FINAL INTERVIEW

To prepare for the final interview, the instructor reviews the student's portfolio and decides finally whether the student has earned the grade requested. Experience indicates that about eight of ten students will have compiled portfolios that justify grades higher than C. On a successful portfolio, the instructor writes a summary comment congratulating the student on the quality of the portfolio and stressing one particular strength the student should continue to develop. Instructors mentally register one or two areas still needing development and mention these during the final interview. Occasionally instructors report raising a grade because a student has been too modest or conservative in his or her grade request. For students who have overshot the mark in their requests, brief summary comments explain the grades given. The comments note three or four instances where the grade arguments are faulty or incomplete, or the revisions or examples of good writing inadequate. Since this final review of each portfolio should come immediately before the meeting with the student, interviews should be scheduled to guarantee some private time to the instructor between students.

Interviews themselves are generally pleasant. Successful students often ask how they can continue their development, and instructors advise these students on which literature or writing course might be useful for them to take next. Instructors stress that the freshman course is the beginning, not the culmination, of students' development as writers, that they need more exposure and practice to realize their complete potential. We recommend specific courses and explain why they would be helpful.

Interviews with students whose arguments are inflated and unsuccessful vary. The students who knew they were asking for too much generally understand their final grades and are often able to explain their shortcomings as writers quite specifically. Sometimes students know that the problem is the normal time-lag between understanding and performance. They know they need more time and practice, and ask what their next course should be.

The other, less pleasant, interviews involve students who want to argue. Since instructors have already prepared rationales for their evaluations, they can respond specifically, and cut off those students who want to continue the argument for the sole sake of arguing. There are better ways to use time.

Of the steps in the portfolio procedure, the final interview is the most problematic. The interview demands interpersonal skills as well as competence in evaluating writing. Instructors using the portfolio system for the first time report a tendency to "cave in" during the final interviews. The source of the cave-in can be student pressure or the instructor's lack of confidence. These combine with the fondness for students that instructors develop through the highly interactive process of teaching writing and may lead to compromised standards.

For these reasons, inexperienced instructors are encouraged to discuss interviewing techniques with experienced portfolio users. A workshop where instructors discuss their experiences, anticipate and solve certain common interview problems, and simulate an interview or two helps new instructors build confidence. In addition, those using the portfolio with interview for the first time must have absolute confidence that the administration will support them by being available to solve problems when they arise, and by being ready to defend their decisions to students, parents, or higher administration should that become necessary.

Though the final interview sometimes causes a problem or two, it is the most effective way to complete a portfolio evaluation. The interview fosters communication between instructor and student, reinforcing the goals of the writing program as a whole.

RECAPITULATION

Portfolio evaluation is not an easy way to grade student writing. The procedure makes demands on the program, on the students, and especially on individual instructors. It requires an elaborate and individualized style of response/evaluation. It asks students to strive for excellence and long-term development rather than settling for the immediate gratification available through traditional grading. It demands the commitment of considerable time and psychic energy from instructors. But all of these challenges are manageable in light of the benefits that portfolio evaluation offers:

1. Portfolio evaluation reinforces a program's commitment to the teaching of writing as a process involving multiple drafting, and emphasizes the need for revision.

2. Portfolio evaluation establishes a writing course as an organic sequence of assignments, each building consciously upon the one before, and culminating in the development of "whole," process-aware writers rather than skillful hurdlers over unrelated individual assignments.

3. Portfolio evaluation establishes a writing environment rather than a grading environment in the classroom, encouraging instructors to become respondents providing feedback of the same kind as the feedback students get from their peers, though perhaps of a more sophisticated quality.

4. Portfolio evaluation encourages students to assume responsibility for the quality of their work. Students develop and apply a critical sense to their own writing, fostering the development of their potential and avoiding the problem of depending on the instructor for approval. This reflective critical sense may be the most valuable skill with which students leave the writing course. Portfolio evaluation creates independent writers and learners.

5. Portfolio evaluation frustrates the lowest-common-denominator, "get by," or survivalist mentality that some students bring into the classroom. They find no reward in doing only the minimum required. They are not competing with peers or contending with an instructor. Rather they must collaborate with peers and instructor and strive to realize their potential.

6. By postponing summative evaluation, portfolio evaluation avoids or at least tempers the frustration students feel when they do not succeed in early assignments, while allowing the instructor to begin a semester without feeling any pressure to compromise standards to avoid that frustration. The system encourages high standards from the start, thereby encouraging maximum development.

7. Most important, portfolio evaluation establishes an evaluation system that encourages instructors to focus on specific aspects of writing and to develop responsive skills. The system fosters a healthy trial-and-error attitude toward response/evaluation. Instructors and students confer and discuss reactions to writing rather than debating grades. Instructors individualize rather than pigeonhole students.

In sum, as reported by one novice instructor who had been particularly nervous about using the system, portfolio evaluation gives students and instructors "plenty of room to breathe and grow and enjoy the scenes along the way."

Ranking, Evaluating, and Liking: Sorting Out Three Forms of Judgment

PETER ELBOW *University of Massachusetts at Amherst*

This essay is my attempt to sort out different acts we call assessment—some different ways in which we express or frame our judgments of value. I have been working on this tangle not just because it is interesting and important in itself but because assessment tends so much to drive and control *teaching*. Much of what we do in the classroom is determined by the assessment structures we work under.

Assessment is a large and technical area and I'm not a professional. But my main premise or subtext in this essay is that we nonprofessionals can and should work on it because professionals have not reached definitive conclusions about the problem of how to assess writing (or anything else, I'd say). Also, decisions about assessment are often made by people even less professional than we, namely legislators. Pat Belanoff and I realized that the field of assessment was open when we saw the harmful effects of a writing proficiency exam at Stony Brook and worked out a collaborative portfolio assessment system in its place (Belanoff and Elbow; Elbow and Belanoff). Professionals keep changing their minds about large-scale testing and assessment. And as for classroom grading, psychometricians provide little support or defense of it.

THE PROBLEMS WITH RANKING AND THE BENEFITS OF EVALUATING

By ranking I mean the act of summing up one's judgment of a performance or person into a single, holistic number or score. We rank every time we give a grade or holistic score. Ranking implies a single scale or continuum or dimension along which all performances are hung.

By evaluating I mean the act of expressing one's judgment of a performance or person by pointing out the strengths and weaknesses of different features or dimensions We evaluate every time we write a comment on a paper or have a conversation about its value. Evaluation implies the recognition of different criteria or dimensions—and by implication different contexts and audiences for the same performance. Evaluation requires going *beyond* a first response that may be nothing but a kind of ranking ("I like it" or "This is better than that"), and instead looking carefully enough at the performance or person to make distinctions between parts or features or criteria.

It's obvious, thus, that I am troubled by ranking. But I will resist any temptation to argue that we can get rid of all ranking—or even should. Instead I will try to show how we can have *less* ranking and *more* evaluation in its place.

I see three distinct problems with ranking: it is inaccurate or unreliable; it gives no substantive feedback; and it is harmful to the atmosphere for teaching and learning.

(1) First the unreliability. To rank reliably means to give a *fair* number, to find the single quantitative score that readers will agree on. But readers don't agree.

This is not news—this unavailability of agreement. We have long seen it on many fronts. For example, research in evaluation has shown many times that if we give a paper to a set of readers, those readers tend to give it the full range of grades (Diederich). I've recently come across new research to this effect—new to me because it was published in 1912. The investigators carefully showed how high school English teachers gave different grades to the same paper. In response to criticism that this was a local problem in English, they went on the next year to discover an even greater variation among grades given by high school geometry teachers and history teachers to papers in their subjects. (See the summary of Daniel Starch and Edward Elliott's 1913 *School Review* articles in Kirschenbaum, Sidney, and Napier 258–59.)

We know the same thing from literary criticism and theory. If the best critics can't agree about what a text means, how can we be surprised that they disagree even more about the quality or value of texts? And we know that nothing in literary or philosophical theory gives us any agreed-upon rules for settling such disputes.

Students have shown us the same inconsistency with their own controlled experiments of handing the same paper to different teachers and getting different grades. This helps explain why we hate it so when students ask us their favorite question, "What do you want for an A?": it rubs our noses in the unreliability of our grades.

Of course champions of holistic scoring argue that they get *can* get agreement among readers—and they often do (White). But they get that agreement by "training" the readers before and during the scoring sessions. What "training" means is getting those scorers to stop reading the way they normally read—getting them to stop using the conflicting criteria and standards they normally use outside the scoring sessions. (In an impressive and powerful book, Barbara Herrnstein Smith argues that whenever we have widespread inter-reader reliability, we have reason to suspect that difference has been suppressed and homogeneity imposed—almost always at the expense of certain groups.) In short, the reliability in holistic scoring is not a measure of how texts are valued by real readers in natural settings, but only of how they are valued in artificial settings with imposed agreements.

Defenders of holistic scoring might reply (as one anonymous reviewer did) that holistic scores are not perfect or absolutely objective readings but just "judgments that most readers will agree are the appropriate ones given the purpose of the assessment and the system of communication." But I have been in and even conducted enough holistic scoring sessions to know that even that degree of agreement doesn't occur unless "purpose" and "appropriateness" are defined to mean acceptance of the single set of standards imposed on that session. We know too much about the differences among readers and the highly variable nature of the reading process. Supposing we get readings only from academics, or only from people in English, or only from respected critics, or only from respected writing programs, or only from feminists, or only from sound readers of my tribe (white, male, middle-class, full professors between the ages of fifty and sixty). We *still* don't get agreement. We can sometimes get agreement among readers from some subset, a particular community that has developed a strong set of common values, perhaps *one* English department or *one* writing program. But what is the value of such a rare agreement? It tells us nothing about how readers from other English departments or writing programs will judge—much less how readers from other domains will judge.

(From the opposite ideological direction, some skeptics might object to my skeptical train of thought: "So what else is new?" they might reply. "Of *course* my grades are biased, 'interested' or 'situated'—always partial to my interests or the values of my community or culture. There's no other possibility." But how can people consent to give grades if they feel that way? A single teacher's grade for a student is liable to have substantial consequences—for example on eligibility for a scholarship or a job or entrance into professional school. In grading, surely we must not take anything less than genuine fairness as our goal.)

It won't be long before we see these issues argued in a court of law, when a student who has been disqualified from playing on a team or rejected from a professional school sues, charging that the basis for his plight—teacher grades—is not reliable. I wonder if lawyers will be able to make our grades stick.

(2) Ranking or grading is woefully uncommunicative. Grades and holistic scores are nothing but points on a continuum from "yea" to "boo"—with no information or clues about the criteria behind these noises. They are 100 percent evaluation and 0 percent description or information. They quantify the degree of approval or disapproval in readers but tell nothing at all about what the readers actually approve or disapprove of. They say nothing that couldn't be said with gold stars or black marks or smiley-faces. Of course our first reactions are often nothing but global holistic feelings of approval or disapproval, but we need a system for communicating our judgments that nudges us to move beyond these holistic feelings and to articulate the basis of our feeling—a process that often leads us to change our feeling. (Holistic scoring sessions sometimes use rubrics that explain the criteria—though these are rarely passed along to students—and even in these situations, the rubrics fail to fit many papers.) As C. S. Lewis says, "People are obviously far more anxious to express their approval and disapproval of things than to describe them" (7).

(3) Ranking leads students to get so hung up on these oversimple quantitative verdicts that they care more about scores than about learning—more about the grade we put on the paper than about the comment we have written on it. Have you noticed how grading often forces us to write comments to justify our grades?—and how these are often *not* the comment we would make if we were just trying to help the student writer better? ("Just try writing several favorable comments on a paper and then giving it a grade of D" [Diederich 21]).

Grades and holistic scores give too much encouragement to those students who score high—making them too apt to think they are already fine—and too little encouragement to those students who do badly. Unsuccessful students often come to doubt their intelligence. But oddly enough, many "A" students also end up doubting their true ability and feeling like frauds—because they have sold out on their own judgment and simply given teachers whatever yields an A. They have too often been rewarded for what they don't really believe in. (Notice that there's more cheating by students who get high grades than by those who get low ones. There would be less incentive to cheat if there were no ranking.)

We might be tempted to put up with the inaccuracy or unfairness of grades if they gave good diagnostic feedback or helped the learning climate; or we might put up with the damage they do to the learning climate if they gave a fair or reliable measure of how skilled or knowledgeable students are. But since they fail dismally on both counts, we are faced with the striking question of why grading has persisted so long.

There must be many reasons. It is obviously easier and quicker to express a global feeling with a single number than to figure out what the strengths and weaknesses are and what one's criteria are. (Though I'm heartened to discover, as I pursue this issue, how troubled teachers are by grading and how difficult they find it.) But perhaps more important, we see around us a deep *hunger to rank*—to create pecking orders: to see who we can look down on and who we must look up to, or in the military metaphor, who we can kick and who we must salute. Psychologists tell us that this taste for pecking orders or ranking is associated with the authoritarian personality. We see this hunger graphically in the case of IQ scores. It is plain that IQ scoring does not represent a commitment to looking carefully at people's intelligence; when we do that, we see different and frequently uncorrelated *kinds* or *dimensions* of intelligence (Gardner). The persistent use of IQ scores represents the hunger to have a number so that everyone can have a rank. ("Ten!" mutter the guys when they see a pretty woman.)

Because ranking or grading has caused so much discomfort to so many students and teachers, I think we see a lot of confusion about the process. It is hard to think clearly about something that has given so many of us such anxiety and distress. The most notable confusion I notice is the tendency to think that if we renounce ranking or grading, we are renouncing the very possibility of judgment and discrimination—that we are embracing the idea that there is no way to distinguish or talk about the difference between what works well and what works badly.

So, the most important point, then, is that *I am not arguing against judgment or evaluation.* I'm just arguing against that crude, oversimple way of *representing* judgment—distorting it, really—into a single number, which means ranking people and performances along a single continuum.

In fact I am arguing *for evaluation.* Evaluation means looking hard and thoughtfully at a piece of writing in order to make distinctions as to the quality of different features or dimensions. For example, the process of evaluation permits us to make the following kinds of statements about a piece of writing:

- The thinking and ideas seem interesting and creative.
- The overall structure or sequence seems confusing.
- The writing is perfectly clear at the level of individual sentences and even paragraphs.
- There is an odd, angry tone of voice that seems unrelated or inappropriate to what the writer is saying.
- Yet this same voice is strong and memorable and makes one listen even if one is irritated.
- There are a fair number of mistakes in grammar or spelling: more than "a sprinkling" but less than "riddled with."

To rank, on the other hand, is to be forced to translate those discriminations into a single number. What grade or holistic score do these judgments add up to? It's likely, by the way, that more readers would agree with those separate "analytic" statements than would agree on a holistic score.

I've conducted many assessment sessions where we were not trying to impose a set of standards but rather to find out how experienced teachers read and evaluate, and I've had many opportunities to see that good readers give grades or scores right down through the range of possibilities. Of course good readers sometimes agree—especially on papers that are strikingly good or bad or conventional, but I think I see difference more frequently than agreement when readers really speak up.

The process of evaluation, because it invites us to articulate our criteria and to make distinctions among parts or features or dimensions of a performance, thereby invites us further to acknowledge the main fact about evaluation: that different readers have different priorities, values, and standards.

The conclusion I am drawing, then, in this first train of thought is that we should do less ranking and more evaluation. Instead of using grades or holistic scores—single number verdicts that try to sum up complex performances along only one scale—we should give some kind of written or spoken evaluation that discriminates among criteria and dimensions of the writing—and if possible that takes account of the complex context for writing: who the writer is, what the writer's audience and goals are, who we are as readers and how we read, and how we might differ in our reading from other readers the writer might be addressing.

But how can we put this principle into practice? The pressure for ranking seems implacable. Evaluation takes more time, effort, and money. It seems as though we couldn't get along without scores on writing exams. Most teachers are obliged to give grades at the end of each course. And many students—given that they have become conditioned or even addicted to ranking over the years and must continue to inhabit a ranking culture in most of their courses—will object if we don't put grades on papers. Some students, in the absence of that crude gold star or black mark, may not try hard enough (though how hard is "enough"—and is it really our job to stimulate motivation artificially with grades—and is grading the best source of motivation?).

It is important to note that there are certain schools and colleges that do not use single-number grades or scores, and they function successfully. I taught for nine years at Evergreen State College, which uses only written evaluations. This system works fine, even down to getting students accepted into high quality graduate and professional schools.

Nevertheless we have an intractable dilemma: that grading is unfair and counterproductive but that students and institutions tend to want grades. In the face of this dilemma there is a need for creativity and pragmatism. Here are some ways in which I and others use *less ranking* and *more evaluation* in teaching—and they suggest some adjustments in how we score large-scale assessments. What follows is an assortment of experimental compromises—sometimes crude, seldom ideal or utopian—but they help.

(a) Portfolios. Just because conventional institutions oblige us to turn in a single quantitative course grade at the end of every marking period, it doesn't follow that we need to grade individual papers. Course grades are more trustworthy and less damaging because they are based on so many performances over so many weeks. By avoiding frequent ranking or grading, we make it *somewhat* less likely for students to become addicted to oversimple numerical rankings—to think that evaluation always translates into a simple number— in short, to mistake ranking for evaluation. (I'm not trying to defend conventional course grades since they are still uncommunicative and they still feed the hunger for ranking.) Portfolios permit me to refrain from grading individual papers and limit myself to writerly evaluative comments—and help students see this as a positive rather than a negative thing, a chance to be graded on a body of their best work that can be judged more fairly. Portfolios have many other advantages as well. They are particularly valuable as occasions for asking students to write extensive and thoughtful explorations of their own strengths and weaknesses.

A midsemester portfolio is usually an informal affair, but it is a good occasion for giving anxious students a ballpark estimate of how well they are doing in the course so far. I find it helpful to tell students that I'm perfectly willing to tell them my best estimate of their course grade—but only if they come to me in conference and only during the second half of the semester. This serves somewhat to quiet their anxiety while they go through seven weeks of drying out from grades. By midsemester, most of them have come to enjoy not getting those numbers and thus being able to think better about more writerly comments from me and their classmates.

Portfolios are now used extensively and productively in larger assessments, and there is constant experimentation with new applications (Belanoff and Dickson; *Portfolio Assessment Newsletter; Portfolio News*).

(b) Another useful option is to make a strategic retreat from a wholly negative position. That is, I sometimes do a *bit* of ranking even on individual papers, using two "bottom-line" grades: H and U for "Honors" and "Unsatisfactory." I tell students that these translate to about A or A- and D or F. This practice may seem theoretically inconsistent with all the arguments I've just made, but (at the moment, anyway) I justify it for the following reasons.

First, I sympathize with a *part* of the students' anxiety about not getting grades: their fear that they might be failing and not know about it—or doing an excellent job and not get any recognition. Second, I'm not giving *many* grades; only a small proportion of papers get these H's or U's. The system creates a "non-bottom-line" or "non-quantified" atmosphere. Third, these holistic judgments about best and worst do not seem as arbitrary and questionable as most grades. There is usually a *bit* more agreement among readers about the best and worst papers. What seems most dubious is the process of trying to rank that whole middle range of papers—papers that have a mixture of better and worse qualities so that the numerical grade depends enormously on a reader's priorities or mood or temperament. My willingness to give these few grades goes a long way toward helping my students forgo most bottom-line grading.

I'm not trying to pretend that these minimal "grades" are truly reliable. But they represent a very small amount of ranking. Yes, someone could insist that I'm really ranking every single paper (and indeed if it seemed politically necessary, I could put an OK or S [for satisfactory] on all those middle range papers and brag, "Yes, I grade everything"). But the fact is that I am doing *much less sorting* since I don't have to sort them into five or even twelve piles. Thus there is a huge reduction in the total amount of unreliability I produce.

(It might seem that if I use only these few minimal grades I have no good way for figuring out a final grade for the course—since that requires a more fine-grained set of ranks. But I don't find that to be the case. For I also give these same minimal grades to the many other important parts of my course such as attendance, meeting deadlines, peer responding, and journal writing. If I want a mathematically computed grade on a scale of six or A through E, I can easily compute it when I have such a large number of grades to work from—even though they are only along a three-point scale.)

This same practice of crude or minimal ranking is a big help on larger assessments outside classrooms, and needs to be applied to the process of assessment in general. There are two important principles to emphasize. On the one hand we must be prudent or accommodating enough to admit that despite all the arguments against ranking, there *are* situations when we need that bottom-line verdict along one scale: which student has not done satisfactory work and should be denied credit for the course? which student gets the scholarship? which candidate to hire or fire? We often operate with scarce resources. But on the other hand we must be bold enough to insist that we do far more ranking than is really needed. We can get along not only with fewer occasions for assessment but also with fewer gradations in scoring. If we decide what the real bottom-line is on a given occasion—perhaps just "failing" or perhaps "honors" too—then the reading of papers or portfolios is enormously quick and cheap. It leaves time and money for evaluation—perhaps for analytic scoring or some comment.

At Stony Brook we worked out a portfolio system where multiple readers had only to make a binary decision: acceptable or not. Then individual teachers could decide the actual course grade and give comments for their own students—so long as those students passed in the eyes of an independent rater (Elbow and Belanoff; Belanoff and Elbow). The best way to begin to wean our society from its addiction to ranking may be to permit a tiny bit of it (which also means less unreliability)—rather than trying to go "cold turkey."

(c) Sometimes I use an analytic grid for evaluating and commenting on student papers. An example is given in Figure 1.

Figure 1

Strong   OK   Weak

			CONTENT, INSIGHTS, THINKING, GRAPPLING WITH TOPIC
			GENUINE REVISION, SUBSTANTIVE CHANGES, NOT JUST EDITING
			ORGANIZATION, STRUCTURE, GUIDING THE READER
			LANGUAGE: SYNTAX, SENTENCES, WORDING, VOICE
			MECHANICS: SPELLING, GRAMMAR, PUNCTUATION, PROOFREADING
			OVERALL [Note: this is not a sum of the other scores.]

I often vary the criteria in my grid (e.g. "connecting with readers" or "investment") depending on the assignment or the point in the semester.

Grids are a way I can satisfy the students' hunger for ranking but still not give in to conventional grades on individual papers. Sometimes I provide nothing but a grid (especially on final drafts), and this is a very quick way to provide a response. Or on midprocess drafts I sometimes use a grid in addition to a comment: a more readerly comment that often doesn't so much tell them what's wrong or right or how to improve things but rather tries to give them an account of what is *happening to me* as I read their words. I think this kind of comment is really the most useful thing of all for students, but it frustrates some students for a while. The grid can help these students feel less anxious and thus pay better attention to my comment.

I find grids extremely helpful at the end of the semester for telling students their strengths and weaknesses in the course—or what they've done well and not so well. Besides categories like the ones above, I use categories like these: "skill in giving feedback to others," "ability to meet deadlines," "effort," and "improvement." This practice makes my final grade much more communicative.

(d) I also help make up for the absence of ranking—gold stars and black marks—by having students share their writing with each other a great deal both orally and through frequent publication in class magazines. Also, where possible, I try to get students to give or send writing to audiences outside the class. At the University of Massachusetts at Amherst, freshmen pay a ten dollar lab fee for the writing course, and every teacher publishes four or five class magazines of final drafts a semester. The effects are striking. Sharing, peer feedback, and publication give the best reward and motivation for writing, namely, getting your words out to many readers.

(e) I sometimes use a kind of modified *contract grading*. That is, at the start of the course I pass out a long list of all the things that I most want students to do—the concrete activities that I think most lead to learning—and I promise students that if they do them *all* they are guaranteed a certain final grade. Currently, I say it's a B—it could be lower or higher. My list includes these items: not missing more than a week's worth of classes; not having more than one late major assignment; *substantive* revising on all major revisions; good copy editing on all final revisions; good effort on peer feedback work; keeping up the journal; and substantial effort and investment on each draft.

I like the way this system changes the "bottom-line" for a course: the intersection where my authority crosses their self-interest. I can tell them, "You have to work very hard in this course, but you can stop worrying about grades." The crux is no longer that commodity I've always hated and never trusted: a numerical ranking of the quality of their writing along a single continuum. Instead the crux becomes what I care about most: the *concrete behaviors* that I most want students to engage in because they produce more learning and help me teach better. Admittedly, effort and investment are not concrete observable behaviors, but they are no harder to judge than overall quality of writing. And since I care about effort and investment, I don't mind the few arguments I get into about them; they seem fruitful. ("Let's try and figure out why it looked to me as though you didn't put any effort in here.") In contrast, I hate discussions about grades on a paper and find such arguments fruitless. Besides, I'm not making fine distinctions about effort and investment—just letting a bell go off when they fall palpably low.

It's crucial to note that I am *not* fighting evaluation with this system. I am just fighting ranking or grading. I still write evaluative comments and often use an evaluative grid to tell my students what I see as strengths and weaknesses in their papers. My goal is not to get rid of evaluation but in fact to emphasize it, enhance it. I'm trying to get students to listen *better* to my evaluations—by uncoupling them from a grade. In effect, I'm doing this because I'm so fed up with students *following* or *obeying* my evaluations too blindly—making whatever changes my comments suggest but doing it for the sake of a grade; not really taking the time to make up their own minds about whether they think my judgments or suggestions really make sense to them. The worst part of grades is that they make students obey us without carefully thinking about the merits of what we say. I love the situation this system so often puts students in: I make a criticism or suggestion about their paper, but it doesn't matter to their grade whether they go along with me or not (so long as they genuinely revise in some fashion). They have to think; to decide.

Admittedly this system is crude and impure. Some of the really skilled students who are used to getting A's and desperate to get one in this course remain unhelpfully hung up about getting those H's on their papers. But a good number of these students discover that they can't get them, and they soon settle down to accepting a B and having less anxiety and more of a learning voyage.

THE LIMITATIONS OF EVALUATION AND THE BENEFITS OF EVALUATION-FREE ZONES

Everything I've said so far has been in praise of evaluation as a substitute for ranking. But I need to turn a corner here and speak about the *limits* or *problems* of evaluation. Evaluating may be better than ranking, but it still carries some of the same problems. That is, even though I've praised evaluation for inviting us to acknowledge that readers and contexts are different, nevertheless the very word *evaluation* tends to imply fairness or reliability or getting beyond personal or subjective preferences. Also, of course, evaluation takes a lot more time and work. To rank you just have to put down a number; holistic scoring of exams is cheaper than analytic scoring.

Most important of all, evaluation harms the climate for learning and teaching—or rather *too much* evaluation has this effect. That is, if we evaluate *everything* students write, they tend to remain tangled up in the assumption that their whole job in school is to give teachers "what they want."

Constant evaluation makes students worry more about psyching out the teacher than about what they are really learning. Students fall into a kind of defensive or on-guard stance toward the teacher: a desire to hide what they don't understand and try to impress. This stance gets in the way of learning. (Think of the patient trying to hide symptoms from the doctor.) Most of all, constant evaluation by someone in authority makes students reluctant to take the risks that are needed for good learning—to try out hunches and trust their own judgment. Face it: if our goal is to get students to exercise their own judgment, that means exercising an immature and undeveloped judgment and making choices that are obviously wrong to us.

We see around us a widespread hunger to be evaluated that is often just as strong as the hunger to rank. Countless conditions make many of us walk around in the world wanting to ask others (especially those in authority), "How am I doing, did I do OK?" I don't think the hunger to be evaluated is as harmful as the hunger to rank, but it can get in the way of learning. For I find that the greatest and most powerful breakthroughs in learning occur when I can get myself and others to *put aside* this nagging, self-doubting question ("How am I doing? How am I doing?")—and instead to take some chances, trust our instincts or hungers. When everything is evaluated, everything counts. Often the most powerful arena for deep learning is a kind of "time out" zone from the pressures of normal evaluated reality: make-believe, play dreams—in effect, the Shakespearean forest.

In my attempts to get away from too much evaluation (not from all evaluation, just from too much of it), I have drifted into a set of teaching practices which now feel to me like the *best* part of my teaching. I realize now what I've been unconsciously doing for a number of years: creating "evaluation-free zones."

(a) The paradigm evaluation-free zone is the ten minute, nonstop freewrite. When I get students to freewrite, I am using my authority to create unusual conditions in order to contradict or interrupt our pervasive habit of always evaluating our writing. What is essential here are the two central features of freewriting: that it be private (thus I don't collect it or have students share it with anyone else); and that it be nonstop (thus there isn't time for planning, and control is usually diminished). Students quickly catch on and enter into the spirit. At the end of the course, they often tell me that freewriting is the most useful thing I've taught them (see Belanoff, Elbow, and Fontaine).

(b) A larger evaluation-free zone is the single unevaluated assignment—what people sometimes call the "quickwrite" or sketch. This is a piece of writing that I ask students to do—either in class or for homework—without any or much revising. It is meant to be low stakes writing. There is a bit of pressure, nevertheless, since I usually ask them to share it with others and *I* usually collect it and read it. But I don't write any comments at all—except perhaps to put straight lines along some passages I like or to write a phrase of appreciation at the end. And I ask students to refrain from giving evaluative feedback to each other—and instead just to say "thank you" or mention a couple of phrases or ideas that stick in mind. (However, this writing-without-feedback can be a good occasion for students to discuss the *topic* they have written about—and thus serve as an excellent kick-off for discussions of what I am teaching.)

(c) These experiments have led me to my next and largest evaluation-free zone—what I sometimes call a "jump start" for my whole course. For the last few semesters I've been devoting the first three weeks *entirely* to the two evaluation-free activities I've just described: freewriting (and also more leisurely private writing in a journal) and quickwrites or sketches. Since the stakes are low and I'm not asking for much revising, I ask for *much more* writing homework per week than usual. And every day we write in class: various exercises or games. The emphasis is on getting rolling, getting fluent, taking risks. And every day all students read out loud something they've written—sometimes a short passage even to the whole class. So despite the absence of feedback, it is a very audience-filled and sociable three weeks.

At first I only dared do this for two weeks, but when I discovered how fast the writing improves, how good it is for building community, and what a pleasure this period is for me, I went to three weeks. I'm curious to try an experiment with teaching a whole course this way. I wonder, that is, whether all that evaluation we work so hard to give really does any more good than the constant writing and sharing (Zak).

I need to pause here to address an obvious rejoinder: "But withholding evaluation is not normal!" Indeed, it is *not* normal—certainly not normal in school. We normally tend to emphasize evaluations—even bottom-line ranking kinds of evaluations. But I resist the argument that if it's not normal we shouldn't do it.

The best argument for evaluation-free zones is from experience. If you try them, I suspect you'll discover that they are satisfying and bring out good writing. Students have a better time writing these unevaluated pieces; they enjoy hearing and appreciating these pieces when they don't have to evaluate. And *I* have a much better time when I engage in this astonishing activity: reading student work when I don't have to evaluate and respond. And yet the writing improves. I see students investing and risking more, writing more fluently, and using livelier, more interesting voices. This writing gives me and them a higher standard of clarity and voice for when we move on to more careful and revised writing tasks that involve more intellectual pushing—tasks that sometimes make their writing go tangled or sodden.

THE BENEFITS AND FEASIBILITY OF LIKING

Liking and disliking seem like unpromising topics in an exploration of assessment. They seem to represent the worst kind of subjectivity, the merest accident of personal taste. But I've recently come to think that the phenomenon of liking is perhaps the most important evaluative response for writers and teachers to think about. In effect, I'm turning another corner in my argument. In the first section I argued against ranking—with evaluating being the solution. Next I argued not *against* evaluating—but for no-evaluation zones in *addition* to evaluating. Now I will argue neither against evaluating nor against no-evaluation zones, but for something very different in addition, or perhaps underneath, as a foundation: liking.

Let me start with the germ story. I was in a workshop and we were going around the circle with everyone telling a piece of good news about their writing in the last six months. It got to Wendy Bishop, a good poet (who has also written two good books about the teaching of writing), and she said, "In the last six months, I've learned to *like* everything I write." Our jaws dropped; we were startled—in a way scandalized. But I've been chewing on her words ever since, and they have led me into a retelling of the story of how people learn to write better.

The old story goes like this: We write something. We read it over and we say, "This is terrible. I *hate* it. I've got to work on it and improve it." And we do, and it gets better, and this happens again and again, and before long we have become a wonderful writer. But that's not really what happens. Yes, we vow to work on it—but we don't. And next time we have the impulse to write, we're just a *bit* less likely to start.

What really happens when people learn to write better is more like this: We write something. We read it over and we say, "This is terrible . . . But I *like* it. Damn it, I'm going to get it good enough so that others will like it too." And this time we don't just put it in a drawer, we actually work hard on it. And we try it out on other people too—not just to get feedback and advice but, perhaps more important, to find someone else who will like it.

Notice the two stories here—two hypotheses. (a) "First you improve the faults and then you like it." (b) "First you like it and then you improve faults." The second story may sound odd when stated so baldly, but really it's common sense. Only if we like something will we get involved enough to work and struggle with it. Only if we like what we write will we write again and again by choice—which is the only way we get better.

This hypothesis sheds light on the process of how people get to be published writers. Conventional wisdom assumes a Darwinian model: poor writers are unread; then they get better; as a result, they get a wider audience; finally they turn into Norman Mailer. But now I'd say the process is more complicated. People who get better and get published really tend to be driven by how much *they* care about their writing. Yes, they have a small audience at first—after all, they're not very good. But they try reader after reader until finally they can find people who like and appreciate their writing. I certainly did this. If someone doesn't like her writing enough to be pushy and hungry about finding a few people who also like it, she probably won't get better.

It may sound so far as though all the effort and drive comes from the lonely driven writer—and sometimes it does (Norman Mailer is no joke). But, often enough, readers play the crucially active role in this story of how writers get better. That is, the way writers *learn* to like their writing is by the grace of having a reader or two who likes it—even though it's not good. Having at least a few appreciative readers is probably indispensable to getting better.

When I apply this story to our situation as teachers I come up with this interesting hypothesis: *good writing teachers like student writing* (and like students). I think I see this borne out—and it is really nothing but common sense. Teachers who hate student writing and hate students are grouchy all the time. How could we stand our work and do a decent job if we hated their writing? Good teachers see what is only *potentially* good, they get a kick out of mere possibility—and they encourage it. When I manage to do this, I teach well.

Thus, I've begun to notice a turning point in my courses—two or three weeks into the semester: "Am I going to like these folks or is this going to be a battle, a struggle?" When I like them everything seems to go better—and it seems to me they learn more by the end. When I don't and we stay tangled up in struggle, we all suffer—and they seem to learn less.

So what am I saying? That we should like bad writing? How can we see all the weaknesses and criticize student writing if we just like it? But here's the interesting point: if I *like* someone's writing it's *easier* to criticize it.

I first noticed this when I was trying to gather essays for the book on freewriting that Pat Belanoff and Sheryl Fontaine and I edited. I would read an essay someone had written, I would want it for the book, but I had some serious criticism. I'd get excited and write, "I really like this, and I hope we can use it in our book, but you've got to get rid of this and change that, and I got really mad at this other thing." I usually find it hard to criticize, but I began to notice that I was a much more critical and pushy reader when I liked something. It's even fun to criticize in those conditions.

It's the same with student writing. If I like a piece, I don't have to pussyfoot around with my criticism. It's when I don't like their writing that I find myself tiptoeing: trying to soften my criticism, trying to find something nice to say—and usually sounding fake, often unclear. I see the same thing with my own writing. If I like it, I can criticize it better. I have faith that there'll still be something good left, even if I train my full critical guns on it.

In short—and to highlight how this section relates to the other two sections of this essay— liking is not the same as ranking or evaluating. Naturally, people get them mixed up: when they like something, they assume it's good; when they hate it, they assume it's bad. But it's helpful to uncouple the two domains and realize that it makes perfectly good sense to say, "This is terrible, but I like it." Or, "This is good, but I hate it." In short, I am not arguing here *against* criticizing or evaluating. I'm merely arguing *for* liking.

Let me sum up my clump of hypotheses so far:

- It's not improvement that leads to liking, but rather liking that leads to improvement.
- It's the mark of good writers to like their writing.
- Liking is not the same as evaluating. We can often criticize something better when we like it.
- We learn to like our writing when we have a respected reader who likes it.
- Therefore, it's the mark of good teachers to like students and their writing.

If this set of hypotheses is true, what practical consequences follow from it? How can we be better at liking? It feels as though we have no choice—as though liking and not-liking just happen to us. I don't really understand this business. I'd love to hear discussion about the mystery of liking—the phenomenology of liking. I sense it's some kind of putting oneself out—or holding oneself open—but I can't see it clearly. I have a hunch, however, that we're not so helpless about liking as we tend to feel.

For in fact I can suggest some practical concrete activities that I have found fairly reliable at increasing the chances of liking student writing:

(a) I ask for lots of private writing and merely shared writing, that is, writing that I don't read at all, and writing that I read but don't comment on. This makes me more cheerful because it's so much easier. Students get *better* without me. Having to evaluate writing—especially bad writing— makes me more likely to hate it. This throws light on grading: it's hard to like something if we know we have to give it a D.

(b) I have students share lots of writing with each other—and after a while respond to each other. It's easier to like their writing when I don't feel myself as the only reader and judge. And so it helps to build community in general: it takes pressure off me. Thus I try to use peer groups not only for feedback, but for other activities too, such as collaborative writing, brainstorming, putting class magazines together, and working out other decisions.

(c) I increase the chances of my liking their writing when I get better at finding what is good— or *potentially* good—and learn to praise it. This is a skill. It requires a good eye, a good nose. We tend—especially in the academic world—to assume that a good eye or fine discrimination means *criticizing*. Academics are sometimes proud of their tendency to be bothered by what is bad. Thus I find I am sometimes looked down on as dumb and undiscriminating: "He likes bad writing. He must have no taste, no discrimination." But I've finally become angry rather than defensive. It's an act of discrimination to see what's good in bad writing. Maybe, in fact, this is the secret of the mystery of liking: to be able to see potential goodness underneath badness.

Put it this way. We tend to stereotype liking as a "soft" and sentimental activity. Mr. Rogers is our model. Fine. There's nothing wrong with softness and sentiment—and I love Mr. Rogers. But liking can also be hard-assed. Let me suggest an alternative to Mr. Rogers: B. F. Skinner. Skinner taught pigeons to play ping-pong. How did he do it? Not by moaning, "Pigeon standards are falling. The pigeons they send us these days are no good. When I was a pigeon . . ." He did it by a careful, disciplined method that involved close analytic observation. He put pigeons on a ping-pong table with a ball, and every time a pigeon turned his head 30 degrees toward the ball, he gave a reward (see my "Danger of Softness").

What would this approach require in the teaching of writing? It's very simple . . . but not easy. Imagine that we want to teach students an ability they badly lack, for example how to organize their writing or how to make their sentences clearer. Skinner's insight is that we get nowhere in this task by just telling them how much they lack this skill: "It's disorganized. Organize it!" "It's unclear. Make it clear!"

No, what we must learn to do is to read closely and carefully enough to show the student little bits of *proto*-organization or *sort of* clarity in what they've already written. We don't have to pretend the writing is wonderful. We could even say, "This is a terrible paper and the worst part about it is the lack of organization. But I will teach you how to organize. Look here at this little organizational move you made in this sentence. Read it out loud and try to feel how it pulls together this stuff here and distinguishes it from that stuff there. Try to remember what it felt like writing that sentence—creating that piece of organization. Do it some more." Notice how much more helpful it is if we can say, "Do *more* of what you've done here," than if we say, "Do something *different* from anything you've done in the whole paper."

When academics criticize behaviorism as crude it often means that they aren't willing to do the close careful reading of student writing that is required. They'd rather give a cursory reading and turn up their nose and give a low grade and complain about falling standards. No one has undermined behaviorism's main principle of learning: that reward produces learning more effectively than punishment.

(d) I improve my chances of liking student writing when I take steps to get to know them a bit as people. I do this partly through the assignments I give. That is, I always ask them to write a letter or two to me and to each other (for example about their history with writing). I base at least a couple of assignments on their own experiences, memories, or histories. And I make sure some of the assignments are free choice pieces—which also helps me know them.

In addition, I make sure to have at least three conferences with each student each semester—the first one very early. I often call off some classes in order to keep conferences from being too onerous (insisting nevertheless that students meet with their partner or small group when class is called off). Some teachers have mini-conferences with students during class—while students are engaged in writing or peer group meetings. I've found that when I deal only with my classes as a whole—as a large group—I sometimes experience them as a herd or lump—as stereotyped "adolescents"; I fail to experience them as individuals. For me, personally, this is disastrous since it often leads me to experience them as that scary tribe that I felt rejected by when *I* was an eighteen-year-old—and thus, at times, as "the enemy." But when I sit down with them face to face, they are not so stereotyped or alien or threatening—they are just eighteen-year-olds.

Getting a glimpse of them as individual people is particularly helpful in cases where their writing is not just bad, but somehow offensive—perhaps violent or cruelly racist or homophobic or sexist—or frighteningly vacuous. When I know them just a bit I can often see behind their awful attitude to the person and the life situation that spawned it, and not hate their writing so much. When I know students I can see that they are smart behind that dumb behavior; they are doing the best they can behind that bad behavior. Conditions are keeping them from acting decently; something is holding them back.

(e) It's odd, but the more I let myself show, the easier it is to like them and their writing. I need to share some of my own writing—show some of my own feelings. I need to write the letter to them that they write to me—about my past experiences and what I want and don't want to happen.

(f) It helps to work on my own writing—and work on learning to *like* it. Teachers who are most critical and sour about student writing are often having trouble with their own writing. They are bitter or unforgiving or hurting toward their own work. (I think I've noticed that failed PhDs are often the most severe and difficult with students.) When we are stuck or sour in our own writing, what helps us most is to find spaces free from evaluation such as those provided by freewriting and journal writing. Also, activities like reading out loud and finding a supportive reader or two. I would insist, then, that if only for the sake of our teaching, we need to learn to be charitable and to like our own writing.

A final word. I fear that this sermon about liking might seem an invitation to guilt. There is enough pressure on us as teachers that we don't need someone coming along and calling us inadequate if we don't *like* our students and their writing. That is, even though I think I am right to make this foray into the realm of feeling, I also acknowledge that it is dangerous—and paradoxical. It strikes me that we also need to have permission to hate the dirty bastards and their stupid writing.

After all, the conditions under which they go to school bring out some awful behavior on their part, and the conditions under which we teach sometimes make it difficult for us to like them and their writing. Writing wasn't meant to be read in stacks of twenty-five, fifty, or seventy-five. And we are handicapped as teachers when students are in our classes against their will. (Thus high school teachers have the worst problem here, since their students tend to be the most sour and resentful about school.)

Indeed, one of the best aids to liking students and their writing is to be somewhat charitable toward ourselves about the opposite feelings that we inevitably have. I used to think it was terrible for teachers to tell those sarcastic stories and hostile jokes about their students: "teacher room talk." But now I've come to think that people who spend their lives teaching *need* an arena to let off this unhappy steam. And certainly it's better to vent this sarcasm and hostility with our buddies than on the students themselves. The question, then, becomes this: do we help this behavior function as a venting so that we can move past it and not be trapped in our inevitable resentment of students? Or do we tell these stories and jokes as a way of staying stuck in the hurt, hostile, or bitter feelings—year after year—as so many sad teachers do?

In short I'm not trying to invite guilt, I'm trying to invite hope. I'm trying to suggest that if we do a sophisticated analysis of the difference between liking and evaluating, we will see that it's possible (if not always easy) to like students and their writing—without having to give up our intelligence, sophistication, or judgment.

Let me sum up the points I'm trying to make about ranking, evaluating, and liking:

- Let's do as little ranking and grading as we can. They are never fair and they undermine learning and teaching.

- Let's use evaluation instead—a more careful, more discriminating, fairer mode of assessment.

- But because evaluating is harder than ranking, and because too much evaluating also undermines learning, let's establish small but important evaluation-free zones.

- And underneath it all—suffusing the whole evaluative enterprise—let's learn to be better likers: liking our own and our students' writing, and realizing that liking need not get in the way of clear-eyed evaluation.

REFERENCES

Belanoff, Pat, and Peter Elbow. "Using Portfolios to Increase Collaboration and Community in a Writing Program." *WPA: Journal of Writing Program Administration* 9(3) (Spring 1986): 27–40. (Also in *Portfolios: Process and Product*. Ed. Pat Belanoff and Marcia Dickson. Portsmouth, NH: Boynton/Cook-Heinemann, 1991.)

Belanoff, Pat, Peter Elbow, and Sheryl Fontaine, eds. *Nothing Begins with N: New Investigations of Freewriting*. Carbondale: Southern Illinois UP, 1991.

Bishop, Wendy. *Something Old, Something New: College Writing Teachers and Classroom Change*. Carbondale: Southern Illinois UP, 1990.

————. *Released into Language: Options for Teaching Creative Writing*. Urbana: NCTE, 1990.

Diederich, Paul. *Measuring Growth in English*. Urbana: NCTE, 1974.

Elbow, Peter. "The Danger of Softness." *What is English?* New York: MLA, 1990. 197–210.

Elbow, Peter, and Pat Belanoff. "State University of New York: Portfolio-Based Evaluation Program." *New Methods in College Writing Programs: Theory into Practice*. Ed. Paul Connolly and Teresa Vilardi. New York: MLA, 1986. 95–105. (Also in *Portfolios: Process and Product*. Ed. Pat Belanoff and Marcia Dickson. Portsmouth, NH: Boynton/Cook-Heinemann, 1991.)

Gardner, Howard. *Frames of Mind: The Theory of Multiple Intelligences*. New York: Basic Books, 1983.

Kirschenbaum, Howard, Simon Sidney, and Rodney Napier. *Wad-Ja-Get? The Grading Game in American Education*. New York: Hart Publishing, 1971.

Lewis, C. S. *Studies in Words*. 2d ed. London: Cambridge UP, 1967.

Portfolio Assessment Newsletter. Five Centerpointe Drive, Suite 100, Lake Oswego, Oregon 97035.

Portfolio News. c/o San Dieguito Union High School District, 710 Encinitas Boulevard, Encinitas, CA 92024.

Smith, Barbara Herrnstein. *Contingencies of Value: Alternative Perspectives for Criticism Theory*. Cambridge: Harvard UP, 1988.

White, Edward M. *Teaching and Assessing Writing*. San Francisco: Jossey-Bass, 1985.

Zak, Frances. "Exclusively Positive Responses to Student Writing." *Journal of Basic Writing* 9(2) (1990): 40–53.

Follow-Up Questions and Activities

1. Using criteria that you create in class or those of a standard holistic scoring procedure such as the Test of Written English (TWE), conduct a holistic reading of a series of student essays and then analyze and discuss your scores.

2. Analyze a standard form of holistic scoring, such as the TWE, in terms of its underlying assumptions about what constitutes "good" writing.

3. Construct a course syllabus that incorporates the use of portfolios, explaining your choices with reference to the literature on the use of portfolios.

4. Discuss the relationship between a portfolio approach to assessment and other aspects of the writing process discussed in previous chapters, such as revision and response to student writing.

5. Burnham states that "portfolio evaluation requires the careful planning and execution not only of the individual course but also of a training program to support teachers using the system, thereby encouraging staff development." Imagine you are a teacher trainer and have been asked to help ESL/EFL teachers learn the portfolio system of evaluation. In an essay, explain how you would conduct such a training program and the reasons for your suggestions.

6. Devise an analytic grid such as the one suggested by Elbow and discuss its effectiveness. You may want to do this with classmates in the evaluation of sample student papers.

7. Do you agree that "liking" is important to the learning and teaching of writing? Discuss this from the point of view of your personal experience and explain how you might put this philosophy into practice.

8. Elbow writes, "Good teachers see what is only *potentially* good, they get a kick out of mere possibility—and they encourage it." Write an essay in which you outline specific ways in which teachers can be trained to look only for what is potentially good in their students' writing. It may be helpful to conduct conferences in which your strategies can be tested. These conferences could be taped and then played for class discussion.

INDEX